TOM FINNEY's FORGOTTEN SEASON

By J. Paul Harrison

The story of the 1959/60 season when Tom Finney captained Preston North End to the top of English Football for the last time

Published by LizLin Publishing

Paperback ISBN 978-0-9564803-0-9

A catalogue record for this book is available from the British Library.

Covers prepared by Philip Harrison.

Prepared and printed by:
B & D Print Services Ltd.
Marathon Place
Leyland
Lancashire
PR26 7QN
Tel. 01772 435050
Website: www.bdprints.co.uk

ACKNOWLEDGEMENTS

Firstly and foremost I would like to thank my wife Margaret, for her patience and tenacity in typing the manuscript for my book. Without her help I could never have completed the task.
Next I would like to thank Mike Hill at the Lancashire Evening Post for his general help and advice and also for allowing me to use articles and photographs from the newspaper.
The National Football Museum have been very helpful giving me access to research material regarding Preston North End and in this respect I would thank Peter Holme.
The covers for the book were designed by my brother Philip Harrison and his efforts are much appreciated.
My good friend Jack Fahey had the painstaking job of proof-reading most of the book and I thank him sincerely.
Finally thanks to John Nickson at St. Catherine's Hospice for his support in this project, the profits from which will be donated to this most worthy organisation.

PHOTOGRAPHS

Many of the photographs in the book have had to be taken from original newspapers as the 'photoplates' were no longer available and this has naturally reduced the quality. I still feel that this has not diminished their impact in depicting the game from fifty years ago.
Whilst the majority of the photographs come from the Lancashire Evening Post, the origin of some are unknown.

INTRODUCTION

Over the years a number of books have been written about the career of Sir Tom Finney, who was an outstanding footballer both with his home town club Preston North End and England. His ability to be equally as strong with his left or right foot resulted in him being selected to play in all five forward positions.

Numerous newspaper football columns and magazine articles have been devoted to his goalscoring feats and his silky footballing skills creating scoring opportunities for other players. Tommy Thompson, the former Preston forward (now called a striker) has always stated that one of the reasons he left Aston Villa to join Preston in 1955 was to have the opportunity to play in the same forward line as Finney. Thompson soon became a prolific scorer with North End and Finney provided many of the final passes.

I have tried within this book not to go over old ground regarding the career of Sir Tom but instead to concentrate on the 1959/60 Division 1 football season in the days prior to the creation of the Premier League. The maximum wage was still in existence and there was not a lot of point in moving from one team to another except to play at a higher level or receive a ‘signing on fee’. This was to be Tom Finney’s final season in the Football League and the loss of such an iconic player was to have a devastating effect on the club over the next fifty years.

1958/59 SEASON

In order to set the scene for his final season it is worthwhile firstly reviewing what happened both to Tom Finney and Preston during the 1958/59 football season.
In the summer of 1958 Finney was in the England World Cup squad in Sweden and played at outside left in the opening Group 4 game against Russia on 8th June in Gothenburg. The Russians led 2-0 with about 20 minutes left, when Derek Kevan pulled a goal back and then England were awarded a penalty.
It did not appear that anyone other than Tom Finney wanted to take it and he was left with the task of trying to secure a draw. Although he was naturally stronger on his left side, Finney decided to hit the ball with his right foot to Yashin's right side, and to the relief of the England players and supporters the ball hit the back of the net to make the final score 2-2.
Unfortunately during the game, Finney had been on the wrong end of a number of crunching tackles and awoke the following morning to find his right knee badly swollen and he was unable to take any further part in the rest of the Competition. England, without the Busby Babes-Edwards, Byrne and Taylor-tragically killed in the Munich air crash four months earlier, only managed two draws in their other group games and were then eliminated in a play-off match losing 1-0 against Russia.
Since his Football League debut against Leeds United in August 1946, Finney had the misfortune to miss many games due to injury and other medical problems. The worst was probably the chronic back problem he endured during the mid 1950's which resulted in him having over a year trying to play when he was not fully fit.
To the relief of all the North End fans and the club Tom Finney, who was then 36 years of age, was fit again to play competitive football at the start of the 1958/59 season. He played outside left in the opening game, which was a 2-1 victory over Arsenal at Deepdale in front of 30,000 spectators. This result raised the expectations of the Deepdale faithful that after finishing 3rd in 1956/57 and second in 1957/58 then perhaps this was the season when P.N.E. would finally clinch first spot.

Finney played in the same position in the next eight games, scoring four goals, with the 3-1 win over Leicester City on Monday 22nd September pushing them top of Division 1 after nine games. The following Saturday they were well-beaten 4-1 at Luton Town (with Finney in the team) to allow Luton to go top and Preston had to settle for second place at the end of September.

On the first Saturday in October Finney was selected as outside left in the England team which played Northern Ireland at Windsor Park. He scored in the 3-3 draw along with Bobby Charlton who, playing at centre forward, scored the other two goals. This was Finney's 30th goal for England, creating a new all time England scoring record (and was to be his last). Finney played a further 2 games for P.N.E. in October scoring two goals in the 4-3 home defeat to Newcastle United and then missed two games through injury. These goals were to be the last that he would score during 1958/59.On 22nd October he played his 76th and final international for England at Wembley in the 5-0 demolition of Russia. Then the injury problems started and from 1st November 1958 until Christmas Day Finney only managed to play two games at centre forward for North End with the team winning one and losing one at home. Even without Finney North End's form was still very good, and prior to the Christmas Day game against Blackpool at Bloomfield Road, North End were in 3rd position with a record of

P 23 W 12 D 4 L 7 F 42 A 34 Pts 28

Stanley Matthews was in the Blackpool line up and to everyone's surprise Finney was named in the Preston side. Blackpool took an early lead but Tommy Thompson equalised for North End and then in the 42nd minute, Finney headed a cross into the goalmouth and Thompson scored his second with a header to put P.N.E. 2-1 up at half-time.

Matthews then came into his own in the second half, and lead the North End defenders a merry dance creating numerous chances and Blackpool ran out easy winners by 4-2. During the second half, Finney had a recurrence of the groin injury that continued to plague him, and ended up a 'passenger' on the wing before leaving the field just before full-time. The following day in the return match at Deepdale, both Matthews and Finney were missing from the line-ups and a crowd of over 36,000 saw Blackpool complete the double over P.N.E. with a 3-0 win. The spectators wondered whether or not they would ever see the two players in opposition again in a football league match.

Finney had suffered internal bleeding as a consequence of the groin injury and was told to rest. He took no further part in North End's season for four months until the final match at home to Tottenham Hotspur on the 25th April when he made a surprise return at outside right in a 2-2 draw.

During his absence, Preston had still reached the 5th Round of the F.A. Cup, before losing 1-0 to Bolton Wanderers in a second replay at Ewood Park.

Unfortunately their league form suffered during Finney's absence and they eventually finished in 12th position with 41 points with the worst home attendance during that period being only 10,545 for the game against Luton Town on the 6th April, 1959.

Finney had played just 16 league games during the 1958/59 season scoring six goals-his lowest number of appearances in a season since his debut in 1946/47.

A new season beckoned, but would Finney be fit enough to make a real contribution to the team?

Back row left to right- F. O'Farrell, W. Cunningham, J. Dunn, F. Else, J. Walton, J. Smith, J. O'Neill.

Front row-D. Mayers, T. Thompson, T. Finney, D. Hatsell, D. Sneddon, S. Taylor.

PRESTON NORTH END FIXTURES
1959/60

Date	Opponent	Venue
Aug-22	Chelsea	a
25	WEST HAM UNITED	h
29	WEST BROMWICH ALBION	h
31	West Ham United	a
Sep-05	Newcastle United	a
8	Burnley	a
12	BIRMINGHAM CITY	h
15	BURNLEY	h
19	Tottenham Hotspur	a
26	MANCHESTER UNITED	h
Oct-03	Blackburn Rovers	a
10	MANCHESTER CITY	h
17	Arsenal	a
24	WOLVERHAMPTON WANDERERS	h
31	Blackpool	a
Nov-07	NOTTINGHAM FOREST	h
14	Fulham	a
21	BOLTON WANDERERS	h
28	Luton Town	a
Dec-05	EVERTON	h
12	Sheffield Wednesday	a
19	CHELSEA	h
26	Leicester City	a
28	LEICESTER CITY	h
1960		
Jan-02	West Bromwich Albion	a
9	F.A.CUP 3rd ROUND	
16	NEWCASTLE UNITED	h
23	Birmingham City	a
30	F.A.CUP 4th ROUND	
Feb-06	TOTTENHAM HOTSPUR	h
13	Manchester United	a
20	BLACKBURN ROVERS	h
27	Everton	a
Mar-05	ARSENAL	h
12	Wolverhampton Wanderers	a
19	SHEFFIELD WEDNESDAY	h
26	Nottingham Forest	a
Apr-02	FULHAM	h
9	Bolton Wanderers	a
16	BLACKPOOL	h
18	LEEDS UNITED	h
19	Leeds United	a
23	Manchester City	a
30	LUTON TOWN	h
May-07	F.A.Cup Final	

AUGUST 1959

The fixtures have been released and North End will start the season on 22nd August with an away fixture at Stamford Bridge against Chelsea. The night for home games at Deepdale has been changed from Monday, an experiment for the first time last season, to Tuesday. The kick-off time will be put back from 7pm to 7.15pm to give the home supporters more time to travel to the ground after a day at work.

Ground season ticket prices for standing on the Town End and Spion Kop remain the same as last season at £2-2s-0d. The most expensive season ticket for a seat in the Pavillion Stand including refreshments is £9-18s-0d.

Monday 3rd August and Cliff Britton, the P.N.E. manager, stated that pre-season training started with three days of roadwork followed by general field and track work before the players became fully involved in practice matches against each other. Tom Finney reported back feeling great after a summer break in the Mediterranean sunshine. He said that he had given his groin a really thorough test over the summer months and felt fitter than he had done for some considerable time.

In mid-August the Preston players were well beaten in the annual cricket match against Palace Shield side Fulwood and Broughton. Fulwood made 195 for 7 declared with Dennis Hatsell taking 3 wickets and Fred Else 2. North End only scored 74 all out and only three players-Cunningham, Else and Dagger-managed to achieve double figures. Finney did not play in the game.

Ten days prior to the commencement of the season, Cliff Britton gave a press statement announcing that three players-Kelly, Thompson and Finney-were suffering from minor injury problems. He expected Kelly and Thompson to be fit enough to play in the public practice match at Deepdale on Saturday 15th between the 1st and 2nd teams but Finney has a slight 'thigh problem' and will not be risked in the game. Mr Britton also announced that Finney will captain the Club again in the new season.

Over 5000 spectators attended the practice match with the Whites (1st team) beating the Blues (2nd team) by 4 goals to 3. The game was played at a very low tempo with tackling virtually non-existent. David Sneddon, who signed from Dundee for £10,000 in April, was the most impressive player on view. His distribution and general ball play throughout the game was outstanding and he also got his name on the score sheet.
In the week leading up to the opening league match, North End supporters kept checking the local paper (The Lancashire Evening Post) for news of Finney's fitness. Early reports indicated that he was back in training and the troublesome thigh had withstood a full fitness test. Then the news that all the Deepdale faithful had been hoping to hear, Finney was fit and will play at centre-forward against Chelsea. Sammy Taylor has been given the number 11 shirt and a chance to prove his worth again in the first team, plus an opportunity to strike up a strong early partnership with Sneddon.
Ted Drake, the Chelsea manager, told the London press that, although he has the youngest side in the First Division (known as Drake's Ducklings), he still intended to put the emphasis on attack. Charles Livesey, a £12,000 summer signing from Southampton, will lead the Chelsea attack together with 19 year old Jimmy Greaves who scored a phenomenal 32 League goals last season.

PEN PICTURES OF P.N.E. PLAYERS
(Statistics complete to the start of the 1959/60 season)

ALEC ALSTON
Forward
Born Preston 26th Feb. 1937

Signed from non-league football with Netherfield before making his debut during the 1957/8 season.

League App.	**9**
Goals	**3**

LES CAMPBELL
Winger
Born Wigan 26th July 1935

Joined Preston from non-league Wigan Athletic making his debut at outside-right in October 1953 at Wolverhampton. Has made a limited number of appearances over the last 6 seasons, mainly as a replacement on either wing (did not appear at all in 1957/8).

League App.	**56**
Goals	**4**

LES DAGGER
Winger
Born Preston 25th April 1933

Started his career in non-league football with West Auckland and made his P.N.E. debut in November 1956 in a 6-0 victory at home to Sunderland. He went on to play 25 games on the right-wing during the 1956/7 season. His appearances have since been limited due to the good form of Derek Mayers.

League App.	**41**
Goals	**3**

WILLIE CUNNINGHAM
Full-back
Born Cowdenbeath 22nd February 1925

Began his career as an 18 year-old with Dunfermline Athletic before moving on to Airdrie. In the summer of 1949 Preston paid £5,000 for his services and he made his debut in August 1949 in a Division 2 home game against Grimsby Town. He has remained the regular right-back over the last 10 seasons and 3 times has been an ever present in the team. In 2 other seasons he only missed 1 game.
The very popular tough tackling defender has been capped 8 times by Scotland and was captain of the side at the 1954 World Cup in Switzerland.

League App.	**347**
Goals	**2**

FRANK 0'FARRELL
Wing-half
Born Cork 9th October 1927

Started his career with Cork United before signing for West Ham in 1948. Did not make his League debut until 1950 and went on to play 197 games for the 'Hammers' scoring 6 goals.
Has played on 9 occasions for the Republic of Ireland and has scored 2 goals.
Joined Preston in November 1956 in a straight swap deal for Eddie Lewis and a few days later scored on his debut in a 3-1 win at Deepdale against Manchester City. This remains his only goal for the club up to this season.
His powerful displays at wing-half have made him an automatic choice.

League App.	**91**
Goals	**1**

TOM FINNEY
Forward
Born Preston 5th April 1922

Tom Finney is one of the most famous footballers in the Country having played 76 games for England scoring 30 goals.
Although he played for Preston in the 1941 War Cup Final against Arsenal at Wembley and subsequent replay at Ewood Park, he did not make his Football League debut until August 1946 because of the war. He scored on his debut in a 3-2 victory against Leeds United at Deepdale. The following month he made his International debut in Belfast scoring a goal in England's 7-2 win against Northern Ireland. He has not played for England since the 5-0 win against Russia at Wembley in October 1958.
He was selected as 'Footballer of the Year' in 1954 and 1957 and although now aged 37 is still a feared opponent.
He has been selected in 3 forward positions for England but has played in all five forward positions for North End.
In May 1950 Finney scored 4 goals for England in the 5-3 victory over Portugal in Lisbon but has not yet scored a hat-trick in a League or Cup game for Preston.
During his career he has been unlucky with injuries and last season only played 16 League games.
A good header of the ball with the ability to shoot with either foot, he is presently enjoying his new role at centre-forward.

League App.	**396**
Goals	**170**

GIL LAMBERT
Outside-left
Born Preston 16th March 1937

Gil Lambert progressed as a junior with North End and after a number of good performances in the Central League side he made his debut in the 3-0 home victory against Birmingham City last season.

League App. 13
Goals 2

GORDON MILNE
Wing-half
Born Preston 29th March 1937

Son of former Preston player and now North End's trainer Jimmy Milne, started his career in non-league football with Morecambe. After appearing for the Youth Team and reserve side, Milne became a part-time professional in January 1956 making his debut later the same year. After making just 10 appearances over 2 seasons he became 'first choice' right-half after Tommy Docherty moved to Arsenal at the start of the 1958/9 season. Outside football he has trained as a joiner.

League App. 40
Goals 1

FRED ELSE
Goalkeeper
Born Golborne 31st March 1933

Came into prominence when on National Service stationed at Newcastle, he played for Axwell Park Colliery Welfare F.C. and signed amateur forms for Preston in July 1951.
Made his League debut in March 1954 following an injury to George Thompson. He played 13 League games over the next 2 seasons before becoming an automatic selection in the 1956/7 season when he played every game with North End finishing in 3rd position.
Has played for the England 'B' team and should have won a full cap with his consistent, impressive performances.

League App. 133

DEREK MAYERS
Winger
Born Liverpool 24th January 1935

Derek Mayers started his career at Goodison Park where he made 18 appearances scoring 7 goals before transferring to Deepdale in the summer of 1957. Scored on his debut against Tottenham Hotspur in September 1957 and over the last 2 seasons has made the outside-right slot his own.

League App. 71
Goals 19

DENNIS HATSELL
Centre-forward
Born Sheffield 9th June 1930

Progressed through the junior ranks at Deepdale with a good scoring ratio per game before playing in the Division 1 game at Old Trafford in September 1953 when Preston lost 1-0. During the season he went on to score 12 goals in 19 games and the following season played for an F.A. XI at Highbury as a reward for his good club form.
He has always been a crowd favourite despite the fact that during his first 5 seasons he was unable to command a first team spot. Last season he played 39 games scoring 18 goals.

League App.	112
Goals	54

JIMMY HUMES
Winger
Born Carlisle 6th August 1942

The youngster has impressed in the 'A' and 'B' teams and looks likely to play in the Reserves this season.

JOHN FULLAM
Wing-half
Born Dublin 22nd March 1940

Joined the club from Irish junior football in September 1958 and has regularly played in the Central League side. Awaiting his first team debut.

KEN HEYES
Full-back
Born Haydock 4th January 1936

An England Youth International who regularly played in the Everton Reserve team and joined North End in the summer of 1957. Has not yet appeared in the League side due to the good form of Cunningham, Walton and Wilson.

GARBUTT RICHARDSON
Centre-half
Born Wallsend 24th October 1938

Joined P.N.E. in the summer of 1957 after being released by Bill Shankly, the Huddersfield Town manager.
Was a regular in the Reserve side last season and is waiting for his First Team opportunity.

ALEC FARRALL
Wing-half/Inside-forward
Born Liverpool 3rd March 1936

Played 5 League games for Everton before joining North End in 1957.
Made his debut in the 1957/8 season against Sunderland and went on to play 6 games. His appearances have been limited but he did score in 3 consecutive games last season whilst making 11 appearances.

League App.	**17**
Goals	**5**

JOE DUNN
Centre-half
Born Glasgow 20th September 1925

Started his career at Clyde before joining Preston for £1,500 in the summer of 1951. Although he made his debut in February 1952 in a 2-1 home defeat against Manchester United he was unable to command a place every week due to the form of Forbes and Marston.
He only played 83 games over the first 5 seasons before becoming the first choice centre-half in 1956/7.
A strong, forceful player, and a good header of the ball Joe Dunn is regarded as one of the best centre-halves in the country.

League App.	**191**
Goals	**2**

TOMMY THOMPSON
Inside-forward
Born Fencehouses, County Durham 10th November 1928

Started his career with Newcastle United and played 20 games scoring 6 goals during the period from 1947 to 1950. He could not hold a regular first team place and when manager George Martin left to take charge of Aston Villa he took Thompson with him for a fee of £12,500.
He went on to play 166 League and Cup games for Villa scoring 76 goals (including 3 hat-tricks) from 1950 to 1955 and was recognised throughout football as an outstanding goal scorer. He won his first cap for England v Wales in 1951.
Joined North End at the start of the 1955/6 season for a fee of £25,000 and scored on his debut in a 4-0 win over Everton.
In 1957 he won his second cap in the game against Scotland and went on to score 34 League goals in the 1957/8 season.
Has formed a prolific scoring partnership with Tom Finney in the Preston forward line and, in the 4 seasons the pair have been together, they have scored a total of 186 League and Cup goals with Thompson scoring 2 more hat-tricks.

League App.	**155**
Goals	**102**

JOE WALTON
Full-back
Born Manchester 5th June 1925

Made his debut for Manchester United in the 1946/7 season, playing 21 games before moving to North End the following season.
In 1948/9 he established himself as the regular first team full-back but during the promotion season of 1950/1 was replaced in the team by Scott and struggled to gain his place back.
Eventually in 1953/4 he re-established himself into the team and played in the losing Cup Final team against West Bromwich Albion.
He played for England v Scotland in the 'Victory' International of 1946 and was also selected for the Football League against the League of Ireland in 1948.

League App.	**353**
Goals	**3**

SAMMY TAYLOR
Winger
Born Glasgow 23rd September 1933

Joined Falkirk in the 1954/5 season from Cowie F.C. junior team. Moved to North End in May 1955 for £8,500 plus the guarantee of a floodlit friendly match against the Scottish side. Plays equally well on either wing but has now made the outside-left spot his own.
Made his debut in August 1955 against Newcastle United and played 15 games in his first season. Has a very good scoring record for a winger and has scored a hat-trick on three occasions.

League App. 105
Goals 31

JIM SMITH
Wing-half
Born Arbroath 16th October 1937

Arrived at Deepdale from Arbroath Lads making his debut in December 1958 against Manchester United. Is determined to make the left-half spot his own this season despite a call-up to undertake his National Service.

League App. 18
Goals 1

BOB WILSON
Full-back
Born Liverpool 8th September 1928

Played for Clitheroe then Burscough before joining North End in April 1950. Did not make his debut until March 1953 because of the consistent form of Willie Cunningham.
Played 24 games in the 1955/6 season, which is his best season to date.
Has found it almost impossible to oust Scottish International Cunningham from the right-back 'slot' and has only played 5 games over the last three seasons but remains a capable deputy.

League App. 55
Goals 0

DAVID SNEDDON
Inside-forward
Born Kilwinning 24th April 1936

Signed from Dundee in April 1959 and unusually made his debut in the last game of the 1958/9 season giving an encouraging display in the 2-2 home draw against Tottenham Hotspur.
Will hope to replace Jimmy Baxter in the number 10 shirt this season.

League App. 1
Goals 0

SATURDAY 22ND AUGUST

CHELSEA 4 **PRESTON NORTH END 4**

Greaves 3, Blunstone Finney, Thompson, Mayers,O'Farrell

Att. 42,891

The P.N.E. players arrived in London to find the sun beating down at Stamford Bridge and temperatures in the mid 8o's. The pitch was dry, hard and flat, similar to those found at the end of the season.

In the early stages of the game Finney found himself very tightly marked by Mortimore and was struggling to make any impression on the game in his role at centre-forward. Suddenly, after 13 minutes, he finally found a few yards of space and after good work by Mayers, FINNEY slotted home to put North End in the lead.

Within a few minutes of the restart GREAVES pulled a goal back for Chelsea with a fantastic volley and then almost immediately the same player scored again, beating Else with a crisp shot. Blunstone, Brabrook and Greaves continued to torment the Preston defence and it was no surprise when BLUNSTONE hit a strong shot, clipping the post, before nestling in the back of the net. 3-1 to Chelsea.

The Chelsea defenders continually fouled Finney, but the referee seemed reluctant to take any firm action. Just before Chelsea scored their third goal Finney had, what appeared to be, a stonewall appeal for a penalty following a trip by the goalkeeper turned down by the referee. Things were just not going Preston's way.

Tommy Thompson was also unlucky with a header that hit the crossbar and fell to safety and continued to cause plenty of problems in the Chelsea penalty area.

David Sneddon, in only his second game for P.N.E., seemed to be having difficulty in adapting to the pace of the game as compared to his previous experience in Scottish football. He had a couple of half chances and could easily have scored if he had reacted quicker.

Chelsea extended their lead when teenager GREAVES completed his hat-trick midway through the second half after out running the somewhat older North End defenders and lobbing the ball over the advancing Fred Else into the empty net. Chelsea 4 P.N.E. 1

At this stage, the travelling North End fans feared the side was heading for a heavy defeat but with about 20 minutes to go they saw the team pull a goal back when Finney threaded a ball through the Chelsea defence for THOMPSON to score with a powerful shot. Preston were now playing some wonderful football and Finney had switched to the right wing with Mayers moving to centre-forward. Finney was causing havoc down the right flank and after 80 minutes he created a chance for Sammy Taylor whose shot hit DEREK MAYERS and then the keeper before crossing the line.

Chelsea 4-P.N.E. 3

During the last ten minutes, time and time again Finney created openings for players, and eventually, in the final minute he found O'FARRELL with a pass and the midfield player slotted home.

What a start to the new season, a goal with virtually the last kick of the game giving North End a 4-4 draw after having trailed by three goals.

Both sets of fans had witnessed a great game and the journey back home for the Preston supporters was so much sweeter than it might have been.

CHELSEA

Colours—Shirts: Royal Blue (White Collars). Knickers: White. Stockings: Navy Blue, Blue and White Tops.

1. (Goal) **Matthews**

2. (Right-back) **Sillett (P.)** — 3. (Left-back) **Whittaker**

4. (Right-half) **Anderton** — 5. (Centre-half) **Mortimore** — 6. (Left-half) ~~Crowther~~ Compton

7. (Outside-right) **Brabrook** — 8. (Inside-right) **Greaves** — 9. (Centre-forward) **Livesey** — 10. (Inside-left) **Nicholas** — 11. (Outside-left) **Blunstone**

Referee: Mr. K. HOWLEY [Middlesbrough]

Linesmen: Mr. D. A. G. BAKER [Bournemouth] [Red Flag]; Mr. W. T. CASTLE [Colchester] [Yellow Flag]

Taylor 11. (Outside-left) — **Sneddon** 10. (Inside-left) — **Finney** 9. (Centre-forward) — **Thompson** 8. (Inside-right) — **Mayers** 7. (Outside-right)

Smith 6. (Left-half) — **Dunn** 5. (Centre-half) — **O'Farrell** 4. (Right-half)

Walton 3. (Left-back) — **Cunningham** 2. (Right-back)

Else 1. (Goal)

PRESTON NORTH END

Colours—Shirts: White. Knickers: Blue. Stockings: Blue and White Rings

Frank O'Farrell

POST MATCH COMMENTS

Cliff Britton said that North End had played some beautiful football and in the end had virtually brought Chelsea to their knees. He was also pleased with the staying power of his team, especially the older players.

DIVISION 1 RESULTS

ARSENAL	*0*	*SHEFFIELD WED.*	*1*
BIRMINGHAM C.	*0*	*WOLVES*	*1*
BLACKBURN R.	*4*	*FULHAM*	*0*
BLACKPOOL	*3*	*BOLTON W.*	*2*
CHELSEA	*4*	*PRESTON N. E.*	*4*
EVERTON	*2*	*LUTON TOWN*	*2*
LEEDS UNITED	*2*	*BURNLEY*	*3*
MANCHESTER C.	*2*	*NOTTINGHAM F.*	*1*
NEWCASTLE U.	*1*	*TOTTENHAM H.*	*5*
WEST BROM. ALB	*.3*	*MANCHESTER U.*	*2*
WEST HAM UTD.	*3*	*LEICESTER C.*	*0*

Dunn and Mayers said that they found the weather hotter than that which they had encountered on the 1958 tour to South Africa. Sammy Taylor thought the ball could already have been over the line from his shot for the third goal before Mayers touched it. He conceded however, that the goal could not be credited to him as the referee would probably not have given it.

On Saturday North End Reserves drew 2-2 in the Central League game against Bury Reserves at Deepdale.

Tues.-25th Cliff Britton informed the press that Preston will be unchanged for the home game that evening against West Ham United. Finney will remain at centre-forward despite many fans feeling that he should return to the right wing position following his outstanding success in that role during the last ten minutes of the game at Chelsea when he created two goals.

TUESDAY 25TH AUGUST

PRESTON NORTH END 1 WEST HAM UNITED 1

Thompson Musgrove

Att. 29,489

P.N.E.-*Else, Cunningham, Walton, O'Farrell, Dunn, Smith, Mayers, Thompson, Finney, Sneddon, Taylor.*

W.H.U.-*Dwyer, Bond, Cantwell, Malcolm, Brown, Smith, Grice, Woosnam, Keeble, Dick, Musgrove.*

Although an evening kick-off the weather was still warm and humid, just like it had been at Stamford Bridge on Saturday.

North End dominated the early part of the game and on a number of occasions Mayers and Taylor found room down the wings but their crosses failed to create any clear cut chances. At times their final distribution of the ball was disappointing.

West Ham defended tightly and gave the North End forwards little room or time to create any space.

Finney tried to link up with his colleagues 'up front' but they were playing too close to each other and making the job easier for the West Ham defenders. Unfortunately for P.N.E., Finney's passing was not up to his usual high standards and the opposition intercepted a number of them.

Thompson had an early chance for North End but 'snapped' at it too quickly and shot wide.

West Ham had not looked too threatening going forward and, except for a shot from Grice, Preston's defence had looked very comfortable. However, after 32 minutes, that all changed when MUSGROVE was given too much room and scored with a strong shot which gave Fred Else no chance.

In the 35th minute Preston drew level when Brown, the W.H.U. centre-half, slipped and the ball broke loose for Mayers. He could have shot but instead passed the ball to THOMPSON who scored from close range. Almost immediately, Mayers had a chance to score himself, but his shot was well saved by Dwyer and the teams finished the half level at 1-1.

During the second half, North End had by far the better chances with Sneddon in particular having two efforts on target. The first was

TOMMY THOMPSON

cleared off the line by a defender and the second was saved by Dwyer who had an outstanding game in goal for the 'Hammers'.
On another occasion an opportunity arose for Finney to run clear of the West Ham defence, but his pace for once let him down, and he ended up passing the ball and the chance came to nothing.
There were no further clear cut chances in the game for either side and the score remained 1-1.
It had been a disappointing display by the Preston team, as they should have won the game easily considering the number of chances created. This result brought two draws from the first two opening games.

North End Reserves won 2-1 at Leeds United to maintain their unbeaten start to the season.

The Friday night team news for tomorrow's home game against West Bromwich Albion was that Gordon Milne will play his first game of the season at inside-right in place of the injured Thompson.
Milne has scored in the opening two reserve games and will provide support to Finney in the forward line.

GORDON MILNE

SATURDAY 29TH AUGUST

PRESTON NORTH END 1 WEST BROM. ALB. 1

Milne Kevan

Att. 24,876

P.N.E. - *Else, Cunningham, Walton, O'Farrell, Dunn, Smith, Mayers, Milne, Finney, Sneddon, Taylor.*

W.B.A.-*Potter, Howe, Williams, Setters, Kennedy, Barlow, Hogg, Burnside, Robson, Kevan, Dixon.*

Once again North End created enough chances to have won the game easily but the lack of a killer instinct in the opposition penalty area resulted in just one goal and the third drawn game in succession.

Walter Pilkington writing in the Lancashire Evening Post, questioned whether centre-forward was really the best position for Tom Finney. He stated in his report that, 'Opposing centre-halves are finding it is not necessarily fatal to allow him room to manoeuvre, as long as he is closely marked when the moment comes for the final thrust and other forwards are covered.'

He went on to write, ' The familiar dart which made this versatile artist a terror to defences alas has gone, otherwise he would have had two or three goals at Deepdale on Saturday.'

It is clear that perhaps North End have relied too much on Finney to create chances and also expected him to score goals when there are other players who also need to take on more responsibility.

Both the wingers, Mayers and Taylor, have at times 'waltzed past' their respective full-backs, only then to over elaborate and fail to deliver the final telling ball into the penalty area.

North End fans have seen the same problems develop in both home games, when good approach work has tended to 'fizzle out' when reaching the opposition danger area.

Gordon Milne in his first start this season was easily North End's most effective player. He found room to move into scoring positions whenever possible and it was no surprise when he opened the scoring for P.N.E. Milne also provided a superb cross from which Finney just failed to score with a header.

Cunningham and Dunn were the pick of the Preston defence but were unable to prevent DEREK KEVAN equalising for West Brom. with a diving header. Maurice Setters, the Albion mid-field player, was injured early in the game but still caused problems for the North End defence whilst playing as a 'passenger' up front and was the best opposition player on view.

DIVISION 1 RESULTS

BOLTON WANDERERS	*2*	*EVERTON*	*1*
BURNLEY	*1*	*WEST HAM UNITED*	*3*
FULHAM	*1*	*BLACKPOOL*	*0*
LEICESTER CITY	*3*	*CHELSEA*	*1*
LUTON TOWN	*0*	*LEEDS UNITED*	*1*
MANCHESTER UNITED	*3*	*NEWCASTLE UNITED*	*2*
NOTTINGHAM FOREST	*2*	*BLACKBURN ROVERS*	*2*
PRESTON NORTH END	*1*	*WEST BROM. ALBION*	*1*
SHEFFIELD WED.	*1*	*MANCHESTER CITY*	*0*
TOTTENHAM HOTSPUR	*0*	*BIRMINGHAM CITY*	*0*
WOLVERHAMPTON W.	*3*	*ARSENAL*	*3*

North End Reserves continued their unbeaten run after drawing 1-1 away to Barnsley thanks to an Alec Alston goal. Alan Kelly was unlucky when he dived to save a penalty but Barnsley equalised from the rebound.

FURNIVAL CARTOON FROM THE LANCASHIRE EVENING POST – 31ST AUGUST 1959

"THE THROSTLES"

MONDAY 31ST AUGUST

For the second time in ten days, North End are in London for tonight's match against West Ham United. The two teams drew at Deepdale 1-1 last Tuesday and both remain undefeated after three games.
The team news is that Finney will play at outside-right in place of the injured Mayers in what will be his 400th league game for the club. Dennis Hatsell will play at centre-forward in his first outing in Division 1 this season. Frank O'Farrell will captain the side against his former club for whom he played 197 league games from 1950-56 scoring six goals.
The Hammers line-up will include 18 year old Andy Smillie at inside-left in place of John Dick for his first home game of the season. Smillie scored in the 3-1 win at Burnley last Saturday.

WEST HAM UNITED 2 PRESTON NORTH END 1

Smillie, Keeble Smith

Att. 31,916

W.H.U.-*Dwyer, Bond, Cantwell, Malcolm, Brown, Smith, Grice, Woosnam, Keeble, Smillie, Musgrove.*
P.N.E.-*Else, Cunningham, Walton, O'Farrell, Dunn, Smith, Finney, Milne, Hatsell, Sneddon, Taylor.*

West Ham United started the game at a frenetic pace and the North End defenders had a tough time just trying to keep them away from the penalty area.
A number of the moves were started by Dwyer, the Hammer's keeper, who threw the ball out to the full-backs Bond and Cantwell for them to quickly move forward and build up an attack with the United mid-field players. Even Brown, the centre-half, wanted the ball played to his feet and on one occasion in the first half, ran the length of the pitch before hitting the North End woodwork with a 30 yard thunderbolt shot.
This method of attacking from the rear by the defenders seemed to give the West Ham forwards far more room as the Preston players did not know who to 'pick up'.

Despite the constant barrage from West Ham, the North End mid-field kept trying to play their own brand of attacking football and had the better chances in the first half.
Hatsell shot over the bar from a pass by Milne. Then Taylor shot tamely at goal following a header by Smith from a Finney corner. The same player almost immediately shot wide from a chance created by Milne following good work by Sneddon, O'Farrell and Finney. Sneddon then had a snap shot cleared off the line.
West Ham did have the ball in the net after 26 minutes but an off-side flag ruled the goal out. In the last minute of the first half, Musgrove had a great chance when put clean through with only Else to beat, but somehow shot wide. Half-time 0-0.
The second-half started just like the first had done, with West Ham camped out in the North End half of the pitch. Grice shot wide and then Else saved another effort from him. Eventually the deadlock was broken when after 53 minutes SMILLIE squeezed between two North End defenders and shot hard and low into the net.
P.N.E. almost equalised immediately when a clever ball from Sneddon found Milne but his shot was cleared off the line by Cantwell. Then Brown had his second effort of the game saved by Else.
In the 67th minute W.H.U. doubled their lead when KEEBLE charged Fred Else and the ball over the line. Else fatally had tried to catch a cross instead of punching it over the bar and Keeble waited for him to hit the ground with both feet, before fairly charging him into the net. West Ham then hit the bar.
Surprisingly Finney, who was having a quiet game on the right-wing, switched to centre-forward and Hatsell moved to his position at outside-right. Within minutes, Hatsell created some space down the right hand side, and hit a beautiful cross for SMITH to score with a great header. North End were unable to create any more clear-cut chances and suffered their first loss of the season.
The crowd of over 31,000 had witnessed a great game of football and left the ground expecting to find West Ham at the top of Division 1. Unfortunately, Blackburn Rovers also won their game 1-0 against Bolton Wanderers, to go top of the table with 7 points ahead of West Ham United on goal average.

SEPTEMBER 1959

Tues.1st-North End Reserves beat Leeds United Reserves 3-0 at Deepdale with goals from Byrne 2 and Alston. Their record to date in the Central League is

P 4 W 2 D 2 L 0 F 8 A 4 Pts 6

Wed.2nd – Garbutt Richardson, who was signed from Huddersfield Town two years ago as cover for the centre-half position, has asked for a transfer after being kept out of the reserve team by young Tony Singleton.

****

Shown below are the Division 1 leading goal-scorers and league table following the mid-week games:-

THE LEAGUE—DIV. I
(Including 2nd September)

	P	W	D	L	Goals F	Goals A	W	D	L	Goals F	Goals A	Pts
Blackburn	4	2	0	0	5	0	1	1	0	5	2	7
W. Ham	4	2	0	0	5	1	1	1	0	4	2	7
'Spurs	4	0	2	0	2	2	2	0	0	7	2	6
Wolves	4	1	1	0	6	4	1	1	0	3	2	6
Burnley	4	1	0	1	6	5	2	0	0	5	3	6
Blackpool	4	1	1	0	3	2	1	0	1	1	1	5
Leicester	4	2	0	0	6	3	0	1	1	1	4	5
Sheff. Wd.	4	1	1	0	3	2	1	0	1	2	3	5
Arsenal	4	0	1	1	1	2	1	1	0	6	3	4
Man. Utd.	4	1	0	1	3	3	1	0	1	8	6	4
W.B.A.	4	1	0	1	4	4	0	2	0	3	3	4
Man. City	**4**	**2**	**0**	**0**	**5**	**2**	**0**	**0**	**2**	**2**	**6**	**4**
Fulham	4	2	0	0	6	2	0	0	2	1	7	4
Preston	4	0	2	0	2	2	0	1	1	5	6	3
Leeds U.	4	0	1	1	3	4	1	0	1	3	3	3
Birminghm	4	1	0	1	4	4	0	1	1	0	1	3
Chelsea	4	0	1	1	7	10	1	0	1	2	3	3
Newcastle	4	1	0	1	2	5	0	0	2	5	7	2
Bolton	4	1	0	1	2	4	0	0	2	2	4	2
Luton	4	0	0	2	0	2	0	2	0	2	2	2
Nttm For.	4	0	1	1	2	5	0	1	1	2	3	2
Everton	4	0	1	1	3	4	0	0	2	3	7	1

Leading goal scorers

VIOLLET (Man. Utd)	6
GREAVES (Spurs)	5
CLAPTON (Arsenal)	4
CONNELLY (Burnley)	4
DOBING (Blackburn Rov.)	4
MURRAY (Wolves.)	4
POINTER (Burnley)	4
CHARNLEY (Blackpool)	3
EASTHAM (Newcastle Utd)	3
HERD (Arsenal)	3
JONES (Spurs)	3
LEGGAT (Fulham)	3
VERNON (Blackburn Rov.)	3
WHITE (Newcastle Utd.)	3

Fri.4th- Jim Smith, North End's wing-half, has received his deferred Army call up papers and will begin two years National Service at Oswestry immediately. This will cause a break in the young Scots promising football career. He will now only occasionally be available to play for the club. North End have decided to give a Football League debut to John Fullam at right-half in place of Smith for the game at Newcastle. Mayers and Thompson are both unfit.

SATURDAY 5TH SEPTEMBER

NEWCASTLE UTD 1 PRESTON NORTH END 2

Eastham Finney, Milne Att. 37,683

NEWCASTLE U.-*Harvey, Keith, McMichael, Scoular, Stokoe, Mitchell, Taylor, Allchurch, Tait, Eastham, White.*

P.N.E.-*Else, Cunningham, Walton, Fullam, Dunn, O'Farrell, Finney, Milne, Hatsell, Sneddon, Taylor.*

ELSE GREAT IN DEPENDABLE DEFENCE

North End had the better chances

By Walter Pilkington

(L.E.P. article Monday 7th September 1959)

Preston were generally accounted lucky to win at Newcastle, but this assumption needs qualifying. Both sides had escapes. There were two instances when I thought that North End were a trifle fortunate. In neither was the let-off the outcome of a schemed move, or due to a lapse. Thus a hopeful deflection by White, when Else was moving the other way to keep out another forward's shot, almost scraped in, but Preston were leading at the time. It was another illustration of how much depends on mere chance rather than calculated effort.

North End came back with two points-a victory at last in their fifth match and their fourth in succession at St. James's Park-and I reckon these points were earned.

No doubt the psychological aspect of playing on a ground where Preston has seldom failed in recent years, gave the team a more buoyant confident feeling but that alone will not win matches. Team work is needed and Preston possessed this priceless asset in good measure.

Better chances

Newcastle United, it is true, had about two thirds of the play, but the objective way to look at this is to estimate the number of actual scoring chances, the times a forward was through unmarked with no one but the goalkeeper to beat.

Preston were at an advantage in this respect.

United had a clear sight of the target in two or three of their many raids and scored once. Else, who was in great form, foiled them with fine saves on the other occasions.

His anticipation and alacrity and judgement greatly impressed Newcastle people. He soon got over early signs of being jumpy and gave a brilliant exhibition of high class goalkeeping, especially in the last 20 minutes, when Newcastle were trying desperately hard to save the match.

Good covering

They could not beat Else: in fact they seldom beat the other defenders either. The Preston covering system functioned splendidly with especial credit to what one may term the "old

Brigade."

I think the Newcastle forwards would agree with me that the Preston defence was a good deal harder to penetrate than the Newcastle rearguard.

Certainly with a lot less flurry and expenditure of effort and many fewer attacks Preston created more gaps and scoring opportunities. Only two of them were accepted but when I point out that Hatsell, through a second's fatal dallying with the goalkeeper out of position, missed what should have been a gift goal; and that Finney with time and room to aim straight twice narrowly shot wide; it will be realised that Preston could have had at least four goals instead of only two.

Promising start

The steadiness under pressure of Cunningham, Walton, Dunn and O'Farrell, their coolness in covering and minimising danger, were all the more gratifying because young Fullam, in making his League debut at right-half, naturally was feeling his way and obviously wanting in experience.

Cunningham and Dunn nursed and protected him unselfishly and made the youngster feel less nervous in what is always a trying experience for a comparative novice.

Fullam, of course, has plenty to learn. The defensive side of his role, such as how and when to tackle, and heading a man off, as Cunningham does so cleverly, offers room for improvement. But the stamp of a likely prospect was apparent in his approach to his game, and markedly so in his constructive distribution.

He was in no sense a disappointment and appealed to me as the type of lad, thoughtful and modest, who will profit from his first experience of a higher class of football.

The Preston forwards took a long time to get going. They were too casual at the outset, then over-impetuous. After half an hour they began to hold the ball more and draw the opposition, to play with the precision needed in their style of game.

At once there was a transformation. United were flung back on defence with an abruptness which startled them.

They sacrificed only one goal, but just as easily could have been three down at half-time and it would have been all over. The only thing lacking was thrust and decisiveness when good chances were there for the taking.

Hidden menace

Although Finney was seldom conspicuous his quietness was deceptive. He kept one or two defenders occupied and was always on the alert for a sudden opening. His periodic switch with Hatsell revealed distinct possibilities by the ease with which Newcastle were thrown into confusion. Without being in any way spectacular Finney might have had three neatly taken goals instead of only the one which settled the issue. It would have been his first 'hat-trick' for Preston. He will not always be as kind in erring slightly with his marksmanship.

Sneddon's perception and good passing contributed to both goals. He did a lot of useful work, but I would like to see him up the field more, playing closer with his partner and emulating Milne in being in the right spot to take possible chances.

It was Milne, who again opened North End's scoring and once more he played an energetic, decidedly serviceable game. He earned his place.

Newcastle are no mean team. There was some fine, mature talent on view and with one or two changes, such as finding a different outside-right and putting the opportunist White back at centre-forward, they should soon be among the goals and points.

I was greatly taken by the tall, smooth, polished Mitchell in his new position at left-half, especially, when backing up the attack. White, a perpetual motion type who takes the shortest possible route for goal was always a menace. Things happen through his drive and unquenchable enthusiasm, when he is in the vicinity of goal.

NEWCASTLE UNITED

Back row left to right-R. Stokoe, A. McMichael, R. Simpson, R. Whitehead, J. Bell.

Front row-G. Hughes, I. Allchurch, L. White, J. Scoular, G. Eastham, R. Mitchell.

SEPT. 5TH DIVISION 1 RESULTS

ARSENAL	*1*	*TOTTENHAM H.*	*1*
BIRMINGHAM C.	*1*	*MANCHESTER UTD*	*1*
BLACKBURN ROV.	*3*	*SHEFFIELD WED.*	*1*
BLACKPOOL	*0*	*NOTTINGHAM F.*	*1*
CHELSEA	*4*	*BURNLEY*	*1*
EVERTON	*0*	*FULHAM*	*0*
LUTON TOWN	*0*	*BOLTON WAN.*	*0*
MANCHESTER C.	*4*	*WOLVERHAMPTON*	*6*
NEWCASTLE U.	*1*	*PRESTON N.E.*	*2*
WEST BROM. ALB.	*5*	*LEICESTER CITY*	*0*
WEST HAM UTD.	*1*	*LEEDS UNITED*	*2*

Mon.7th Sept.-North End Reserves beat Blackpool Reserves 3-1 at Bloomfield Road with goals from Alston, Kerry and Lambert. This game followed the Reserves 3-3 draw with W.B.A. Reserves at Deepdale last Saturday.

P.N.E. Reserves record P6 W3 D3 L0 F14 A8 Pts 9

……………………..

The early team news for the Division 1 game at Turf Moor tomorrow evening is that Burnley will be unchanged for the sixth consecutive game. Danger men Connelly and Pointer have scored nine goals between them.

North End will field the same team that won 2-1 at Newcastle on Saturday.

TUESDAY 8TH SEPTEMBER

BURNLEY 2 PRESTON NORTH END 1

Pointer, Robson Sneddon Att. 29,195

BURNLEY-*Blacklaw, Angus, Cummings, Seith, Miller, Adamson, Connelly, McIlroy, Pointer, Robson, Pilkington.*

P.N.E.-*Else, Cunningham, Walton, Fullam, Dunn, O'Farrell, Finney, Milne, Hatsell, Sneddon, Taylor.*

The first local derby of the season saw North End start the game in an impressive manner. They moved the ball around by passing and running into space creating anxious moments for the Burnley defenders.

Burnley tried to take the game to Preston but Fred Else had little difficulty in dealing with a couple of crosses from Connelly.

Finney was proving dangerous down the right-wing and easily had the better of Cummings but for some reason, the ball was not being played wide to him on enough occasions. In fact Preston kept trying to play the ball down the middle of the pitch but Miller, the Burnley centre-half, was too strong and dealt easily with any attack along that route.

After 19 minutes, a cross from Finney, found Taylor whose pass was hooked into the net by SNEDDON. Sneddon was then foiled by Blacklaw who made a sharp save from him and then saved again from the rebound.

Burnley never looked dangerous and McIlroy was at fault for continuously slowing the game down by dithering whilst on the ball and not playing colleagues into space. Half Time Burnley 0 P.N.E.1

In the second half, Connelly continued to be dangerous down the right side, but his crosses failed to penetrate the Preston defence.

Finney was becoming more and more a spectator as the ball was just not being played to him.

It was inevitable that eventually one of Connelly's crosses would find a Burnley forward. After 70 minutes he again beat Walton and his cross was headed into the net by POINTER.

Although Blacklaw in the 'Clarets' goal had to save shots from Sneddon and Hatsell, the game had now swung in Burnley's favour.

They continued to press forward and four minutes from time Connelly again beat Joe Walton and crossed for ROBSON to score the winning goal with a header.
North End had been guilty of thinking they could just sit back and keep their one goal lead and paid the penalty with their second defeat of the season.
The Preston supporters again left the ground feeling that the team could have achieved a better result.
The two teams meet again at Deepdale next Tuesday in the return fixture.

Sneddon hooks the ball over the diving Blacklaw to score North End's goal from a very narrow angle.

Fri.11th-The Friday night team news is that Hatsell has been dropped by North End after failing to impress or score in the last three games. He will be replaced at centre-forward by Alec Alston who has scored four goals in six games for the Reserves. Gordon Milne will switch from inside-right to right-half in place of Fullam and Gil Lambert will play at inside-left in his first game of the season. Sneddon moves to inside-right.
Birmingham City who, like North End, have only won one game so far this season, will remain unchanged from the team that drew 1-1 at home to Chelsea on Wednesday.

SATURDAY 12TH SEPTEMBER

PRESTON NORTH END 3 BIRMINGHAM CITY 2

Taylor 2, Lambert — Stubbs, Neal — Att. 19,134

"THE FACE-SAVER"

As can be seen from the Furnival Cartoon from the L.E.P.-North End came from 2-1 down to win the game against Birmingham City through a late goal from Sammy Taylor.
The crowd - which was below 20,000 for the first time this season - witnessed an early onslaught from Birmingham, which resulted in Fred Else making four excellent saves. The pressure eventually lead to STUBBS opening the scoring after 25 minutes when his shot entered the net off Cunningham who was trying to cover on the line. North End were guilty of moves breaking down because of poor passing and also partly due to the inexperience of Alston and Lambert. Finney was marked by two defenders but after 34 minutes managed to find some space and played the ball out to Alston on the right wing who then centred for LAMBERT to head home.
Only a few minutes later, Birmingham restored their lead when NEAL scored from close range after Walton had given away a needless free kick. Half Time P.N.E. 1 Birmingham City 2.

SAMMY TAYLOR

In the second half P.N.E. came more into the game and Sneddon and Milne combined with Finney to cause havoc in the City defence. Over and over again, North End pushed forward with swift passing movements and looked likely to score at any moment. Alston and Lambert at last managed to get more involved in the game and Finney showed he had lost none of his powers providing the final telling pass.
Finney had a hand in both the second and third goals which were well taken by by TAYLOR (pictured left).

If it had not been for Schofield in the Birmingham goal then Preston would have won by a much bigger margin than one goal.
P.N.E.-*Else, Cunningham, Walton, Milne, Dunn, O'Farrell, Finney, Sneddon, Alston, Lambert, Taylor.*
BIRMINGHAM CITY-*Schofield, Farmer, Allen, Watts, Smith, Neal, Hooper, Gordon, Stubbs, Larkin, Orritt.*

SEPT 12TH DIVISION 1 RESULTS			
ARSENAL	*3*	*MANCHESTER C.*	*1*
BOLTON W.	*5*	*WEST HAM UTD.*	*1*
BURNLEY	*2*	*WEST BROM. ALB*	*1*
FULHAM	*4*	*LUTON TOWN*	*2*
LEEDS UNITED	*2*	*CHELSEA*	*1*
LEICESTER CITY	*0*	*NEWCASTLE UTD.*	*2*
MANCHESTER U.	*1*	*TOTTENHAM H.*	*5*
NOTTINGHAM F.	*1*	*EVERTON*	*1*
PRESTON N. E.	*3*	*BIRMINGHAM CITY*	*2*
SHEFFIELD WED.	*5*	*BLACKPOOL*	*0*
WOLVES.	*3*	*BLACKBURN ROV.*	*1*

North End Reserves suffered their first defeat of the season when they were comprehensively beaten 4-0 away against Newcastle United Reserves.

HIGHEST ATTENDANCE 55,641 AT OLD TRAFFORD

Mon.14th Sept- North End Reserves again conceded four goals after being beaten 4-1 away to Liverpool Reserves. Thompson scored the only goal.

On the same evening, North End announced that the team will be unchanged for tomorrow night's home game with Burnley following Saturday's great fight back against Birmingham City.
Burnley have injury problems for the first time this season with both Bobby Seith and Jimmy McIlroy unfit to play. Billy White will start in the forward line and 18 year old Alex Elder (pictured left) will make his league debut at left-back facing up against Tom Finney.

TUESDAY 15TH SEPTEMBER

PRESTON NORTH END 1 BURNLEY 0

Finney Att. 27,299

P.N.E.-*Else, Cunningham, Walton, Milne, Dunn, O'Farrell, Finney, Sneddon, Alston, Lambert, Taylor.*

BURNLEY-*Blacklaw, Angus, Elder, Adamson, Cummings, Miller, Connelly, White, Pointer, Robson, Pilkington.*

Preston made a great start when FINNEY opened the scoring after just 5 minutes. Taylor centred the ball and Finney out jumped the defenders to head the ball into the net. Young debutante, Alex Elder, was guilty of giving him far too much room.

The game was being played at a fast and furious pace with tackles flying in from all sides as you would expect in a local derby. There was no time for any player to linger on the ball.

North End's experienced defenders had the better of the early exchanges with the younger 'Clarets' attack and certainly the ball skills of McIlroy were badly missed.

P.N.E. created a number of chances:

Sneddon shot a fraction wide from a pass by Finney;
Blacklaw saved from Lambert;
Alston headed over the bar from a centre by Taylor;
Sneddon had a further shot that was too high;
Finney missed the target with a wide shot.

At the other end, an effort by Robson drifted just wide of the post and Else saved an attempt by Adamson.

Cunningham was having a great game in the Preston defence, never giving Pilkington a yard of space although he was cautioned for a late tackle on the same player. Dunn and Walton also had impressive games with their strong forceful defending giving the Burnley forwards a frustrating time by denying them room to manoeuvre. After his earlier mistake, Elder followed Finney all over the pitch, preventing him from having any opportunity to create clear cut chances for any Preston forwards. Half time P.N.E.1 Burnley 0

Connelly opened the second half by creating problems for the North End defenders and Burnley started to impose themselves more on the

THE FINNEY HEADER. — Up goes Finney to meet this centre, at Deepdale, last night. He rose above Miller and Elder to head the North End goal by which Burnley were beaten.

MISS BY LAMBERT FROM FINNEY PASS

game. Pilkington, for once, beat Cunningham down the line and crossed to Pointer whose attempt at goal went wide. Else looked a little uncertain when he dropped the ball from a high cross but fortunately regained possession quickly. He made amends a few minutes later by making a superb save from White.

Burnley's determination to win the ball was not appreciated by referee Mr Hamer who cautioned Pilkington and White for late tackles.

Finney and Alston again swapped positions mid-way through the second half and this change certainly had the desired effect of upsetting the Burnley defenders. Walter Pilkington, writing in the L.E.P. said, 'Finney was easily their best forward, always moving to a purpose and using the ball to advantage. Gradually, without concerning himself much with speed, he is finding his assured touch and revealing his familiar guile'.

In the final minutes, Finney provided a perfect pass to Lambert who somehow rushed his shot and mis-kicked the ball from a perfect position with only Blacklaw to beat. In the ensuing panic, the ball landed at the feet of Alston who shot wide.

North End had won their second consecutive game and avenged the 2-1 defeat at Turf Moor the previous week.

Wed.16th- Wolves beat Fulham 9-0 at Molineux in front of over 41,000 spectators with goals from Deeley 4, Flowers, Broadbent, Mason, Murray and Clamp. Tony Macedo, the Fulham goalkeeper, had just heard that he had been selected for England under 23's!!

At Stamford Bridge, Chelsea beat Birmingham 4-2 with Jimmy Greaves scoring his second hat-trick of the season.

In an F.A. Youth Cup tie at Deepdale, North End beat Wigan 4-0. The youngsters put on a sparkling display of football and could have won by an even bigger margin. Laing 2, Spavin and Peter Thompson scored the goals.

Tues.15th

P.N.E. BOARD MEETING

It was reported that Lincoln City had offered £1,500 for Garbutt Richardson. The Board decided that no decision should be made at the present time.

Fri.18th Sept-North End are in London for the third time this season for tomorrow's game at White Hart Lane against top of the League, big spending, Tottenham Hotspur. Spurs are unbeaten, having drawn their three home games, but their away record of four wins and one draw including 5-1 victories at Newcastle United and Manchester United is outstanding.
They have spent over £200,000 on assembling a 'star studded' team including-Brown £20,000, Norman £15,000, Mackay £30,000, Medwin £28,000, Smith £16,000, Jones £35,000, Marchie £30,000 and Blanchflower £30,000.
The news from the North End 'camp' is that Mayers is fit again and will play on the right-wing with Finney moving to centre-forward. Alston has been left out. Tommy Thompson is still unfit despite scoring for the Reserves at Liverpool on Monday. He has had a recurrence of knee trouble and will undergo hospital treatment.
Joe Dunn will make his 200th appearance for P.N.E. and Frank O'Farrell his 100th, whilst for Spurs Danny Blanchflower will play his 200th game since his move from Aston Villa in December 1954.

TOP 6 OF DIVISION 1

	P.	W.	D.	L.	F.	A.	Pts.
1 TOTTENHAM H.	**8**	**4**	**4**	**0**	**19**	**9**	**12**
2 WOLVERHAMPTON W.	**8**	**5**	**2**	**1**	**28**	**14**	**12**
3 ARSENAL	**8**	**4**	**3**	**1**	**14**	**8**	**11**
4 BURNLEY	**8**	**5**	**0**	**3**	**16**	**15**	**10**
5 BLACKBURN ROVERS	**8**	**4**	**1**	**3**	**14**	**10**	**9**
6 PRESTON NORTH END	**8**	**3**	**3**	**2**	**14**	**13**	**9**

++++++++++++++++++++++++

<u>SATURDAY 19TH SEPTEMBER</u>

TOTTENHAM HOTSPUR 5 PRESTON N. E. 1

Jones 2, Mackay, Smith, Dunmore Lambert Att. 51,776

SPURS-*Brown, Baker, Hopkins, Blanchflower, Norman, Mackay, Medwin, Harmer, Smith, Dunmore, Jones.*

P.N.E.-*Else, Cunningham, Walton, Milne, Dunn, O'Farrell, Mayers, Sneddon, Finney, Lambert, Taylor.*

Any neutral supporter seeing the final score would naturally assume that this must have been a one sided game with Preston well and truly beaten. This could not be further from the truth and only in the final 20 minutes, when North End were playing with only nine fit men did Spurs take control of the game scoring three goals.

SATURDAY, SEPT. 19th, 1959 VOL. LII. No. 8
COPYRIGHT ALL RIGHTS RESERVED
TOTTENHAM HOTSPUR
FOOTBALL AND ATHLETIC COMPANY LIMITED
Official Programme
AND RECORD OF THE CLUB
WELCOME TO "PROUD PRESTON"
PRICE TWOPENCE

The game started with Tottenham taking the lead after only 2 minutes when they were awarded a free kick on the edge of the North End penalty area. Dunmore stepped over the ball, Blanchflower then clipped a square pass in front of the defensive wall and Mackay hit a thunderbolt 20 yard shot against the post and JONES was on hand to tap the ball into the net.

Preston soon fought back and Finney caused all sorts of problems by continuing to drag Norman out of his position in the centre of the defence. After 14 minutes, Finney was put clean through on goal following a glorious pass from Lambert, but somehow shot straight at Brown. A minute later P.N.E. deservedly drew level when Brown dropped the ball from a cross by Taylor and LAMBERT took advantage to side foot home from close range.

North End continued to attack the Spurs defence and Finney created an opening for Taylor but his driven shot, heading for the top corner, was turned away by Brown.

The first half was developing into a terrific game of exciting, flowing football for the crowd of over 51,000, contested by two evenly matched teams with different strengths.
The Preston team played the ball on the ground, passing and moving with everything revolving around Tom Finney. Balls played into him were held and then neatly played off to left or right.
Spurs had a more direct approach with all the moves emanating through Blanchflower, Mackay and Harmer.
Some enthralling head to head battles were developing involving Mackay and Sneddon, O'Farrell and Harmer as well as Taylor and Baker. There were also strong individual performances from Else and Milne in the North End defence.
As half time approached, and with the score at 1-1 there was little to choose between the two teams, although Preston were possibly slightly ahead on points. Then came the first incident that would change the course of the game. Finney was laid low by a fierce tackle from Mackay and hit his head on the rock like pitch. Finney continued on the field for the last few minutes until the half time whistle blew. During the interval it was found that he may have concussion and was taken to hospital accompanied by Preston's manager Cliff Britton.
On the resumption of the second half, the crowd were surprised to see Preston restart the game with only 10 men and would only find out later what had happened to Finney.
Spurs soon took advantage of the extra man and after 50 minutes, neat inter-passing between Smith and Dunmore, resulted in DUNMORE volleying the ball at pace past Else to go 2-1 up.
P.N.E. were forced onto the back foot and had to encounter wave after wave of attack. Else and the defenders, together with help from the forwards, stood firm. In fact, North End, would not give up the game and Milne was unlucky on one occasion not to score.
After 70 minutes, this determination to take the game to Tottenham, resulted in a further injury. Lambert, whilst trying to escape the clutches of Baker, was injured in a tackle and went down with an ankle injury. As the game continued, with Lambert writhing in agony, Spurs hit the ball forward and JONES headed the ball into the Preston net from a cross.

Lambert then received attention from the trainer who determined that he had suffered a serious ankle injury and he was stretchered from the pitch.

Cliff Jones rises above the P.N.E. defence to head home the third goal.

The nine men of Preston gallantly fought on but could not withstand the Spurs barrage any longer and in the last few minutes, conceded two further goals scored by SMITH and MACKAY.
How it could all have been so different if North End had not suffered the two injuries and had completed the game with all eleven players.

SEPT 19TH DIVISION 1 RESULTS			
BIRMINGHAM C.	*3*	*LEICESTER CITY*	*4*
BLACKBURN ROV.	*1*	*ARSENAL*	*1*
BLACKPOOL	*3*	*WOLVES*	*1*
BOLTON W.	*3*	*FULHAM*	*2*
CHELSEA	*2*	*WEST HAM UTD.*	*4*
EVERTON	*2*	*SHEFFIELD W.*	*1*
LUTON TOWN	*1*	*NOTTINGHAM F.*	*0*
MANCHESTER C.	*3*	*MANCHESTER U.*	*0*
NEWCASTLE U.	*1*	*BURNLEY*	*3*
TOTTENHAM H.	*5*	*PRESTON N.E.*	*1*
WEST BROM. A.	*3*	*LEEDS UNITED*	*0*

Macedo, the Fulham 'keeper, after conceding nine goals at Wolves in mid-week, was injured during the 3-2 defeat at Bolton. He spent much time of the second half on the wing after having three stitches in a head wound and must now be considered doubtful for the England Under 23's match against Hungary at Everton on Wednesday night.

Burgin, the Leeds United goalkeeper, saved two penalty kicks from Allen and Howe at West Brom. but still finished on the losing side.

CENTRAL LEAGUE TOP 5

	P	W	D	L	F	A	Pts
MANCHESTER UNITED	9	7	1	1	26	12	15
LIVERPOOL	8	5	3	0	21	6	13
WOLVERHAMPTON W.	7	5	1	1	27	11	11
SHEFFIELD UNITED	9	4	3	2	15	10	11
PRESTON NORTH END	**9**	**4**	**3**	**2**	**16**	**16**	**11**

North End Reserves beat Sheffield United Reserves 1-0 at Deepdale with a goal from Hatsell to move into fifth position in the Central League. Jim Smith was available from his National Service.
Team- Kelly, Nettleton, O'Neill, Fullam, Richardson, Smith, Dagger, Byrne, Hatsell, Farrall , Campbell.

****

Mon.21st – The injury news from Deepdale is both good and bad. Twenty-two years old Gil Lambert has a fractured ankle and torn ligaments and is likely to be absent for some time.
Fortunately, Tom Finney, who was concussed during the game and attended the Prince of Wales hospital in London, was feeling fine and should be fit for Saturday's game against Manchester United. Both players managed to catch the 6.30 train from Euston with the rest of the team.
Joe Dunn and Willie Cunningham reported that during the game on Saturday they had also banged their heads on the bone hard pitch at White Hart Lane and suffered mild concussion. They could not understand why the pitch had not been watered to counteract the problem.

Tues.22nd – **North End Reserves beat Blackpool Reserves 5-0 at Deepdale.**

Tues.22nd(continued)- ***P.N.E. BOARD MEETING-Reported that Lincoln City had increased their offer for Richardson to £4,000 and that they wanted to take Mattinson on a trial basis-decision left to the Manager.***
Fri.25th Sept.-A major surprise in the early team news from Manchester United is that Dennis Viollet, who has scored eight goals at centre-forward this season, will switch to right-half. This is an attempt to bolster a defence which has conceded 14 goals in the last four games. Alex Dawson, the burly 19 year old Aberdeen born centre-forward, will play his second game of the season.
North End will make two changes with Farrall replacing the injured Lambert and Jim Smith, available again from National Service, replacing O'Farrell. Sneddon switches to inside-left from the number 8 spot. Finney is passed fit to play following his concussion in the game last Saturday.
Manchester United have an impressive record at Deepdale, having won six and drawn one over the last eight seasons. A bumper crowd of over 30,000 is expected and no doubt hoping to see P.N.E. improve on this record.

MANCHESTER UNITED 1959-60

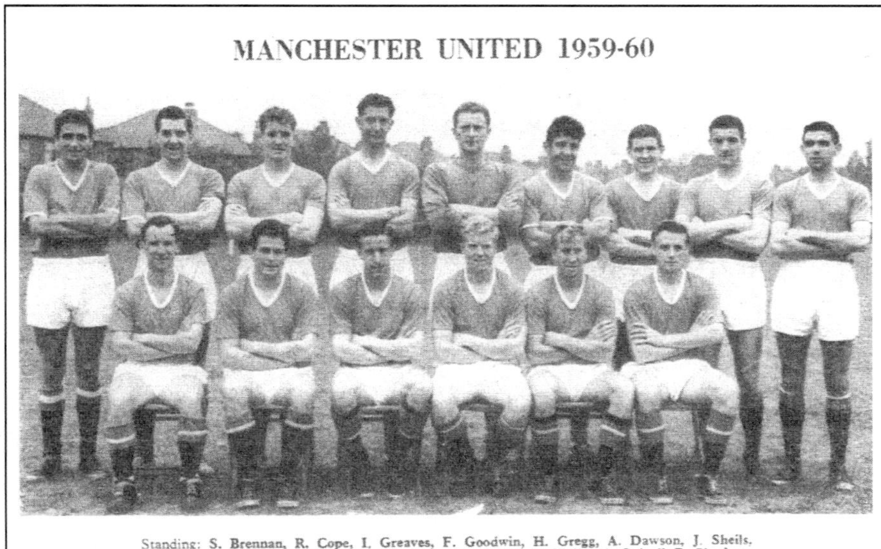

Standing: S. Brennan, R. Cope, I. Greaves, F. Goodwin, H. Gregg, A. Dawson, J. Sheils, W. Foulkes, J. Carolan. Seated: W. Bradley, W. McGuinness, D. Viollet, A. Quixall, R. Charlton, A. Scanlon.

SATURDAY 26TH SEPTEMBER

PRESTON NORTH END 4 MANCHESTER UTD. 0

Finney 2 (1 pen), Sneddon, Taylor Att. 35,016

P.N.E.-*Else, Cunningham, Walton, Milne, Dunn, Smith, Mayers, Farrall, Finney, Sneddon, Taylor.*

MAN. UTD.-*Gregg, Foulkes, Carolan, Viollet, Cope, McGuinness, Bradley, Quixall, Dawson, Charlton, Scanlon.*

FINNEY MASTER-MIND IN FINE ATTACK

North End triumph fruit of team work

By Walter Pilkington

(L.E.P. article Monday 28th September 1959)

Painfully used to taking chastening knocks from Manchester United, Preston North End have waited a long time to twist the tails of the famed Red Devils. Thus the long deferred pleasure of decisive revenge for the worst of numerous defeats –a 0-5 thrashing at home-was all the sweeter.

It was the more satisfying because not even fervent partisans in the usual big following from Manchester could find any excuse for their favourites sharp defeat.

A number were noticed, on leaving the ground fairly subdued to be discreetly putting out of sight the red scarves and berets which were so much in evidence two hours earlier.

Those in the official party and probably the humbled United players, too were thankful that this further set-back to a still ambitious club was no worse than a 0-4 trouncing.

They knew perfectly well how often mere inches had come between Preston's irresistible attack and a truly bountiful harvest of goals.

Hard on Farrall

For instance, young Farrall missed a 'sitter' when Preston had first got on top. He did the right thing in trying to place a side-footed shot instead of recklessly blazing away. Unfortunately his aim was inaccurate.

Farrall had my sympathy; I know what these lapses can mean to youngsters. They so often become afraid to have a go the next time through fear of missing again.

A goal at that juncture would have given this enthusiastic Irishman, who put 100% endeavour into his game and was not selfish, the confidence he needed.

It will console him to know that his industry was appreciated and that his promise did not pass unnoticed. Farrall's unconcealed joy when Taylor opened the score left no doubt about where his heart lies.

Finney scores from the penalty spot

Teamwork rewarded

This instinctive expression of delight reflected the greatest factor of North End's fine performance-their wholehearted team spirit.

Farrall's miss was far from being United's only escape. There was one on the goal line with Gregg missing and someone coming to the rescue: then Gregg, who was at fault with the first goal through coming too far out, saved gloriously from Milne when no one would have reproached him for being beaten.

Two other simple looking chances among many skilfully created were wasted: Milne hit the crossbar with another fierce shot: Smith had a beauty desperately saved in the final minutes when United were overwhelmed and he shot narrowly wide the next moment with Gregg helpless.

A bewildered, out-manoeuvred defence had other frights. In between a rampant North End piled up four goals without reply to gain a victory convincing in every respect.

Enduring style

Preston played the kind of football which, over the years, has earned the club an enviable reputation. It was good to see the ingrained style still there and better to see it given tangible expression through a combination of zest, purpose, intelligent moves and first class craftsmanship.

A display of high intrinsic merit was the logical outcome. To the discriminating eye it was delightful. A supporter who is not easily pleased enthused to me yesterday in this manner about North End's achievement:

"Beautiful, absolutely beautiful and 35,000 saw it. That's the way to pack them in and pull the crowds back. Real entertainment, goals or no goals."

Forward rhythm

How often have I written that the players have the answer to falling "gates" in their own brains and feet? This clearly was the kind of football the public want and will gladly pay to see. It was captivating, not least because there was no heedless booting and fruitless scuffling, little or no dallying and bunching. The Preston forward pattern flowed smoothly along the well grassed turf, often starting at full-back. Everyone got on with it, moving with rhythm and harmony, linking to a plan and finding each other with a stream of precision passes. The wings functioned at last with economy, directness and speed.

It was the kind of football Preston supporters have been waiting and hoping to see for a long time, perfectly co-ordinated with the team coming before any individuals.

Certainly it made Manchester United, even allowing for their obvious lack of confidence, look a mediocre side indeed. There luminaries were dimmed. Their only prominent players were those of whom not too much fuss is made, excluding Viollet. Although this versatile artist looked out of place at right-half and might have been able to pull the loose ends of a ragged attack together as leader or schemer, he strove as hard as anyone to save his side from a complete eclipse.

Cope too, never gave up, bewildered as he was at times by Finney's subtleties and instinctive sense of positioning. The plucky efforts of McGuinness, Carolan and Foulkes also merit a mention. Like the others they were often lost but at least they fought.

I cannot say the same for all the forwards. Charlton and Quixall not only were obliterated, but left their overworked defenders to fend for themselves.

Consequently their masters-North End's energetic wing-halves Milne and Smith-often were able to go through unchallenged as extra forwards. Both played exceptionally well.

Brilliant Finney

Only Scanlon and Bradley caught the eye in United's attack and neither looked like scoring. The only real alarm was when Charlton shot over from short range. As there was only one goal between the teams this lapse may be described as the turning point. United had been markedly inferior up to then: afterwards they wilted under an avalanche.

Preston again drew inspiration from the command of the rugged, skilful Cunningham, the composure and sureness of Dunn, the resource of Walton, the shrewd generalship of Finney and the intelligent play of tireless Sneddon, whose sagacity left a distinct imprint on the game.

Along with Finney, whose display was masterly, Sneddon shaped North End's ultimate triumph. Both drew defenders artfully out of position to open a clear path many time for wing men who responded with verve and determination. Taylor used his undoubted foot-craft to positive advantage without loss of time and Mayers neat and incisive has never played better. He contributed to all Preston's four goals and won many new admirers.

SEPT 26TH DIVISION 1 RESULTS			
ARSENAL	*2*	*BLACKPOOL*	*1*
BURNLEY	*3*	*BIRMINGHAM C.*	*1*
FULHAM	*1*	*CHELSEA*	*3*
LEEDS UNITED	*2*	*NEWCASTLE UTD.*	*3*
LEICESTER CITY	*1*	*TOTTENHAM H.*	*1*
MANCHESTER C.	*2*	*BLACKBURN ROV.*	*1*
NOTTINGHAM F.	*2*	*BOLTON WAN.*	*0*
PRESTON N.E.	*4*	*MANCHESTER U.*	*0*
SHEFFIELD W.	*2*	*LUTON TOWN*	*0*
WEST HAM UTD.	*4*	*WEST BROM. ALB.*	*1*
WOLVES.	*2*	*EVERTON*	*0*

North End Reserves lost 2-1 at Derby County Reserves with defensive errors proving very costly. Hatsell scored the only goal.

Les Dagger fractured his left arm when he crashed over a low wall surrounding the pitch after a heavy tackle.

DIVISION 1-LEADING CLUBS

	P	W	D	L	F	A	Pts
TOTTENHAM H.	10	5	5	0	25	11	15
ARSENAL	10	5	4	1	17	10	14
WOLVERHAMPTON W.	10	6	2	2	31	17	14
BURNLEY	10	7	0	3	22	17	14
BLACKBURN ROVERS	10	5	2	3	19	12	12
WEST HAM UNITED	10	5	2	3	22	17	12
NOTTINGHAM FOREST	10	4	3	3	11	11	11
PRESTON NORTH END	10	4	3	3	19	18	11

....

LEADING GOAL SCORERS

GREAVES	CHELSEA	11
DEELEY	WOLVERHAMPTON W.	10
CONNELLY	BURNLEY	8
VIOLLET	MANCHESTER UNITED	8
CROWE	LEEDS UNITED	7
HERD	ARSENAL	7
JONES	TOTTENHAM HOTSPUR	7
McADAMS	MANCHESTER CITY	7
MUDIE	BLACKPOOL	7
MURRAY	WOLVERHAMPTON W.	7
SMITH	TOTTENHAM HOTSPUR	7
DOUGAN	BLACKBURN ROVERS	6

OCTOBER 1959

Thurs.1st Oct-The Football Association informed North End that Derek Mayers was suspended for 14 days following his sending off in the Reserve fixture at Newcastle United.

Fri.2nd Oct-The team news from Blackburn is that Ronnie Clayton is injured and will be replaced by 17 year old Mike England. It will be his League debut. Peter Dobing will play after having his transfer request refused by manager Dally Duncan. The forward, who despite scoring seven goals, has been barracked by a section of the crowd and has been told by Mr Duncan to be less 'thin-skinned'. Derek Dougan will be absent on International duty playing in Belfast for Ireland against Scotland. Roy Vernon returns to the side.
North End have named an unchanged team but have been surprised by Frank O'Farrell submitting a transfer request stating that he wishes to move back south. He has been told that because Milne and Smith are not always available due to their National Service duties, his request cannot be granted at the present time.
O'Farrell will play in the Reserves at home to Manchester United tomorrow alongside Tommy Thompson who will try out his injured knee for the third time in the second team. It is understood that Sheffield United will watch Hatsell at the game with a view to making an official approach for his transfer.

SATURDAY 3RD OCTOBER

BLACKBURN ROV. 1 PRESTON NORTH END 4

Dobing — Finney, Farrall, Sneddon, Taylor

Att. 41,694

BLACKBURN ROV-*Leyland, Taylor, Smith, England, Woods, McGrath, Isherwood, Douglas, Dobing, Vernon, MacLeod.*
P.N.E.-*Else, Cunningham, Walton, Milne, Dunn, Smith, Mayers, Farrall, Finney, Sneddon, Taylor.*
The third local derby of the season saw North End travel the short distance to Ewood Park hoping to avenge last season's heavy 4-1 loss.
The Blackburn programme notes stated 'This season, North End have improved from a moderate start and last week brought off a great performance in adding to Manchester United's present worries by putting four more goals past their defence. Their shining star was the incomparable Tom Finney, back at his best again. We look forward to seeing him in action again for the first time on this ground for nine years'.After the game many Rovers fans must have wished that Finney had also not been available for this game.
Blackburn started strongly and in the first minute DOBING opened the scoring with a header.
It went downhill for Rovers from there on. Tom Finney, supposedly playing as centre-forward was everywhere on the pitch and easily the outstanding 'man of the match'. As the Furnival cartoon in the L.E.P. more than once mentioned, he just 'mesmerised' the opposition.
Using both wings, his outstanding ball control enabled him to emerge from any encounter with the Blackburn defenders with the ball and freedom to shoot. He equalised with his sixth goal of the season and then 'laid on' goals for SNEDDON and FARRALL.
Finney's supreme display was inspirational to the rest of his team, who, to a man, gave a smooth skilful performance to thoroughly outclass the opposition.
The fourth goal was scored by TAYLOR and Sneddon then had one disallowed for offside.

"THE MESMERISTS"

In defence, Smith showed his fine ability to tackle and initiate the build up of effective attacks but it was Finney's class performance that had the crowd cheering, applauding and loving every minute of watching a master at work.

Finney 'mesmerises' the Blackburn defence

Blackburn still had their own chances and somehow managed to miss three good goal scoring opportunities either side of half time. Vernon played well and Woods dominated in the air but they lacked a team around them to match the wonderful display of Finney and his team mates.

It had been an unforgettable game providing fine entertainment, excitement and revenge for the North End following.

North End Reserves drew 1-1 with Central League leaders Manchester United at Deepdale with a goal from Hatsell.

FIRST DIVISION

					Goals		
	P.	W.	D.	L.	F.	A.	Pts.
Wolves	11	7	2	2	36	18	16
Tottenham H.......	11	5	6	0	26	12	16
Burnley	11	7	1	3	23	18	15
Arsenal	11	5	4	2	18	13	14
North End	**11**	**5**	**3**	**3**	**23**	**19**	**13**
West Ham	11	5	3	3	22	17	13
Blackburn R.	11	5	2	4	20	16	12
Chelsea	11	5	2	4	27	25	12
Manchester C. ...	11	6	0	5	23	22	12
Notts Forest	11	4	3	4	12	14	11
Fulham...............	11	5	1	5	20	28	11
West Brom.........	11	3	4	4	20	18	10
Manchester U. ...	11	4	2	5	25	25	10
Leicester City ...	11	3	4	4	17	26	10
Sheffield W.	11	4	1	6	15	14	9
Bolton W.	11	4	1	6	14	16	9
Everton	11	3	3	5	15	19	9
Newcastle U.......	11	3	3	5	16	21	9
Blackpool	11	3	3	5	13	19	9
Leeds United	11	3	2	6	14	25	8
Birmingham	11	2	3	6	16	21	7
Luton Town	11	2	3	6	9	18	7

OCT 3RD DIVISION 1 RESULTS

BIRMINGHAM C	*2*	*LEEDS UTD.*	*0*
BLACKBURN R.	*1*	*PRESTON N.E.*	*4*
BLACKPOOL	*1*	*MAN. CITY*	*3*
BOLTON W.	*1*	*SHEFF. WED.*	*0*
EVERTON	*3*	*ARSENAL*	*1*
FULHAM	*3*	*NOTT'M. FOR.*	*1*
LUTON TOWN	*1*	*WOLVES*	*5*
MAN. UNITED	*4*	*LEICESTER C.*	*1*
NEWCASTLE U.	*0*	*WEST HAM U.*	*0*
TOTTENHAM H.	*1*	*BURNLEY*	*1*
WEST BROM. A.	*1*	*CHELSEA*	*3*

INTERNATIONAL MATCH

IRELAND	*0*	*SCOTLAND*	*4*

Tues.6th Oct- A North End 1st team, including Finney, lost 1-0 in a lacklustre, floodlit friendly match at Deepdale against Dundee in front of 11,906 spectators.

Thurs.8th- Spurs signed John White, the Scottish International forward from Falkirk for £20,000.

Fri.9th- Manchester City, having won their previous three games, make one change for tomorrow's game at Deepdale with McAdams returning in place of Kerr.

North End are forced to make one change following the suspension of Derek Mayers with Les Campbell playing outside-right in his first game of the season.

SATURDAY 10TH OCTOBER

PRESTON NORTH END 1 MANCHESTER CITY 5

Finney | McAdams 3, Barlow, Cheetham

Att. 32,546

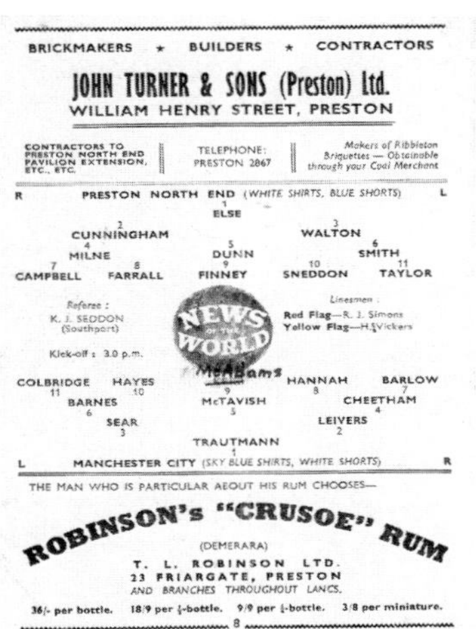

BRICKMAKERS ★ BUILDERS ★ CONTRACTORS

JOHN TURNER & SONS (Preston) Ltd.
WILLIAM HENRY STREET, PRESTON

CONTRACTORS TO PRESTON NORTH END PAVILION EXTENSION, ETC., ETC. | TELEPHONE: PRESTON 2867 | Makers of Ribbleton Briquettes — Obtainable through your Coal Merchant

R PRESTON NORTH END (WHITE SHIRTS, BLUE SHORTS) L

1 ELSE

2 CUNNINGHAM 3 WALTON

4 MILNE 5 DUNN 6 SMITH

7 CAMPBELL 8 FARRALL 9 FINNEY 10 SNEDDON 11 TAYLOR

Referee: K. J. SEDDON (Southport)

Linesmen: Red Flag—R. J. Simons; Yellow Flag—H. Vickers

Kick-off: 3.0 p.m.

COLBRIDGE 11 HAYES 10 McADAMS 9 HANNAH 8 BARLOW 7

BARNES 6 McTAVISH 5 CHEETHAM 4

SEAR 3 LEIVERS 2

TRAUTMANN 1

L MANCHESTER CITY (SKY BLUE SHIRTS, WHITE SHORTS) R

THE MAN WHO IS PARTICULAR ABOUT HIS RUM CHOOSES—

ROBINSON'S "CRUSOE" RUM

(DEMERARA)

T. L. ROBINSON LTD.
23 FRIARGATE, PRESTON
AND BRANCHES THROUGHOUT LANCS.

36/- per bottle. 18/9 per ½-bottle. 9/9 per ¼-bottle. 3/8 per miniature.

8

After winning four games out of the last five, North End came back down to earth following a crushing 5-1 home defeat to a rejuvenated Manchester City.

A good crowd of over 32,000 were surprised to see Preston suffer their first home defeat of the season in such a dramatic fashion.

The main difference between the two teams was the decisive finishing of City in a game where both sides created a similar number of goal scoring opportunities. The away team captain Ken Barnes gave a 'man of the match' performance. Whenever he gained possession of the ball he moved forward smoothly to link with his forwards and had no difficulty in dealing with young Farrall when Preston attacked. In fact Farrall himself was guilty in allowing Barnes far too much room by failing to tackle or otherwise prevent his progress. It was a bad afternoon for Farrall who was at fault for two goals and also missed a sitter at the City end.

Finney was unlucky with a shot which just flashed wide but Sneddon was guilty of a bad miss. FINNEY did guide a spectacular header passed Trautmann just before the interval.

However, the P.N.E. defence struggled to cope with the pressure from City and Joe Dunn had a nightmare game against BILL McADAMS (pictured left) who scored a hat-trick to bring his seasons total to 10 goals in nine games.

Finney beats Trautmann with a great header

City worked extremely hard for the victory and their fitness was evident when they scored a further two goals in the last 3 minutes of the game to produce a somewhat flattering scoreline.
It was difficult to single out any individual North End player for praise and only Milne and Cunningham came out of the game with any credit. Fred Else, who had been the saviour of Preston on a number of occasions already this season, had an off day. His indecision on knowing whether or not to come out for a cross resulted in two City goals for BARLOW and CHEETHAM.
Overall the best team won on the day and P.N.E. will have to improve dramatically at Highbury next week in order to turn the situation around.

North End Reserves were soon in trouble at Ewood Park when Blackburn Reserves took a two goal lead early in the game. Tommy Thompson, again trying out his injured knee, pulled a goal back from a penalty. Alston then hit a perfect centre for Thompson to head home the equaliser. Final score 2-2.

OCT 10TH DIVISION 1 RESULTS			
BIRMINGHAM C.	*0*	*SHEFFIELD W.*	*0*
BURNLEY	*1*	*BLACKPOOL*	*4*
CHELSEA	*0*	*BOLTON WAN.*	*2*
LEEDS UNITED	*3*	*EVERTON*	*3*
LEICESTER CITY	*2*	*BLACKBURN ROV.*	*3*
MANCHESTER U.	*4*	*ARSENAL*	*2*
NEWCASTLE U.	*2*	*NOTTINGHAM F.*	*1*
PRESTON N.E.	*1*	*MANCHESTER C.*	*5*
TOTTENHAM H.	*5*	*WOLVES.*	*1*
WEST BROM. A.	*2*	*FULHAM*	*4*
WEST HAM UTD.	*3*	*LUTON TOWN*	*1*

		Home					Away					
	P.	W.	D.	L.	F.	A.	W.	D.	L.	F.	A.	Pts.
Tottenham H'spur	12	2	4	0	15	7	4	2	0	16	6	18
Wolverhampton	12	4	1	0	20	5	3	1	3	17	18	16
West Ham United	12	4	0	2	14	7	2	3	1	11	11	15
Burnley	12	4	0	2	14	12	3	1	2	10	10	15
Blackburn Rovers	12	4	1	1	13	7	2	1	3	10	11	14
Manchester City	12	4	0	2	15	11	3	0	3	13	12	14
Arsenal	12	3	2	1	9	6	2	2	2	11	11	14
Preston N.E. ..	12	3	2	1	11	9	2	1	3	13	15	13
Fulham	12	5	0	1	17	9	1	1	4	7	21	13
Manchester Utd.	12	4	0	2	18	11	1	2	3	11	16	12
Chelsea	12	2	1	3	17	19	3	1	2	10	8	12
Bolton Wanderers	12	4	0	2	11	8	1	1	4	5	8	11
Blackpool ..	12	2	2	2	10	10	2	1	3	7	10	11
Newcastle United	12	2	2	3	6	11	2	1	2	12	11	11
Nottingham F'rest	12	2	2	1	7	7	2	1	4	6	9	11
Sheffield Wed. ..	12	3	1	1	10	3	1	1	5	5	11	10
West Bromwich A.	12	3	1	3	17	13	0	3	2	5	9	10
Everton	12	3	2	1	10	6	0	2	4	8	16	10
Leicester City ..	12	2	2	2	10	10	1	2	3	9	19	10
Leeds United ..	12	1	3	2	12	13	2	0	4	5	15	9
Birmingham City	12	2	3	2	11	10	0	1	4	5	11	8
Luton Town ..	12	1	1	4	3	9	1	2	3	7	12	7

Wed. 14th- North End Youth team beat Huddersfield Town 3-2 in the First Round of the F.A. Youth Cup at Deepdale watched by a crowd of 3,802. In a hard fought game goals from Peter Thompson and Jimmy Humes 2, together with some wonderful wing play by David Wilson, put Preston through to the next round against Liverpool.

Fri.16th Oct.- North End are again in London for the fourth time in seven away games this season and have yet to win. After missing ten league games Tommy Thompson returns after injury at inside-right in place of Farrall who had a nightmare game against Manchester City last Saturday. Alec Alston is included on the right wing in place of Les Campbell.

Arsenal have made two positional changes to the side that lost 4-2 at Old Trafford and have brought in Julians in place of Clapton.

....

SATURDAY 17TH OCTOBER

ARSENAL 0 PRESTON NORTH END 3

Sneddon, Walton, Alston

Att. 43,941

ARSENAL-*Standen, Wills, McCullough, Docherty, Dodgin, Groves, Henderson, Bloomfield, Julians, Herd, Haverty.*
P.N.E.-*Else, Cunningham, Walton, Milne, Dunn, Smith, Alston, Thompson, Finney, Sneddon, Taylor.*

The 'experts' say that in football, incidents and decisions tend to even themselves out over a season of 42 games. That was certainly the case at Highbury when Arsenal were reduced to ten men after 20 minutes of the game following an injury to Tommy Docherty. North End eventually winning the game quite easily.
Only three weeks earlier, Preston ended the game at White Hart Lane with only nine players and suffered a heavy defeat. In the early stages of the game there was little to choose between the two teams. Preston played a compact, close passing and moving game whereas Arsenal were far more direct using long passes and superb wing play. Arsenal created the early chances and only Fred Else in the Preston goal prevented them from scoring with some outstanding saves. Arsenal were awarded a penalty but somehow Wills contrived to miss his spot kick.
The injury to Docherty occurred as both he and Dodgin tried to intercept a cross from Alston. The two Arsenal players collided and with Docherty lying on the ground, Thompson passed the ball to SNEDDON who scored from close range. North End conceded a goal in similar circumstances at Spurs when Lambert lay injured. Sneddon caused Arsenal all sorts of problems by finding space to break forward through the centre of the home team's defence. Finney, Thompson and Sneddon continually interchanged positions leaving the 'Gunners' marking players bewildered as to whether to

ARSENAL-Back row (left to right) L. Julians, B. McCullough, B. Dodgin, J. Standen, J. Kelsey, M. Charles, G. Ward, J. Petts. Middle row-J. Bloomfield, L. Wills, T. Docherty, V. Groves, D. Herd, D. Clapton, J. Henderson. Front row-J. Barnwell, J. Haverty.

follow them or not. This indecision within the defence was the main reason why Arsenal struggled to cope with the intricate passing and running of the forwards from Lancashire.

At still only 1-0 down, Arsenal were still in the game even with ten men and Herd hit a thunderbolt shot against the post. Henderson and Haverty, on the wings, harassed the North End full-backs but failed to make the final ball into the middle count in terms of goals.

In the end it was left to JOE WALTON to hit a thirty yard screamer against the crossbar and down over the line to make the score 2-0. ALSTON finished the game off by scoring the third.

After last weeks dire performance against Manchester City, this first win in the Capital this season, lifted North End to sixth place in the table. The return of Tommy Thompson and his telepathic understanding with Tom Finney showed that better times might be around the corner.

North End Reserves drew 1-1 at home to Huddersfield Town Reserves, Byrne scoring the only goal.
Team-Kelly, Wilson, O'Neill, Fullam, Richardson, Hart, Ascroft, Byrne, Hatsell, Farrall, Campbell.

October 17th Division 1 Results and Scorers

ARSENAL	0	PRESTON NORTH END	3	
		Sneddon,Walton,Alston		Att.43,941
BLACKBURN ROVERS	3	BURNLEY	2	
Dobing, Dougan, Vernon		Pilkington, Douglas (og)		Att.33,316
BLACKPOOL	3	LEEDS UNITED	3	
Kaye, Durie, Peterson		McCole 2, Francis		Att.22,301
BOLTON WANDERERS	0	WEST BROMWICH ALBION	0	
				Att.22,581
EVERTON	0	WEST HAM UNITED	1	
		Musgrove		Att.30,563
FULHAM	4	NEWCASTLE UNITED	3	
Key, Cook, Hill, Haynes		Hale 2, Eastham		Att.36,293
LUTON TOWN	1	CHELSEA	2	
Brown		Livesey, Pacey (og)		Att.18,831
MANCHESTER CITY	3	LEICESTER CITY	2	
McAdams 2, Hayes		McDonald 2		Att.33,896
NOTTINGHAM FOREST	0	BIRMINGHAM CITY	2	
		Stubbs, Gordon		Att.24,904
SHEFFIELD WEDNESDAY	2	TOTTENHAM HOTSPUR	1	
Wilkinson, Young		White		Att.37,623
WOLVERHAMPTON WANDERERS	3	MANCHESTER UNITED	2	
Murray 2, Broadbent		Viollet, Stuart (og)		Att.45,451

In the International match at Ninian Park, Wales drew 1-1 with England. Jimmy Greaves scored for England in the first half and Graham Moore hit a late equaliser for Wales in a poor game that was hampered by wind and rain.
England Team-*Hopkinson, Howe, Allen, Clayton, Smith, Flowers, Connelly, Greaves, Clough, Charlton, Holliday.*

League Tables

FIRST DIVISION

	P.	W.	D.	L.	Goals F.	Goals A.	Pts.
Tottenham H.......	13	6	6	1	32	15	18
Wolves	13	8	2	3	40	25	18
West Ham Utd....	13	7	3	3	26	18	17
Blackburn R.	13	7	2	4	26	20	16
Manchester C. ...	13	8	0	5	31	25	16
North End	**13**	**6**	**3**	**4**	**27**	**24**	**15**
Burnley	13	7	1	5	26	25	15
Fulham...............	13	7	1	5	24	33	15
Arsenal	13	5	4	4	20	20	14
Chelsea	13	6	2	5	29	28	14
Manchester Utd.	13	5	2	6	31	30	12
Bolton W.	13	5	2	6	16	16	12
Sheffield W.	13	5	2	6	17	15	12
Blackpool	13	4	4	5	20	23	12
Nottingham F. ...	13	4	3	6	13	18	11
Newcastle Utd....	13	4	3	6	21	26	11
West Brom.	13	3	5	5	22	22	11
Birmingham C. ...	13	3	4	6	18	21	10
Everton	13	3	4	6	19	23	10
Leeds Utd.	13	3	4	6	20	31	10
Leicester City......	13	3	4	6	21	32	10
Luton T.	13	2	3	8	11	23	7

CENTRAL LEAGUE

	P.	W.	D.	L.	Goals F.	Goals A.	Pfs.
Liverpool	14	8	5	1	38	18	21
Manchester Utd.	13	9	3	1	38	20	21
Wolves	11	8	2	1	38	13	18
Sheffield Utd.......	14	7	4	3	27	17	18
Bury	14	6	4	4	24	18	16
North End	**14**	**5**	**6**	**3**	**26**	**22**	**16**
Derby C.............	14	6	3	5	18	14	15
Sheffield W.	12	7	2	3	22	19	16
Blackburn R.	13	6	3	4	25	24	15
Everton	14	4	6	4	23	21	14
Burnley	13	6	2	5	21	19	14
Stoke City	14	4	5	5	18	24	13
Chesterfield	13	5	3	6	19	25	13
Newcastle Utd. ...	14	4	4	6	28	24	12
Aston Villa	13	4	4	5	29	22	12
Bolton W.	13	4	3	6	17	27	11
Manchester City...	13	4	2	7	23	26	10
West Brom.	13	4	2	7	24	27	10
Huddersfield T....	13	2	6	5	13	27	10
Blackpool	14	2	4	8	28	37	8
Barnsley	14	3	2	9	13	41	8
Leeds Utd.	13	1	1	11	17	45	3

Tues. 20th-***P.N.E.BOARD MEETING-It was reported that Nottingham Forest had expressed an interest in signing Alston or Campbell. They had offered £12,000 for Alston and £6,500 for Campbell. It was decided to leave the decision to the Manager.***

GARBUTT RICHARDSON

Fri.-23rd Joe Dunn failed a fitness test and will be replaced by Garbutt Richardson for tomorrow's home game with second placed Wolverhampton Wanderers. Richardson will make his debut on his 21st birthday following some impressive performances in the reserves. He has been at Deepdale since the summer of 1957 after he was released by Bill Shankly whilst at Huddersfield Town.

Ron Flowers is back from International duty and will play at left-half for Wolves in place of Kirkham.

SATURDAY 24TH OCTOBER

PRESTON N. E. 4 WOLVERHAMPTON W. 3

Finney (pen), Taylor, Thompson, Alston. — Horne 2, Murray

Att. 22,612

P.N.E.-*Else, Cunningham, Walton, Milne, Richardson, Smith, Alston, Thompson, Finney, Sneddon, Taylor*

WOLVES-*Finlayson, Kelly, Harris, Slater, Stuart, Flowers, Deeley, Durandt, Murray, Broadbent, Horne.*

Deepdale witnessed a wonderful game of football played by two teams solely intent on scoring as many goals as possible in 90 minutes.

Wolves started the game at a blistering pace and soon took the lead. They employed a fast, direct style of play compared to North End's more skilful passing and moving game.

The game was played on the first rainy Saturday of the season resulting in a lower than normal crowd for this top of the table clash.

The game unfolded as follows:-

P.N.E. 0 WOLVES 1-MURRAY scored after 2 minutes with a powerful header after North End had conceded a needless corner.

P.N.E. 1 WOLVES 1-FINNEY was fouled in the penalty area and scored himself from the spot kick.

P.N.E. 1 WOLVES 2-A superb pass from Flowers found HORNE who hit a speculative cross shot from outside the penalty area which completely deceived Else and ended up in the net.

HALF TIME

P.N.E. 2 WOLVES 2-TAYLOR scored an equaliser.

P.N.E. 3 WOLVES 2-Finney flicked a ball onto THOMPSON from

MURRAY

ALSTON

a goal kick. Thompson ran with it from the half way line leaving defenders in his trail and hit a low left foot shot passed Finlayson.
P.N.E. 3 WOLVES 3-Fred Else was at fault once again when he completely miss-judged another attempted cross by HORNE, which put Wolves level.
P.N.E. 4 WOLVES 3-ALSTON outpaced the Wolves defence and hit his shot over the head of the advancing goalkeeper.
There were missed chances by both teams and two disallowed goals including one from Thompson which the crowd thought should have been given but was overruled for off-side.
A number of players had outstanding games. For Wolves, Broadbent, Murray and Horne gave the P.N.E. defence a torrid time in a goal hungry attack. Deeley had a quiet game for once being well marshalled by Joe Walton.
There is no doubt that Preston look a better balanced team when Thompson is playing, giving Finney more time and space to lead the attack with his artistry and pinpoint passing.
Finally Richardson, on debut, coped exceptionally well against the

forceful Wolves attack, growing in stature and self-belief as the game progressed. He showed a good temperament for the step up to the first team despite giving Murray too much room for the first goal. A draw would probably been a fairer result but Preston's sixth victory in the last eight games has given the supporters fresh optimism for the rest of the season. The fans put off by the weather would have been kicking themselves after missing such a feast of goals.

The National papers described the game as the match of the day in Division 1.
Finney was singled out and praised for his role in the team as a deep lying centre-forward.
P. N. E. were described as 'a pleasure to watch' and fully deserving of their fifth place in the League table.

OCT.24

OCT.24TH DIVISION 1 RESULTS			
BIRMINGHAM CITY	*2*	*FULHAM*	*4*
BURNLEY	*4*	*MANCHESTER CITY*	*3*
CHELSEA	*1*	*EVERTON*	*0*
LEEDS UNITED	*0*	*BLACKBURN ROVERS*	*1*
LEICESTER CITY	*2*	*ARSENAL*	*2*
MANCHESTER UTD.	*3*	*SHEFFIELD WED.*	*1*
NEWCASTLE UTD.	*0*	*BOLTON WANDERERS*	*2*
PRESTON NORTH E.	*4*	*WOLVERHAMPTON W.*	*3*
TOTTENHAM H.	*2*	*NOTTINGHAM FOR.*	*1*
WEST BROM. ALB.	*4*	*LUTON TOWN*	*0*
WEST HAM UTD.	*1*	*BLACKPOOL*	*0*

LEADING CLUBS DIVISION 1

		`P	Home W	D	L	F	A	Away W	D	L	F	A	Pts
1	SPURS	14	3	4	0	17	8	4	2	1	17	8	20
2	W.H.U.	14	5	0	2	15	7	3	3	1	12	11	19
3	WOLVES.	14	5	1	0	23	7	3	1	4	20	22	18
4	BLACKBURN	14	5	1	1	16	9	3	1	3	11	11	18
5	P.N.E.	14	4	2	1	15	12	3	1	3	16	15	17
6	BURNLEY	14	5	0	2	18	15	3	1	3	12	13	17
7	FULHAM	14	6	0	1	21	12	2	1	4	11	23	17
8	MAN. CITY	14	5	0	2	18	13	3	0	4	16	16	16
9	CHELSEA	14	3	1	3	18	19	4	1	2	12	9	16
10	ARSENAL	14	3	2	2	9	9	2	3	2	13	13	15

OTHER ITEMS OF NEWS

Dennis Viollet played his 200th league game for Manchester United and celebrated by scoring 2 goals in the 3-1 home win against Sheffield Wednesday. He remains the leading goal scorer in Division 1 with 14 goals.

Stanley Matthews, now 44 years of age, had his first try out of the season in the reserves in a 1-1 draw at home to Derby County in front of 5,139 spectators. His masterful wing play has been sorely missed by the 'Seasiders'.

North End Reserves drew 1-1 away to Bolton Wanderers Reserves with Hatsell scoring early in the game and Bolton responding with a late equaliser.

++++++++++

Tues. 27th-***P.N.E. BOARD MEETING-It was reported that referee Mr. P. Rhodes was only awarded 1 point for the P.N.E. v Wolves game as he "allowed far too much boisterous play and gave no protection to players. He did not apply the advantage rule sensibly". There was no further contact from Nottingham Forest regarding Alston or Campbell.***

Wed. 28th Oct-At Wembley England lost 3-2 to Sweden, the World Cup runners-up in 1958. Connelly and Charlton scored the goals but the partnership of Jimmy Greaves and Brian Clough didn't work as both players were too similar in style resulting in them often being in the same place at the same time. The team was jeered off the pitch at the end of the game.

Fri. 30th-Stanley Matthews passed a fitness test and will play his first Division 1 game of the season against Preston at Bloomfield Road tomorrow in place of Hill. Hauser comes in for Kelly. Mayers will replace Alston for North End.

TRANSFER NEWS- Colin Booth, the Wolves inside-forward who has scored one goal in three games this season, was transferred to Nottingham Forest for £20,000.

SATURDAY 31ST OCTOBER

BLACKPOOL 0 PRESTON NORTH END 2

Taylor, Finney Att.27,796

BLACKPOOL-*Farm, Armfield, Martin, Hauser, Gratrix, Kelly H., Matthews, Peterson, Mudie, Durie, Kaye.*
P.N.E.-*Else, Cunningham, Walton, Milne, Richardson, Smith, Mayers, Thompson, Finney, Sneddon, Taylor.*

'ANOTHER GOOD WIN FOR PRESTON'

Matthews still a weaver of spells

By Walter Pilkington

(L.E.P. article Monday 2nd November 1959)

WITHOUT being a classic, the latest of Blackpool's tussles with their Preston rivals was one to remember, not least because it afforded the 27,796 spectators rich and engrossing entertainment.

It was contested with unspared effort by teams spurred by local rivalry to give their utmost, win or lose. Consequently the play throughout was animated and interest was never allowed to flag.

Some individuals shone more than others, among them Matthews, Armfield, Gratrix, Farm, Durie, Cunningham, Finney, Richardson, Sneddon and Smith, but all the players contributed something to the game's ever-changing phases.

Blackpool had the sort of luck which seems to cling to teams going through a difficult period, in that little, if anything, went right for them. They could also fairly claim that both the goals which consoled Preston for their defeat at Bloomfield Road last Christmas were somewhat fortuitous.

When North End opened the score, Taylor's shot or centre was deflected by Armfield out of Farm's reach. An hour later Finney shot, a second through a bunch of players. Often enough such shots strike a leg, arm or body, but this went straight in with Farm at a disadvantage.

Further, Blackpool had their forward line disorganised to some extent by an injury to Peterson their South African inside-right.

Handicapped

He stayed on the field and did some useful things, but was handicapped by a painful ankle. His limp became worse the more it was aggravated by his plucky efforts to ride it.

Blackpool had two or three good scoring chances before Peterson's effectiveness diminished. They were either spoiled by alert, agile goalkeeping or the forwards did not finish well.

Peterson had as good a reason as anyone to feel embarrassed in this

Blackpool v Preston North End
Is there an England' Selector here?
27,796 MINDS WITH BUT A SINGLE THOUGHT
BECAUSE IF THE WHOLE BOARD OF SELECTORS HAD BEEN WATCHING TWO "STARS" WITH SOME 130 CAPS BETWEEN THEM, THEY MIGHT HAVE LEARNED SOMETHING
They're still Tops!!!
A FAIRLY EVEN FIRST HALF, WITH THE BLACKPOOL ATTACKS BREAKING UP AGAINST THE "SEA-WALL" DEFENCE OF CUNNINGHAM & WALTON, ASSISTED BY—
—A GROWING LAD NAMED RICHARDSON.
A RATHER MORE ONE-SIDED SECOND-HALF, WITH THE 'POOL SUPPORTERS COMPLAINING THAT IT WASN'T THEIR LUCKY DAY
The Ref. both linesmen, AND the ball are playing for 'em!
SOME BRILLIANT ACROBATIC SAVES BY FARM IN THE 'POOL GOAL
AND SOME ENGLAND-CLASS FOOTWORK BY MATTHEWS AND FINNEY
The result?
TAYLOR
FINNEY
BY MAKING THE BALL DO THE WORK, PRESTON FOUND THE OPEN SPACES BETTER
ONE AT EACH END.
FURNIVAL

"THE STARS"

respect. He shared with Thompson the chagrin of missing a simple looking opportunity.

Lapses of this kind were about equally divided, and Else's safe goalkeeping during an anxious first half hour for Preston, was matched by two splendid saves when Farm denied a goal to both Thompson and Mayers. Sneddon shot barely a foot wide with Farm out of position and when it was too late to matter, Mudie dropped a lob onto the Preston crossbar.

But, as a team, Preston were the more impressive and methodical combination, which fact became more evident the longer the game lasted. It took them some time to find the desired touch owing to tenacious and strenuous opposition from defenders never easy to beat but their superiority had become clearly apparent long before the finish.

Team-work

Preston moved with better ideas and understanding, thereby developing a rhythm and command lacking in Blackpool's display. In defence, too, North End were at least Blackpool's equals in keenness and adhesiveness. No one could be faulted in a well knit rearguard, although one or two stood out more than others.

Cunningham, for example, again proved himself a masterly exponent of polished full-back play, so making his admirers wonder anew why Scotland could possibly overlook a player so well endowed with uncommon ability in timing, resource and decision.

Richardson, Preston's powerfully built young centre-half, took his extended opportunity so well that his future indeed looks bright.

He was dominant in every sense of the word even though confronted with a tricky opponent of Mudie's wiles and ripe experience. Furthermore, Richardson did not allow himself to become flustered and thereby, either found or made time to use the ball to a purpose when he had won possession in the tackle or in the air. Attack after attack foundered on the solid bulwark his defiance created.

Richardson's resolute performance was reflected in the strong influence exerted by North End's young half-back line as a whole, and although averaging barely 22 years of age, Milne, Richardson and Smith, played with the assurance and skill of well established players in providing the soundest basis for a successful team-a resilient and capable middle trio. Richardson is to be complimented on the way he has taken his chance as Dunn's deputy.

Imprint of class

Preston's forward line set more problems than Blackpool's, although one never knew what to expect next from the ever youthful educated feet of the inimitable Matthews. I join gladly in the chorus of praise which has greeted the long awaited and certainly overdue return of Blackpool's brilliant veteran.

He was Blackpool's best and most tantalising forward, ever shifting his course, working and gliding the ball so easily and surely, effortlessly making it his servant.

Walton played him well, matching his

wits in a shrewd tactical struggle, but Matthews, nevertheless schemed or found openings for numerous passes of unerring accuracy. With better support in a finishing sense he might well have swung the game in Blackpool's favour.

Finney was some time in getting the measure of Gratrix and had to work hard in the first half for limited scope. Afterwards, in much the same way as Matthews, he exerted a potent sway upon North End's gradually increasing superiority.

To those who ask what is wrong with England's team I would commend a study of these two great players, each an artist in his own sphere. For so patently did they possess the guile, deception, elusiveness, quick thinking and fine craftsmanship which the much trumpeted leading young players of today manifestly lack.

OCT.31ST DIVISION 1 RESULTS

ARSENAL	*3*	*BIRMINGHAM C.*	*0*
BLACKBURN R.	*1*	*MANCHESTER U.*	*1*
BLACKPOOL	*0*	*PRESTON N.E.*	*2*
BOLTON W.	*1*	*LEEDS UTD.*	*1*
EVERTON	*6*	*LEICESTER CITY*	*1*
FULHAM	*1*	*WEST HAM UTD.*	*0*
LUTON TOWN	*1*	*BURNLEY*	*1*
MANCHESTER C.	*1*	*TOTTENHAM H.*	*2*
NOTTINGHAM F.	*3*	*CHELSEA*	*1*
SHEFFIELD W.	*2*	*WEST BROM. ALB*	*0*
WOLVES.	*2*	*NEWCASTLE UTD.*	*0*

		Home					Away					
	P.	W.	D.	L.	F.	A.	W.	D.	L.	F.	A.	Pts
Tottenham H'spur	15	3	4	0	17	8	5	2	1	19	9	22
Wolverhampt'n W.	15	6	1	0	25	7	3	1	4	20	22	20
West Ham U'td.	15	5	0	2	15	7	3	3	2	12	12	19
Blackburn Rovers	15	5	2	1	17	10	3	1	3	11	11	19
Preston N.E. ..	15	4	2	1	15	12	4	1	3	18	15	19
Fulham	15	7	0	1	22	12	2	1	4	11	23	19
Burnley	15	5	0	2	18	15	3	2	3	13	14	18
Arsenal	15	4	2	2	12	9	2	3	2	13	13	17
Manchester City	15	5	0	3	19	15	3	0	4	16	16	16
Chelsea	15	3	1	3	18	19	4	1	3	13	12	16
Bolton W'and. ..	15	4	2	2	12	9	2	1	4	7	8	15
Manchester Utd.	15	5	0	2	21	12	1	3	4	14	20	15
Sheffield W'day ..	15	5	1	1	14	4	1	1	6	6	14	14
West Bromwich A.	15	4	1	3	21	13	0	4	3	5	11	13
Nottingham For.	15	3	2	2	10	10	2	1	5	7	11	13
Everton	15	4	2	2	16	8	0	2	5	8	17	12
Blackpool ..	15	2	3	3	11	15	2	1	4	7	11	12
Newcastle Utd. ..	15	2	2	4	6	13	2	1	4	15	17	11
Leeds United ..	15	1	3	3	12	14	2	2	4	9	19	11
Leicester City ..	15	2	3	2	12	12	1	2	5	12	28	11
Birmingham City	15	2	3	3	13	14	1	1	5	7	14	10
Luton Town ..	15	1	2	5	5	12	1	2	4	7	16	8

LEADING GOAL SCORERS

VIOLLET	Manchester U.	14
SMITH	Tottenham H.	13
DEELEY	Wolverhampton	12
GREAVES	Chelsea	12
McADAMS	Manchester C.	12
MURRAY	Wolverhampton	12
DOBING	Blackburn Rov.	10
FINNEY	**Preston N. E.**	**10**
HERD	Arsenal	9
JONES	Tottenham H.	9

North End Reserves completely outplayed Chesterfield Reserves at Deepdale winning the game emphatically by 5 goals to 2.

Alston scored a hat-trick and Farrell added two more goals to keep the second team in the top six of the Central League.

Tony Singleton had a commanding game in the heart of the defence and looks a promising player for the future.

NOVEMBER 1959

Fri.6th Nov.-Dave Hickson, the Everton centre-forward, who has scored six goals this season was transferred to Second Division rivals Liverpool.

The team news from Deepdale is that Joe Dunn is fit again and will replace Richardson at the heart of the defence for tomorrow's home game against Nottingham Forest. Jim Smith is unable to obtain release from his National Service duties and Frank O'Farrell will play his first game since 19th September.
Nottingham Forest will remain unchanged from the team that beat Chelsea last Saturday.

SATURDAY 7TH NOVEMBER

PRESTON NORTH END 1 NOTTINGHAM FOR. 0

Cunningham Att.21,226

P.N.E.-*Else, Cunningham, Walton, Milne, Dunn, O'Farrell, Mayers, Thompson, Finney, Sneddon, Taylor.*

NOTT'M F.-*Thomson, Whare, Patrick, Iley, McKinlay, Burkitt, Gray, Booth, Wilson, Quigley, Imlach.*

In a game in which North End created numerous chances, it was perhaps fitting that the only goal of the game should be scored by the popular Scottish full-back WILLIE CUNNINGHAM. His shot in the 59th minute from outside the penalty area somehow found it's way through a crowded goal mouth and into the net after wrong footing Thomson in the Forest goal. Cunningham had been involved in a fascinating contest all afternoon with Stuart Imlach which neither player could claim to have won as they were so equally matched.

The goal by Willie Cunningham to win the game for Preston was only his 3rd in 11 seasons at Deepdale.

The goal was a cruel moment for 'Chick' Thomson as he had performed admirably in keeping the Preston forwards at bay almost single-handedly.

He saved efforts from Thompson, Mayers and Taylor and watched helplessly as a shot from Sneddon was cleared off the line by a defender.

At times he seemed to be having a personal duel with Tom Finney who had two half chances saved by the 'keeper and then hit the cross-bar with a header.

Finney was also instrumental in creating other chances for his colleagues which Thomson kept out.

Nottingham Forest never gave up and despite lacking a 'killer touch' in front of goal still managed to create chances for Iley, Imlach and

Quigley. Fortunately for P.N.E., Else in the North End goal was also in good form and had no difficulty in keeping a clean sheet.
Joe Dunn was back to his best in the North End defence and was ably assisted by the vastly experienced Frank O'Farrell
Preston have now scored in every game this season and this win was their fourth in succession. They have also won eight out of the last ten games and only trail Spurs by one point; West Ham edging them out of second place on goal average.
Tottenham Hotspur's first home defeat of the season at home to Bolton was the shock of the day and has given all the other 'chasing' teams belief that they can be caught.

++++++++++

NOV.7TH DIVISION 1 RESULTS

BIRMINGHAM C.	*1*	*LUTON TOWN*	*1*
BURNLEY	*4*	*WOLVES.*	*1*
CHELSEA	*3*	*BLACKBURN R.*	*1*
LEEDS UNITED	*3*	*ARSENAL*	*2*
LEICESTER CITY	*2*	*SHEFFIELD W.*	*0*
MANCHESTER U.	*3*	*FULHAM*	*3*
NEWCASTLE U.	*8*	*EVERTON*	*2*
PRESTON N.E.	*1*	*NOTTINGHAM F.*	*0*
TOTTENHAM H.	*0*	*BOLTON WAND.*	*2*
WEST BROM. A.	*2*	*BLACKPOOL*	*1*
WEST HAM UTD.	*4*	*MANCHESTER C.*	*1*

TOP 6 DIVISION 1

	P	W	D	L	F	A	Pts
SPURS	16	8	6	2	36	19	22
W.H.U.	16	9	3	4	31	20	21
P.N.E.	16	9	3	4	34	27	21
WOLVES.	16	9	2	5	46	33	20
BURNLEY	16	9	2	5	35	30	20
FULHAM	16	9	2	5	36	38	20

In the bottom of the table clash at St. James' Park, Newcastle United demolished Everton 8 – 2, White 3, Allchurch 2, Luke, Hughes and Eastham (pen) scored the goals with Thomas scoring two in reply for Everton.
Blackpool slipped to third from the bottom of the table after losing 2-1 at West Bromwich Albion despite Matthews having another good game following his return from injury.

North End Reserves drew 2-2 with Wolves Reserves at Molineux With Hatsell and Byrne scoring the goals. Lill scored both goals for Wolves including a thirty yard screamer, which gave Alan Kelly no chance in the Preston goal.

....

Thurs.12thNov.-Gil Lambert had the pin removed from his ankle.

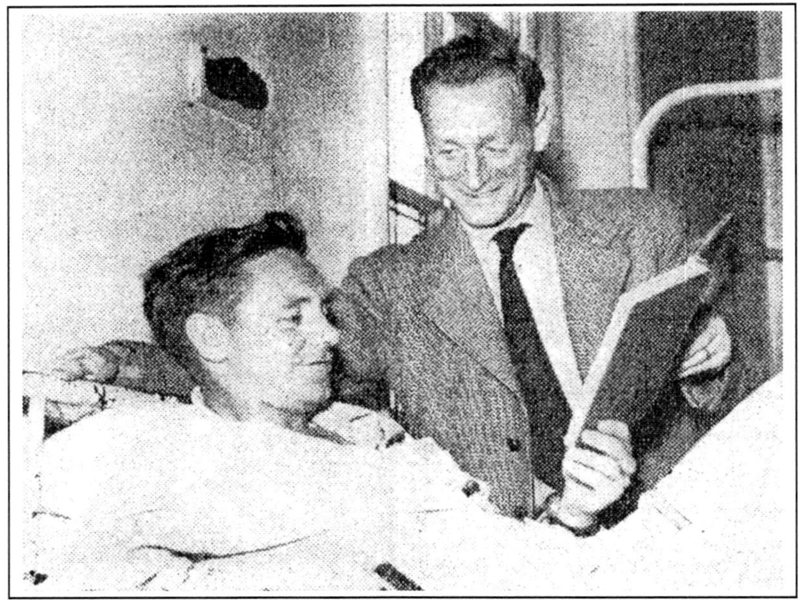

Tom Finney visiting Gil Lambert in hospital

Fri.13th -The early team news for North End's trip to Craven Cottage tomorrow is that Jim Smith is available from National Service and will replace Frank O'Farrell.

Fulham are unchanged from the team that drew 3-3 at Old Trafford last Saturday when Leggat scored a hat-trick on his return to the side after missing five games.

Fred Else will play his 150th game for Preston.

SATURDAY 14TH NOVEMBER

FULHAM 1 PRESTON NORTH END 2

Haynes Mayers, Taylor Att. 26,432

FULHAM-*Macedo, Cohen, Langley, Mullery, Bentley, Lowe, Key, Hill, Leggat, Haynes, Chamberlain.*

P.N.E.-*Else, Cunningham, Walton, Milne, Dunn, Smith, Mayers, Thompson, Finney, Sneddon, Taylor.*

Preston are the form team of the Division after winning their ninth game out of the last eleven to go second only on goal average to West Ham United. This was no easy game for North End as Fulham had won seven of their eight home games.

Fulham started the game brightly and were slightly on top during a goal-less first half with neither team able to create any clear cut chances.

The goals were all scored in the last 20 minutes. Fulham took the lead after 73 minutes when a powerful header from Jimmy Hill was brilliantly saved by Else at the foot of the post but the ball rolled to HAYNES who had the easy task of tapping it into the net. Else comfortably dealt with all the other attempts at goal including two late drives from Haynes, which he tipped over the bar.

The goal seemed to galvanise North End into action and after 76 minutes Thompson centred for the lively winger MAYERS to equalise.

With 5 minutes remaining, Finney on the left side hit a beautiful through ball to SAMMY TAYLOR whose shot was deflected by Langley and went through Macedo's legs for a soft goal that won the game. Macedo otherwise had a good game, fully justifying his recent selection for the England Under 23's team.

North End's defence was outstanding, especially Joe Dunn, who gave his best performance of the season whilst marking Leggat out of the game. The centre-forward was restricted to a long shot at goal and a few simple passes.

Cunningham and Walton also had fine games in nullifying the threat from the two wingers.

Haynes was easily the best player in a Fulham shirt and his passing was a joy to watch. He continually fed accurate passes both to the right and left wings but his colleagues did not make the most of them. Milne had a difficult time trying to stem the flow of balls played from the England player.

Finney 'the master' gave Bentley a torrid time

But the difference between the two teams was Tom Finney. His experience and guile whilst standing with his foot on the ball and crispness of passing never gave his former England colleague, Roy Bentley, any chance to dispossess him. Bentley admitted afterwards that his contest with Finney had been his hardest game of the season. Finney at time showed glimpses of his best form from years gone by and never wasted a ball. He was the inspiration behind North End's fifth consecutive victory. The Sunday Express headline, 'Finney Still The Master,' summed up his performance perfectly.

NOV. 14TH DIVISION 1 RESULTS

ARSENAL	*1 WEST HAM UTD.*	*3*
BLACKBURN R.	*3 WEST BROM. ALB.*	*2*
BLACKPOOL	*2 NEWCASTLE U.*	*0*
BOLTON WAND.	*1 MANCHESTER U.*	*1*
EVERTON	*4 BIRMINGHAM C.*	*0*
FULHAM	*1 PRESTON N.E.*	*2*
LUTON TOWN	*1 TOTTENHAM H.*	*0*
MANCHESTER C.	*1 CHELSEA*	*1*
NOTTINGHAM F.	*1 LEICESTER CITY*	*0*
SHEFFIELD W.	*1 BURNLEY*	*1*
WOLVES.	*4 LEEDS UNITED*	*2*

FIRST DIVISION

					Goals		
	P.	*W.*	*D.*	*L.*	*F.*	*A.*	*Pts.*
West Ham Utd....	17	10	3	4	34	21	23
North End	**17**	**10**	**3**	**4**	**36**	**28**	**23**
Wolves	17	10	2	5	50	35	22
Tottenham H.......	17	8	6	3	36	20	22
Blackburn R.	17	9	3	5	32	26	21
Burnley	17	9	3	5	36	31	21
Fulham..............	17	9	2	6	37	40	20
Chelsea	17	8	3	6	35	33	19
Bolton W.	17	7	4	6	22	18	18
Manchester Utd....	17	6	5	6	39	36	17
Arsenal	17	6	5	6	28	28	17
Manchester C. ...	17	8	1	8	37	36	17
West Brom. A. ...	17	5	5	7	30	28	15
Sheffield Wed. ...	17	6	3	8	21	21	15
Notts. Forest	17	6	3	8	18	22	15
Blackpool	17	5	4	8	23	28	14
Newcastle Utd. ...	17	5	3	9	29	34	13
Leeds Utd.	17	4	5	8	26	39	13
Leicester C..........	17	4	5	8	26	41	13
Everton	17	5	4	8	20	23	14
Birmingham C. ...	17	3	5	8	21	23	11
Luton T.	17	3	5	9	14	29	11

At Bloomfield Road, Stanley Matthews played his 600th league game in the 2-0 win against Newcastle United. He started his career in March 1932 and has now played 262 games for Stoke City and 338 for Blackpool.

Alec Alston scored both goals in North End Reserves 2-0 home win against Sheffield Wednesday Reserves. Garbutt Richardson, the Preston centre-half, was injured during the game and only a superb display from Alan Kelly ensured that the lead was held to the final whistle.

....

Tues.17th Nov.-Third Lanark inside-forward Bobby Craig signed for Sheffield Wednesday for £7,500.

England beat Ireland 2-1 at Wembley with goals from Baker and Parry. Bingham had equalised for Ireland with only 2 minutes left but England responded immediately when Baker, out on the left, crossed for Parry to score the winner.

Wed. 18th-In the F.A. Youth Cup 2nd round Preston beat Liverpool 4-1 at Anfield to cruise into the next round. North End's youth team were far superior in both attack and defence and led 4-1 at half-time following goals from Smith, Spavin and Thompson 2. After the interval they 'eased off' and could easily have won by a far greater margin.
Tom Bush, the Liverpool Youth Team coach said, 'Preston were one of the best youth sides I have seen for a long time and were far too good for Liverpool.'

Thurs.19th-Louis Bimpson, the Liverpool centre-forward, who had scored 37 goals in 102 League and Cup appearances for the club, was transferred to Blackburn Rovers.

Fri.20th-P.N.E. announced an unchanged team for tomorrow's home game against Bolton Wanderers.
Bolton will make one change with Malcolm Edwards replacing Brian Edwards who broke his ankle in training during the week. He now joins Lofthouse, Banks and Hennin on the injury list.

....

SATURDAY 21ST NOVEMBER

PRESTON N. E. 1 BOLTON WANDERERS 0

Mayers Att.28,723

P.N.E-*Else, Cunningham, Walton, Milne, Dunn, Smith, Mayers, Thompson, Finney, Sneddon, Taylor.*

BOLTON W.-*Hopkinson, Hartle, Farrimond, Stanley, Higgins, Edwards M., Birch, Hill, Stevens, Parry, Holden.*

On the day that North End announced a net profit of £10,150 in the last trading year, the team on the pitch maintained their tremendous recent form with a sixth consecutive victory.

Bolton Wanderers arrived at Deepdale unbeaten in the last seven games and were determined to ensure that they stamped their mark on the game in a typical blood and guts local derby. They fought for every ball and battled for every spare inch of space in their effort to extend their run.

The Wanderers tackling was ferocious and frightening at times with the aim seemingly to get the ball or the man. P.N.E. were also not afraid to 'mix it'.

The North End programme described centre-half John Higgins as 'that rugged piece of granite from the Derbyshire village of Little

Longstone, near Buxton who came to Lancashire over nine years ago from Buxton F.C., developed his effective stopper role when in the Army of Occupation in Germany.' The programme description of the powerhouse defender Higgins (pictured left) could not have been more apt. In the early stages of the game he incurred the wrath of the Preston supporters when he scythed down Finney on four occasions. The referee took no action against him. Roy Hartle also got 'stuck in' to the Preston forwards. Finney as usual dusted himself down and got on with the game. He continued to make life awkward for the defenders by shielding the ball close to his body, almost inviting the crunching tackles. In fact, despite his treatment from the colossus Higgins, the longer the game went on the better Finney played.

After a fairly even goal-less first half, Preston were by far the better side in the second period. Every time Finney received the ball he caused panic in the Bolton defence and created two clear cut chances, which were unfortunately wasted by his team mates.

It was Finney who eventually engineered the only goal of the game 4 minutes from time when he hit an inch perfect pass to Taylor on the left-wing. The winger crossed the ball for MAYERS to hit first time into the net.

P.N.E. at times were guilty of over elaborating whilst in possession of the ball and always wanting to make one pass too many. Whereas Bolton, despite overzealous tackling, still had the ability to move the ball forward in a more direct manner with Hill and Parry particularly dangerous. The North End wing-halves Milne and Smith were guilty of giving the ball away too easily and not marking Hill and Parry tightly enough.

Else in goal gave a commanding performance and was well supported by Cunningham, Walton and Dunn.

This win was Preston's tenth in the last twelve games and yet somehow they still can't wrestle the top spot from West Ham United. Next week P.N.E. visit bottom of the table Luton Town whereas West Ham are at Hillsborough for, what appears on paper, a far more difficult game against a Sheffield Wednesday team who have only lost once at home this season.

"THE MARKED MAN"

Furnival Cartoon L.E.P- 23/11/59

NOV. 21ST DIVISION 1 RESULTS

BIRMINGHAM C	*2*	*BLACKPOOL*	*1*
BURNLEY	*8*	*NOTTINGHAM F.*	*0*
CHELSEA	*1*	*ARSENAL*	*3*
LEEDS UNITED	*1*	*SHEFFIELD W.*	*3*
LEICESTER CITY	*0*	*FULHAM*	*1*
MANCHESTER U.	*4*	*LUTON TOWN*	*1*
NEWCASTLE U.	*3*	*BLACKBURN R.*	*1*
PRESTON N. E.	*1*	*BOLTON WAND.*	*0*
TOTTENHAM H.	*3*	*EVERTON*	*0*
WEST BROM. A.	*2*	*MANCHESTER C.*	*0*
WEST HAM UTD.	*3*	*WOLVES*	*2*

		Home					Away					
	P.	W.	D.	L.	F.	A.	W.	D.	L.	F.	A.	Pts.
West Ham United	18	7	0	2	22	10	4	3	2	15	13	25
Preston N.E. ..	18	6	2	1	17	12	5	1	3	20	16	25
Tottenham H'spur	18	4	4	1	20	10	5	2	2	19	10	24
Burnley	18	7	0	2	30	16	3	3	3	14	15	23
Wolverhmptn. W.	18	7	1	0	29	9	3	1	6	23	29	22
Fulham	18	7	0	2	23	14	3	2	4	15	26	22
Blackburn Rovers	18	6	2	1	20	12	3	1	5	13	17	21
Manchester Utd.	18	6	1	2	28	16	1	4	4	15	21	19
Arsenal	18	4	2	3	13	12	3	3	3	18	17	19
Chelsea	18	4	1	4	22	23	4	2	3	14	13	19
Bolton Wanderers	18	4	3	2	13	10	3	1	5	9	9	18
West Bromwich A.	18	6	1	3	25	14	0	4	4	7	14	17
Sheffield Wedn'd'y	18	5	2	1	15	5	2	1	7	9	17	17
Manchester City	18	5	1	3	20	16	3	0	6	17	22	17
Newcastle United	18	4	2	4	17	16	2	1	5	15	19	15
Nottingham F'rest	18	4	2	2	11	10	2	1	7	7	20	15
Everton	18	5	2	2	20	8	0	2	7	10	28	14
Blackpool ..	18	3	3	3	15	15	2	1	6	9	15	14
Birmingham City	18	3	4	3	16	16	1	1	6	7	18	13
Leeds United ..	18	2	3	4	16	19	2	2	5	11	23	13
Leicester City ..	18	3	3	3	14	13	1	2	6	12	29	13
Luton Town ..	18	2	2	5	6	12	1	3	5	9	21	11

At Turf Moor, Burnley hammered Nottingham Forest by 8-0 in front of 24,349 spectators. It was 5-0 at half-time and Jimmy Robson had already scored a hat-trick. In the second-half Robson went on to score two more. Ray Pointer with two goals and Brian Pilkington were the other scorers.

North End Reserves were well beaten 4-2 at Aston Villa despite goals from Farrall and Byrne. The North End full-backs were given the run around by Villa's wingers leaving Richardson in the middle of the defence far too much work to do.

Mon. 23rd Nov.-In the F.A. County Youth Cup 2nd round North End's Peter Thompson and David Wilson played for Lancashire against Manchester at Old Trafford. Lancashire won the game easily 5-0 with Thompson scoring twice in a dazzling display and Wilson also getting his name on the score sheet.

Tues. 24th-***P.N.E. BOARD MEETING-It was reported that Mr Slinger, the referee in the Bolton Wanderers home game, had only been awarded one point for his performance as he had allowed far too much rough play and was not consistent in penalising offences. He had also failed to give a clear penalty. The Board were informed that John Wylie would be going into hospital for disc trouble.***

Fri. 27th -P.N.E. announced an unchanged team for tomorrow's game against Luton Town.

<u>SATURDAY 28TH NOVEMBER</u>

LUTON TOWN 1 PRESTON NORTH END 3
Bingham Thompson 2, Mayers Att.17,174
LUTON TOWN-*Collier, Dunne, Daniel, Groves, Kelly, Brown, Bingham, Kilgannon, Morton, Cummins, Gregory.*
P.N.E.-*Else, Cunningham, Walton, Milne, Dunn, Smith, Mayers, Thompson, Finney, Sneddon, Taylor.*

PRESTON GO TOP

After winning their seventh consecutive game, North End finally achieved top spot in Division 1, but Luton Town provided stubborn opposition. P.N.E. are now two points clear of previous leaders West Ham United following their 7-0 humiliation at Sheffield Wednesday. The first half at Kenilworth Road was anything but an easy ride for Preston. Luton, fighting for their lives at the foot of the table, were easily the better side. They created two early chances but Morton and Bingham wasted the opportunities. Luton continued to play attractive attacking football but their finishing was weak and they found Else in the Preston goal in top form.

Bingham was just too quick for Walton down the right side and should really have created more chances for his colleagues after good footwork allowed him time and space to cross.

It was BINGHAM who eventually opened the scoring for Luton with a clever header on the stroke of half-time. Up to this point Preston had played in a casual lethargic manner giving the ball away too easily.

Within a few minutes of the second half North End looked like a different team, attacking Luton almost at will and it was no surprise when after 10 minutes THOMPSON scored the equaliser. Taylor had done the hard work in providing the chance.

Two minutes later Thompson laid the ball to MAYERS whose shot somehow eluded Collier in the Luton goal and rolled into the net. From this moment onwards P.N.E. were in complete control and

Finney began to weave his magic on the game tormenting Luton with a series of probing passes causing panic in the home defence.

LUTON TOWN
Back row (left to right) A. Brown, B. Morton, S. Dunne, R. Baynham, K. Hawkes, T. Kelly.
Front row B. Bingham, G. Cummins, J. Groves, J. Kilgannon, T. Gregory.

It was Finney who, with 6 minutes remaining, glided down the touch-line drawing the goal-keeper towards him before placing the ball into the path of THOMPSON to tap into the net. Thompson had not scored in the last four games and his two goals were just reward for some outstanding forward play. He had the 'knack' of being in the right place at the right time.

As far as statistics go this was North End's fifth consecutive away win in a sequence of eleven wins in thirteen games. You have to go back to the 1950/51 Division 2 promotion season when Preston won fourteen consecutive games to find a better run than the present seven. North End have also scored in all nineteen league games this season.

The Preston supporters will be wondering if North End can continue the run when struggling Everton visit Deepdale on Saturday.

Poor finishing by North End Reserves in their game at Deepdale against Stoke City Reserves cost them dearly. Dagger and Campbell both missed good opportunities and defensive mistakes resulted in a 2-0 defeat.

SATURDAY 28TH NOVEMBER
DIVISION 1 RESULTS AND SCORERS

Home		Away		Attendance
ARSENAL	2	WEST BROMWICH ALBION	4	
Groves, Bloomfield		Allen 2 (1pen), Robson, Kevan		Att.41,011
BLACKBURN ROVERS	2	BIRMINGHAM CITY	1	
Dobing, MacLeod		Barrett		Att,20,549
BLACKPOOL	2	TOTTENHAM HOTSPUR	2	
Charnley, Durie		Mackay, Smith		Att.17,085
BOLTON WANDERERS	3	LEICESTER CITY	1	
Stevens, Hartle (pen), Parry		Cheesebrough		Att.19,834
EVERTON	2	MANCHESTER UNITED	1	
Collins (pen), Thomas		Viollet		Att.46,095
FULHAM	1	BURNLEY	0	
Hill				Att.29,582
LUTON TOWN	1	PRESTON NORTH END	3	
Bingham		Thompson 2, Mayers		Att.17,174
MANCHESTER CITY	3	NEWCASTLE UNITED	4	
McAdams 3		Allchurch,Bell,White,McTavish (og)		Att.29,416
NOTTINGHAM FOREST	4	LEEDS UNITED	1	
Booth 2, Wilson, Gray (pen)		Revie		Att.21,366
SHEFFIELD WED.	7	WEST HAM UNITED	0	
Fantham 2, Finney2, Craig, Ellis, Wilkinson				Att.36,899
WOLVERHAMPTON W.	3	CHELSEA	1	
Flowers 2, Clamp		Tindall		Att.32,894

TOP OF THE TABLE

	P	W	D	L	F	A	Pts
PRESTON NORTH END	**19**	**12**	**3**	**4**	**40**	**29**	**27**
TOTTENHAM HOTSPUR	19	9	7	3	41	22	25
WEST HAM UNITED	19	11	3	5	37	30	25
WOLVERHAMPTON W.	19	11	2	6	55	39	24
FULHAM	19	11	2	6	39	40	24
BURNLEY	19	10	3	6	44	32	23
BLACKBURN ROVERS	19	10	3	6	35	30	23
BOLTON WANDERERS	19	8	4	7	25	20	20

++++++++++++++++++++++++

Mon 30TH Nov-Nottingham Forest signed winger Tony Barton from Fulham.

DECEMBER 1959

Tues. 1st Dec-Bill Shankly, former P.N.E. wing-half and manager of Huddersfield Town appointed manager of 2nd Division Liverpool in place of Phil Taylor.

P.N.E. BOARD MEETING-It was decided not to accept an offer of £7,500 from Sheffield United for Alec Alston.

Wed.2nd-Maurice Setters, West Bromwich Albion wing-half and England Under 23's captain, suspended for 14 days for being sent off after kicking an opponent in the 2-0 defeat at Sheffield Wednesday on 31st October.

Fri.4th Dec-Manchester United manager Matt Busby surprised the football world by announcing that Gregg, McGuinness, Charlton and Bradley have all been dropped from the team for tomorrow's game at home to Blackpool. Their places will be taken by Gaskell, Brennan, Pearson and Dawson.

The team news from Deepdale was that Preston have been forced to make one change for the home game against Everton due to Joe Dunn injuring his shoulder. His place will be taken by Garbutt Richardson. Everton are unchanged from the side that beat Manchester United 2-1 last Saturday with 19 year old Brian Labone facing Tom Finney.

SATURDAY 5TH DECEMBER 1959

PRESTON NORTH END 0 EVERTON 0

Att.24,463

P. N. E.-*Else, Cunningham, Walton, Milne, Richardson, Smith, Mayers, Thompson, Finney, Sneddon, Taylor.*
EVERTON-*Dunlop, Parker, Jones, King, Labone, Harris B., Harris J., Thomas, Shackleton, Collins, Laverick.*

NORTH END CHECKED

Attack lacked sting or snap

By Walter Pilkington

(L.E.P. article Monday 7th December 1959)

STOP Finney and you stop Preston! Club managers used to say this, and so often were near the mark. Now they are saying it again. The strong man, or rather youth, in Everton's team at Deepdale was 19-year-old Brian Labone, a Merseyside product and ex-captain of Lancashire schools.

The Goodison peoples' high opinion of his possibilities as a stopper centre-half was supported by his commanding display at Deepdale.

Behind him were backs of much better than average quality-the experienced former centre-half Tommy Jones and Scotland's right-back Alex Parker, and a goalkeeper, Dunlop, who knows his job and habitually does it well.

Labone caught the eye almost as much as the brilliant Parker because he put the fetters on Finney and thereby dislocated the North End attack.

Preston's wandering schemer and general seemed as if he could not get from under Labone's feet. He so seldom escaped this mobile quick tackler, that it was obvious North End would have a thin time unless the other forwards did something of a compensating nature. No one did.

Forward flop

The forward line flopped and for the first time this season, Preston failed to score. Thus, on a good day for the other leading First Division teams, and a depressing one for the strugglers, Everton and Birmingham and Luton excepted, North End alone of the top six clubs did not win. Their sequence of victories ended at seven.

Thanks to a good defence in which Else and Cunningham excelled, and some kind hearted shooting by Everton during prolonged first-half dominance, a home defeat was averted.

The measure of strength in the Deepdale side's sound rearguard may be judged from the fact that only six goals have been conceded in eight matches since Manchester City's shock 5-1 win at Preston on October 10th.

Fond of Deepdale

A set back, if only a partial one, was not unexpected. Everton felt good after chastising Manchester United in gaining a much needed tonic the previous week. They came to Deepdale all the more cheerful because Everton seldom return from this ground un-rewarded.

These trends influence the approach of players to a particular match perhaps more than people think.

True the teams change year by year, but there are always five or six who are either optimistic or pessimistic through recollections of past performances on certain grounds.

No doubt the more experienced Everton players told the youngsters they could not go wrong at Preston. So it proved, except that Everton did not take advantage of their best scoring chances.

I am not unduly stressing these points to excuse a disappointing result. Most onlookers would agree that North End, except in defence, did not do anything to justify pride of place in the Championship.

Self-made difficulties

Was it just an off day, a passing phase? There will be an early opportunity at Hillsborough to prove otherwise, remembering that Sheffield Wednesday in their last two games have scored 11 goals to none. I would hate to think that in successive matches North End could be so inept and wasteful in attack as they were against Everton.

Supporters who watch only the home games must have wondered how North End managed to record five consecutive away wins, having seen so much unproductive effort expended at Deepdale to gain a solitary clear cut home win.

The Everton match afforded a further instance of battering against a stone wall or, as I would prefer to put it, of forwards making it easy for the opposition by becoming hopelessly involved in difficulties of their own making.

So involved

The play aptly illustrated the futility of players bunching and getting in each other's way, constantly making two moves when one should suffice, and of generally getting into tangles through not being slick and progressive.

Oftener than not Everton had only to wait for the ball to come into the middle and battle their way out of the fruitless scrimmages that developed.

Preston's lack of nippiness in attack was as much a fatal handicap as one move too many. It was all so laboured and repetitive in character.

Perhaps North End would have fared better if the wing-halves had functioned more satisfactorily. Their effectiveness has declined since powerful displays against Birmingham, Manchester United and Wolves. The passing needs to be brisker and much more accurately directed.

Not much can be said in favour of Preston's inside-forwards on this occasion. They might have been happier at their work and blended better with the others if they had been spared some of the retrieving, fetching and carrying forced upon them by a want of dominance at wing-half.

Finney must have closer support these days to achieve his purpose. He ought not to have to look round and wait for other forwards to come into the picture. They should be there.

Rhythm suffered

The passing as a whole did not impress. It was slipshod rather than lacking in purpose. The wingers were as much at fault as anyone in this respect. Both had a poor game, as had their partners, and short comings were magnified by third rate finishing.

As usual North End became more persistent the longer the game lasted. No one can complain about any want of stamina. But they were never as lively as the Everton forwards and failed to take the few chances wrested from a tough, well organised defence.

They had no one comparable with the twinkling Collins in finding the spaces with a stream of choice passes. If Cunningham had not been in magnificent form Laverick surely must have profited from the fine service laid on for him by the Scottish inside-left. North End's opportunities compared favourably with those gained by Everton during a somewhat one-sided first half, but it is significant that Dunlop had a lot less to do than Else.

So much for the Preston attack in which only Finney, by his initiative, and skilful control tantalised Everton to any appreciable extent, and even he played the kind of game Everton wanted him to play. The rhythm which means so much to North End's style of play was impaired by the failure to produce cohesion and ease of movement.

Once more the defence played a self-reliant, composed game, even though Collins was given too much room. Richardson confirmed his promise by again ably deputising for Dunn.

DEC. 5TH DIVISION 1 RESULTS

BIRMINGHAM C.	*4 MANCHESTER C.*	*2*
BURNLEY	*4 BOLTON WAND.*	*0*
CHELSEA	*0 SHEFFIELD WED.*	*4*
LEEDS UNITED	*1 FULHAM*	*4*
LEICESTER CITY	*3 LUTON TOWN*	*3*
MANCHESTER U.	*3 BLACKPOOL*	*1*
NEWCASTLE U.	*4 ARSENAL*	*1*
PRESTON N. E.	*0 EVERTON*	*0*
TOTTENHAM H.	*2 BLACKBURN ROV.*	*1*
WEST BROM. ALB.	*0 WOLVES.*	*1*
WEST HAM UTD.	*4 NOTTINGHAM F.*	*1*

	P.	W.	L.	D.	F.	A.	Pts.
Preston North End	20	12	4	4	40	29	28
West Ham United	20	12	5	3	41	31	27
Tottenham Hostspur	20	10	3	7	43	23	27
Wolverhampton W.	20	12	6	2	56	39	26
Fulham	20	12	6	2	43	41	26
Burnley	20	11	6	3	48	32	25
Blackburn Rovers	20	10	7	3	36	32	23
Sheffield Wednesday	**20**	**9**	**8**	**3**	**35**	**22**	**21**
Manchester United	20	8	7	5	47	40	21
Bolton Wanderers	20	8	8	4	25	24	20
Newcastle United	20	8	9	3	40	39	19
Arsenal	20	7	8	5	34	37	19
Chelsea	20	8	9	3	37	43	19
West Bromwich Albion	20	7	8	5	36	31	19
Nottingham Forest	20	7	10	3	23	35	17
Everton	20	6	9	5	32	37	17
Manchester City	20	8	11	1	42	46	17
Birmingham City	20	5	10	5	28	38	15
Blackpool	20	5	10	5	27	35	15
Leicester City	20	4	10	6	30	48	14
Leeds United	20	4	11	5	29	50	13
Luton Town	20	3	11	6	19	39	12

(Preston's next opponents in bold)

With the last kick of the game North End Reserves were defeated 3-2 by Manchester City Reserves at Maine Road. When Fagan scored there was only just time to centre the ball when the referee blew full time.
This was unfortunate, for North End had played the much better football with some fine constructive footwork. Had their finishing been as good the result would have been very different.
They took an early lead through Campbell and when City got the equaliser through Fidler they fought back to regain the lead through Wilson who scored a fine goal with a thirty yard drive.
With only 5 minutes to go City got two more by Lister and Fagan to snatch a very lucky victory.
Alston led the line well which showed balance and Duncan, Singleton and O'Farrell were fine prompters. Kelly could not be blamed for any of the goals. North End could play much worse and win. (Extract from L.E. P. report 7/12/59)

Mon.7th Dec-In the F.A. Cup, Preston have drawn Division 2 side Stoke City away in the 3rd Round on 9th January, 1960.

Tues 8th-***P.N.E. BOARD MEETING-it was reported that Norwich City had made an offer of £10,000 for Alec Alston but manager Cliff Britton wanted a fee of £12,000.***

Fri.11th -In an exchange transfer, J. Brooks of Spurs, has signed for Chelsea and L. Allen, the Chelsea forward, will move to White Hart Lane.
West Bromwich Albion have transferred wing-half J. Dudley to Walsall.
North End have announced an unchanged team for the difficult trip to Hillsborough tomorrow as Joe Dunn is still unfit. Sheffield Wednesday have Tony Kay fit again and he is the only change from the team that won 4-0 at Stamford Bridge last Saturday.

SATURDAY 12TH DECEMBER

SHEFFIELD WED. 2 PRESTON NORTH END 2

Wilkinson, Craig Finney 2 Att.41,633

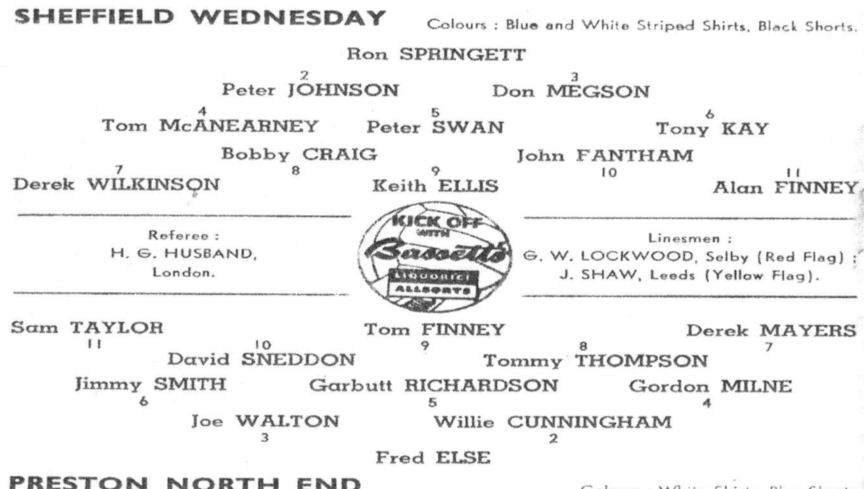

SHEFFIELD WEDNESDAY Colours : Blue and White Striped Shirts, Black Shorts.

Ron SPRINGETT

2 Peter JOHNSON 3 Don MEGSON

4 Tom McANEARNEY 5 Peter SWAN 6 Tony KAY

7 Derek WILKINSON 8 Bobby CRAIG 9 Keith ELLIS 10 John FANTHAM 11 Alan FINNEY

Referee : H. G. HUSBAND, London.

Linesmen : G. W. LOCKWOOD, Selby (Red Flag) ; J. SHAW, Leeds (Yellow Flag).

11 Sam TAYLOR 10 David SNEDDON 9 Tom FINNEY 8 Tommy THOMPSON 7 Derek MAYERS

6 Jimmy SMITH 5 Garbutt RICHARDSON 4 Gordon MILNE

3 Joe WALTON 2 Willie CUNNINGHAM

Fred ELSE

PRESTON NORTH END Colours : White Shirts, Blue Shorts

NORTH END STAY TOP DESPITE SECOND DRAWN GAME

Hillsborough witnessed a glorious game of football with goals, bad misses, goal-line scrambles, thrills, fighting football and 100% endeavour by both teams.

North End were in the lead twice but on each occasion Wednesday struck back almost immediately.

The goals all came in a ten minute spell just before half-time. FINNEY scored in the 31st and 40th minutes then WILKINSON and CRAIG equalised in the 36th and 41st minutes. Preston disputed that the first goal by Wilkinson should have been disallowed as Else was badly impeded when the speculative cross entered the net. Unfortunately these things happen in football and the referee failed to spot any offence.

Sheffield Wednesday employed the same tactics over and over again. These were simply to get the ball down the wings and hit crosses to test out the inexperienced Richardson in the heart of the North End defence. He was given a thorough examination by the robust Ellis and at times seemed out of his depth. It was a credit to Richardson that despite the constant bombardment he prevented Ellis from scoring for only the third time in eight games.

Finney scored both goals to bring his seasons total to 11

For North End, Finney should have had a hat-trick when he rolled a shot wide of the post. Mayers had an attempt deflected wide and Thompson another effort brilliantly saved by Springett.

The league leaders could have been three or four goals clear of their opponents if they had taken their chances but full credit must be given to Wednesday for their 'never say die' spirit in contributing to a thrilling match.

A fog descended on the ground during the second half and at times it was difficult for many in the crowd of almost 42,000 to see clearly what was happening. It was a testament to the quality of the football on display that nearly everyone stayed to the final whistle when both sets of supporters joined together to applaud the teams from the field. With half of the season complete, P.N.E. lead the table by one point from Spurs followed by Burnley, West Ham and Fulham a further point behind. Things could not be any tighter at the top.

DEC. 12TH DIVISION 1 RESULTS

ARSENAL	*2 BURNLEY*	*4*
BLACKBURN R.	*6 WEST HAM U.*	*2*
BLACKPOOL	*3 CHELSEA*	*1*
BOLTON W.	*4 BIRMINGHAM C*	*1*
EVERTON	*2 WEST BROM. A.*	*2*
FULHAM	*1 TOTTENHAM H.*	*1*
LUTON TOWN	*3 NEWCASTLE U.*	*4*
MANCHESTER C.	*3 LEEDS UNITED*	*3*
NOTTINGHAM F.	*1 MANCHESTER U.*	*5*
SHEFFIELD W.	*2 PRESTON N.E.*	*2*

LEADING SCORERS

VIOLLET	Manchester United	23
McADAMS	Manchester City	16
DOBING	Blackburn Rovers	16
MURRAY	Wolverhampton W.	14
SMITH	Tottenham Hotspur	14
CONNELLY	Burnley	13
GREAVES	Chelsea	13
POINTER	Burnley	13
WHITE	Newcastle	13
DEELEY	Wolverhampton W.	12
McCOLE	Leeds United	12
(including 4 for Bradford City)		
FINNEY	**Preston North End**	**11**
ROBSON	Burnley	11

		Home					Away					
	P.	W.	D.	L.	F.	A.	W.	D.	L.	F.	A.	Pts.
Preston North End	21	6	3	1	17	12	6	2	3	25	19	29
Tottenham H'spur	21	5	4	1	22	11	5	4	2	22	13	28
Burnley	21	8	0	2	34	16	4	3	4	18	18	27
West Ham United	21	8	0	2	26	11	4	3	4	17	25	27
Fulham	21	8	1	2	25	15	4	2	4	19	27	27
Wolverhampton W.	21	8	1	1	32	13	4	1	6	24	29	26
Blackburn Rovers	21	8	2	1	28	15	3	1	6	14	19	25
Manchester Utd.	21	7	1	2	31	17	2	4	5	21	24	23
Sheffield Wedn'dy	21	6	3	1	24	7	3	1	7	13	17	22
Bolton Wanderers	21	6	3	2	20	12	3	1	6	9	13	22
Newcastle United	21	5	2	4	21	17	4	1	5	23	25	21
West Bromwich A.	21	6	1	4	25	15	1	5	4	13	18	20
Arsenal	21	4	2	5	17	20	3	3	4	19	21	19
Chelsea	21	4	1	5	22	27	4	2	5	16	19	19
Manchester City	21	5	2	4	26	23	3	0	7	19	26	18
Everton	21	6	3	2	24	11	0	3	7	10	28	18
Blackpool ..	21	4	4	3	20	18	2	1	7	10	18	17
Nottingham For.	21	5	2	3	16	16	2	1	8	8	24	17
Leicester City ..	21	3	4	3	17	16	2	2	7	16	32	16
Birmingham City	21	4	4	3	20	18	1	1	8	9	24	15
Leeds United ..	21	2	3	5	17	23	2	3	6	15	30	14
Luton Town ..	21	2	2	7	10	19	1	4	5	12	24	12

North End Reserves drew 1-1 at Deepdale against Everton Reserves with Alston scoring. Alan Kelly was injured and did not play in the second half but North End comfortably gained a point.

Manchester United, again with four reserve players in the side, won their second game in succession 5-1 away to Nottingham Forest. Viollet 3, Dawson and Scanlon scored the goals.

There were two other hat-tricks in Division 1. At Highbury, John Connelly scored three for Burnley whilst at Ewood Park, Derek Dougan was on target four times for Blackburn in the 6-2 defeat of West Ham United.

In the F.A. Youth Cup 3rd Round, North End beat a very strong Durham side 4-2. Durham had won seventeen games this season before meeting Preston and were surprised at the quality of the P.N.E side. As in the previous tie at Liverpool, North End were far superior to the opposition and could have won by a bigger margin.
Peter Thompson, David Wilson and Alan Spavin were the main architects of the victory. John Barton, in goal, handled everything confidently and could not be blamed for the goals.
P.N.E. Youth team-Barton, Ross, Webb, Baldwin, Will, Hart, Smith, Wilson, Thompson, Spavin, Humes.

North End's share of the gate was £28!

+++++++++++++++

Fri.18th Dec-North End, sitting at the top of the table, face a tricky home game tomorrow against an inconsistent Chelsea side who blow hot and cold. Chelsea have lost their last four games conceding thirteen goals but have also scored three or more goals on seven occasions. Greaves has 13 goals, including a hat-trick in the 4-4 draw on the opening day of the season in the reverse fixture at Stamford Bridge.
Preston are unchanged with Richardson again deputising for Dunn at centre-half. Crowther replaces Compton in the Chelsea defence.

SATURDAY 19TH DECEMBER

PRESTON NORTH END 4 CHELSEA 5

Thompson 3, Sneddon Greaves 5 Att.15,775

PNE-*Else, Cunningham, Walton, Milne, Richardson, Smith, Mayers, Thompson, Finney, Sneddon, Taylor.*

CHELSEA-*Matthews, Sillett J., Sillett P., Anderton, Mortimore, Crowther, Brabrook, Brooks, Livesey, Greaves, Blunstone.*

NORTH END DROP TO SECOND PLACE AFTER 9 GOAL THRILLER

The last Saturday before Christmas usually results in a drop in the attendance at Deepdale due to the last minute Christmas shoppers. This year was no exception and despite the fact that Preston were top of the table, a dank, wet and windy afternoon together with the shoppers, resulted in the lowest attendance so far this season.

What a game the missing thousands missed. North End have been involved in some great matches already this season but this one must rank as the best to date and also perhaps, one of the most intriguing and thrilling games ever seen at the famous old ground.

Jimmy Greaves, the 19-year-old England forward, pulled Preston apart with pace, composure, control and precision finishing to score all five goals for Chelsea. He was almost impossible to mark with his quick push and run style of play. Greaves also had four other chances. One hit the post, another scraped the crossbar and two other powerful shots were saved by Else.

After the game the Chelsea manager, Ted Drake, said 'he might easily have had nine and beat my record of seven goals for Arsenal'. He was referring to the time in December 1935 when he scored seven goals against Aston Villa, a record that still stands for a Division 1 game.

CHELSEA

Back row l. to r. Anderton, Whittaker, Matthews, Mortimore, Livesey, Compton
Front row Greaves, Brabrook, P. Sillett, Nicholas, Blunstone.

How the game unfolded:-
P.N.E. 0 CHELSEA 1- after 14 minutes GREAVES outran a static North End defence to score from a pass by Brooks.
P.N.E. 1 CHELSEA 1- a minute later THOMPSON reacted first to reach a Finney cross to steer the ball home.
P.N.E. 2 CHELSEA 1- SNEDDON scored from a narrow angle after 23 minutes from a ball put through by Thompson.
P.N.E. 2 CHELSEA 2- after half an hour GREAVES received another pass from Brooks and waltzed round Walton and Else before tapping the ball into the net.
P.N.E. 2 CHELSEA 3- three minutes later GREAVES had his hat-trick. Else could not hold a shot from Brabrook and Greaves pounced onto the rebound to score.
HALF TIME

P.N.E. 2 CHELSEA 4- seven minutes into the second half GREAVES scored from a header after a cross by Brooks.
P.N.E. 2 CHELSEA 5- after 64 minutes GREAVES got his fifth goal from a centre by Blunstone.
P.N.E. 3 CHELSEA 5- THOMPSON pulled a goal back from close range.
P.N.E. 4 CHELSEA 5- THOMPSON scored a header from a Finney cross to get his hat trick.
With Preston just one goal behind, the fans urged the team forward and Chelsea hung on desperately against a constant onslaught for the last 10 minutes. Thompson headed over the bar and try as he might, Finney could not just find the space to hit a strong enough shot on goal.
P. N. E. fought tooth and nail to try and extend their unbeaten run to ten games but could not breach the Chelsea defence. Finney was brilliant at times and his tireless efforts could easily have resulted in another goal with just a little more luck.
Both teams had played attractive attacking football and provided the crowd with a thrilling game.

After 21 days at the top of English football this defeat resulted in North End dropping to second place in the table prior to the Christmas double header against Leicester City. Top of the league Spurs will play Leeds United.

+++++++

P.N.E. Reserves drew 1-1 away at Bury Reserves with Farrall scoring their only goal. John Barton, deputising for the injured Kelly, had a very competent game in goal and could not be blamed for the Bury equaliser three minutes from time.

DEC 19TH DIVISION 1 RESULTS

BOLTON W.	*0*	*BLACKPOOL*	*3*
BURNLEY	*0*	*LEEDS UNITED*	*1*
FULHAM	*0*	*BLACKBURN R.*	*1*
LEICESTER CITY	*2*	*WEST HAM U.*	*1*
LUTON TOWN	*2*	*EVERTON*	*1*
MANCHESTER U.	*2*	*WEST BROM. A.*	*3*
NOTTINGHAM F.	*1*	*MANCHESTER C.*	*2*
PRESTON.N.E.	*4*	*CHELSEA*	*5*
SHEFFIELD W.	*5*	*ARSENAL*	*1*
TOTTENHAM H.	*4*	*NEWCASTLE U.*	*0*
WOLVES.	*2*	*BIRMINGHAM C.*	*0*

Top half of Division 1

					Goals		
	P	W	D	L	F	A	Pts.
Spurs	22	11	8	3	48	24	30
P.N.E.	22	12	5	5	46	36	29
Wolves	22	13	2	7	58	42	28
Burnley	22	12	3	7	52	35	27
Blackburn	22	12	3	7	43	34	27
West Ham	22	12	3	7	44	39	27
Fulham	22	12	3	7	44	43	27
Sheff. Wed.	22	10	4	8	42	25	24
Man. Utd.	22	9	5	8	54	44	23
W.B.A.	22	8	6	8	41	35	22
Bolton W.	22	9	4	9	29	28	22

Mon 21st Dec.-North End Youth player David Wilson has been selected to play for England in a trail match at Corby on January 2nd 1960.

Thurs.24th-Christmas Eve-Finney has a torn muscle in his back and will miss the Christmas games against Leicester City. Alec Alston will take his place in the Boxing Day fixture at Filbert Street. Finney has played in every game this season and his twenty-three consecutive league games since last season is one of his longest runs of appearances for the club.
Leicester City are unchanged from the team that won 2-1 at West Ham last Saturday.

Christmas Day-At Ewood Park, Blackburn Rovers beat Blackpool 1-0 with a goal from Dougan in front of over 27,000 spectators.

BOXING DAY SATURDAY 26TH DECEMBER

LEICESTER CITY 2 PRESTON NORTH END 2

Chalmers (pen), Leek   Taylor, Thompson   Att.32,864

LEICESTER CITY-*Banks, Chalmers, Cunningham, White, Knapp, Appleton, McDonald, Cheesebrough, Keyworth, Leek, Wills.*
P.N.E.-*Else, Cunningham, Walton, Milne, Richardson, Smith, Mayers, Thompson, Alston, Sneddon, Taylor.*

INJURY TO WILLIE CUNNINGHAM CHANGES THE GAME

The second highest attendance of the season to date at Leicester for this Boxing Day fixture saw North End start the game very brightly with neat passing movements causing the City defenders all sorts of problems. It was no surprise when after 13 minutes Preston took the lead after TAYLOR lifted the ball over the advancing Gordon Banks to open the scoring.
The 'Whites' continued to press forward and had a further chance cleared off the goal-line. Meanwhile the Leicester attack was well marshalled, particularly by Cunningham and Walton, who gave the forwards no space in which to work.
North End easily had the better of the first half but had created few scoring opportunities.

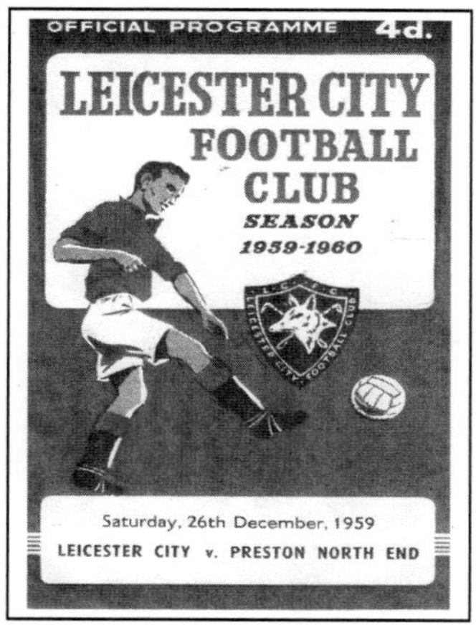

Within 3 minutes of the restart, North End increased their lead after Alston hit a cross and THOMPSON met it perfectly with his head to beat Banks. Then the incident that changed the game completely.
In the 50th minute, Willie Cunningham , the Preston right-back, twisted his left knee in a heavy tackle with Wills and was carried off on a stretcher. At first, North End still looked comfortable, but then after 63 minutes Jim Smith.

covering at full-back, fouled Keyworth in the area and CHALMERS scored from the penalty spot.
Cunningham returned as a passenger on the left-wing with his knee heavily strapped but still managed to steer a header just wide of the post.
Leicester started to dominate the game but found Richardson in the heart of the North End defence determined to head away everything thrown at him. A couple of goal line clearances by defenders kept Leicester at bay and just when it looked like Preston would see the game out the inevitable happened.
In the last minute, following a goal mouth scramble, LEEK was quickest to the ball and beat Else at close range.
Leicester just about deserved the point but it was rough justice for North End having to play nearly half the game with only ten fit players.
Preston remain in second position in the table but are now two points behind Spurs who won 4-2 at Elland Road. Burnley and Blackburn are hot on their heels, one point behind.

....

BOXING DAY RESULTS

ARSENAL	*0*	*LUTON TOWN*	*3*
BIRMINGHAM C.	*2*	*WEST HAM U.*	*0*
BLACKPOOL	*1*	*BLACKBURN R.*	*0*
BOLTON W.	*2*	*WOLVES*	*1*
CHELSEA	*2*	*NEWCASTLE U.*	*2*
EVERTON	*2*	*MANCHESTER C.*	*1*
LEEDS UNITED	*2*	*TOTTENHAM H.*	*4*
LEICESTER CITY	*2*	*PRESTON N.E.*	*2*
MANCHESTER U.	*1*	*BURNLEY*	*2*
SHEFFIELD W.	*1*	*FULHAM*	*1*
WEST BROM. A.	*2*	*NOTTINGHAM F.*	*3*

		Home					Away					
	P.	W.	D.	L.	F.	A.	W.	D.	L.	F.	A.	Pts.
Tottenham H'spur	23	6	4	1	26	11	6	4	2	26	15	32
Preston Nth. End	23	6	3	2	21	17	6	3	3	27	21	30
Burnley	23	8	0	3	34	17	5	3	4	20	19	29
Blackburn Rovers	24	9	2	1	29	15	4	1	7	15	20	29
Wolverh'pton W.	23	9	1	1	34	13	4	1	7	25	31	28
Fulham	23	8	1	3	25	16	4	3	4	20	28	28
West Ham United	23	8	0	2	26	11	4	3	6	18	30	27
Sheffield Wed'day	23	7	4	1	30	9	3	1	7	13	17	25
Bolton Wanderers	23	7	3	3	22	16	3	1	6	9	13	24
Manchester Utd.	23	7	1	4	34	22	2	4	5	21	24	23
West Brom. Alb.	23	6	1	5	27	18	2	5	4	16	20	22
Newcastle United	23	5	2	4	21	17	4	2	6	25	31	22
Chelsea	23	4	2	5	24	29	5	2	5	21	23	22
Blackpool ..	24	5	4	3	21	18	3	1	8	13	19	21
Manchester City	23	5	2	4	26	23	4	0	8	22	29	20
Everton	23	7	3	2	26	12	0	3	8	11	30	20
Arsenal	23	4	2	6	17	23	3	3	5	20	26	19
Leicester City ..	23	4	5	3	21	19	2	2	7	16	32	19
Nottingham For.	23	5	2	4	17	18	3	1	8	11	26	19
Birmingham City	23	5	4	3	22	18	1	1	9	9	26	17
Leeds United ..	23	2	3	6	19	27	3	3	6	16	30	16
Luton Town ..	23	3	2	7	12	20	2	4	5	15	24	16

After being dropped for the last three games, Bobby Charlton returned to the Manchester United side for the home game with Burnley. A crowd of over 62,000 saw Quixall score for United in the 2-1 defeat.

Blackpool avenged their Christmas Day defeat at Ewood Park by beating Blackburn by the same 1-0 score with a goal from Charnley.

At Deepdale North End Reserves beat Liverpool Reserves 4-2 with goals from Byrne 2, and Farrall 2. At one stage Preston led 3-0 but allowed Liverpool to pull two goals back before Byrne scored the best goal of the game to ensure victory.
Barton again had a good game, distinguishing himself with some brilliant saves. Byrne and Campbell were the pick of the P.N.E. players.

Mon.28th-The early news from Deepdale was that both teams are forced to make changes following injuries to players in the Boxing Day game. For Preston, Cunningham and Taylor are out and will be replaced by Wilson and Campbell. Leicester City have Keyworth and Leek side-lined with Lornie and Walsh taking their places.

LEICESTER CITY-Back row l to r- Ogilvie, Cunningham, Baillie, Chalmers, Stephenson Middle row- King, Keyworth, MacLaren, Appleton, Wills Seated- McDonald, Hines, Leek, Cheesebrough, Newman

MONDAY 28TH DECEMBER 1959

PRESTON NORTH END 1 LEICESTER CITY 1

Knapp (own goal) Cheesebrough Att.23,545

P.N.E.-*Else, Wilson, Walton, Milne, Richardson, Smith, Campbell, Thompson, Alston, Sneddon, Mayers.*

LEICESTER CITY-*Banks, Chalmers, Cunningham, White, Knapp, Appleton, McDonald, Cheesebrough, Lornie, Walsh, Wills.*

Anyone arriving at the game late would have missed both goals. Leicester kicked off into a bitterly cold wind, in watery sunshine and took the lead after only 15 SECONDS. A long pass found CHEESEBROUGH who was quicker to the ball than Else and hit a waist high shot into the net.

North End equalised after four minutes when a pass intended for Alston was hooked into his own goal by Leicester centre-half KNAPP.

Preston soon settled down to play in their usual short passing style whereas City relied too much on the long ball. Sneddon and Alston both hit shots wide. Sneddon then had another opportunity but after stroking a crisp low shot, with Banks beaten, Irish full-back Cunningham cleared the ball from the line.

At the other end Walsh missed a chance for Leicester. Thompson then hit the crossbar with a rising shot. In the dying minutes of the first half Alston and Thompson missed further opportunities to extend Preston's lead.

Wilson playing his first game of the season at right back in place of Willie Cunningham looked very composed and allowed Wills no room whatsoever down the wing.

Leicester City continued to struggle to create any cohesive forward play in contrast to North End who had no difficulty slicing through the City defence but could not capitalise on the chances created. Thompson was foiled by Banks yet again after seeing a rasping volley brilliantly saved and then missed an easier chance by shooting wide.

Lornie did have a chance to put Leicester in front but failed to connect with any real power and Walsh headed over.

Finney's guiding and composed influence was badly missed. Sneddon, however, had an outstanding game covering every blade of grass in his efforts to give P.N.E. the two points they deserved based on possession and attempts on goal.
Smith and Richardson gave strong performances in the Preston defence but North End eventually ran out of ideas and the spark disappeared as tired legs took over.
Preston have now drawn four of their last five games but still retain second spot in the table one point behind Spurs who lost at home to Leeds United. Burnley, Blackburn Rovers and West Ham United are a further two points behind.

+++++++++++++

MON. 28TH DEC. DIV. 1 RESULTS

BURNLEY	*1*	*MANCHESTER U.*	*4*
FULHAM	*1*	*SHEFFIELD WED*	*2*
LUTON TOWN	*0*	*ARSENAL*	*1*
MANCHESTER C.	*4*	*EVERTON*	*0*
NEWCASTLE U.	*1*	*CHELSEA*	*1*
NOTTINGHAM F.	*1*	*WEST BROM. ALB.*	*2*
PRESTON N.E.	*1*	*LEICESTER CITY*	*1*
TOTTENHAM H.	*1*	*LEEDS UNITED*	*4*
WEST HAM U.	*3*	*BIRMINGHAM C.*	*1*
WOLVES	*0*	*BOLTON WAND.*	*1*

TOP OF THE TABLE

	P	W	D	L	F	A	Pt
SPURS	24	12	8	4	53	30	32
PRESTON	24	12	7	5	49	39	31
BURNLEY	24	13	3	8	55	40	29
BLACK'N	24	13	3	8	44	35	29
WEST HAM U.	24	13	3	8	47	42	29
WOLVES	24	13	2	9	59	45	28
FULHAM	24	12	4	8	46	46	28
SHEFF. WED	24	11	5	8	45	27	27
BOLTON W.	24	11	4	9	32	29	26
MAN. UTD.	24	10	5	9	59	4	25

Thurs. 31st Dec.-Arsenal made a tentative enquiry about the availability of Frank O'Farrell but after deliberating decided not to proceed with a formal request.
The F.A. Youth Cup tie between North End Youth and Birmingham City Youth will take place at Deepdale on Tuesday 19th January 1960.

JANUARY 1960

SATURDAY 2ND JANUARY

WEST BROMWICH ALBION 4 PRESTON N.E. 0

Richardson (og), Jackson, Kevan, Allen Att. 23,917

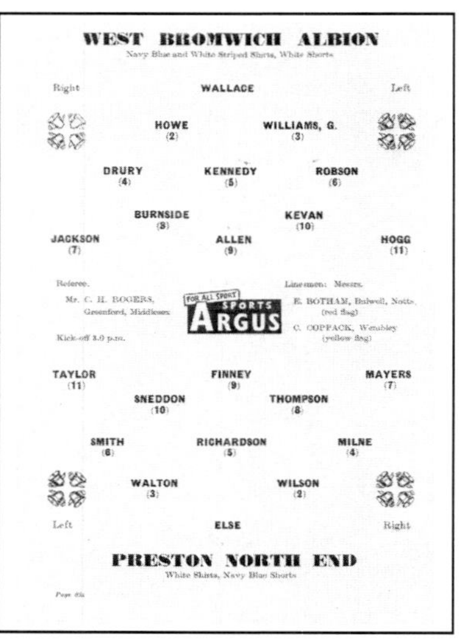

WEST BROMWICH ALBION

Navy Blue and White Striped Shirts, White Shorts

Right WALLACE Left

HOWE (2) WILLIAMS, G. (3)

DRURY (4) KENNEDY (5) ROBSON (6)

BURNSIDE (8) KEVAN (10)

JACKSON (7) ALLEN (9) HOGG (11)

Referee.
Mr. C. H. ROGERS, Greenford, Middlesex

Kick-off 3.0 p.m.

FOR ALL SPORT SPORTS ARGUS

Linesmen: Messrs.
E. BOTHAM, Bulwell, Notts. (red flag)
C. COPPACK, Wembley (yellow flag)

TAYLOR (11) FINNEY (9) MAYERS (7)

SNEDDON (10) THOMPSON (8)

SMITH (6) RICHARDSON (5) MILNE (4)

WALTON (3) WILSON (2)

Left ELSE Right

PRESTON NORTH END

White Shirts, Navy Blue Shorts

After missing two games Tom Finney returned to the P.N.E. team at centre-forward and Sammy Taylor resumed at outside-left. Alston and Cambell were left out from the side that drew 1-1 with Leicester City.

West Bromwich Albion named an unchanged team with Bobby Robson as captain in the continued absence of Setters who had been placed on the transfer list at his own request.

The P.N.E. manager, Cliff Britton, missed the game in order to 'cast his eye' over next week's Cup opponents Stoke City. It was perhaps a good job that he did not see the game as Preston gave their poorest performance of the season in being thrashed 4-0 by West Brom. and it could have been more.

On a grey, misty afternoon at the Hawthorns with a light drizzle falling, Preston were never allowed to settle down and play their neat close passing game.

Finney occasionally showed glimpses of his outstanding talent by gliding passes and swiftly moving from the middle to the wings to put pressure on the Albion defenders to follow him. Unfortunately all the Preston wing-halves and inside-forwards were too busy trying to counteract the constant West Brom. attacks, to provide Finney with any real support.

Surprisingly the first real clear-cut chance fell to North End. A corner was swung into the Albion penalty area and Tommy Thompson reacted quickest to slide a shot goal-wards. With the 'keeper' beaten, Williams stuck out a leg on the line and deflected the ball into the arms of Wallace for a fortunate escape.

West Brom soon responded to this early scare and on three occasions went close to taking the lead. Attempts at goal by Allen, Jackson and Kevan kept Fred Else very busy. The opening goal eventually came in the 34th minute in bizarre circumstances. Jackson crossed the ball into the area and RICHARDSON, the North End centre-half, attempted to kick it upfield. To his horror, the ball ricocheted off his left knee and went backwards, hitting the post before trickling over the line.

DEREK KEVAN
Scored the third W.B.A. goal

BOBBY ROBSON
Was the main architect of the victory

Up until this point, Preston had looked reasonably comfortable, but the goal opened up the flood gates. In the 43rd minute, Allen crossed for JACKSON to score with a powerful volley.

Smith had done a great job 'snuffing out' the dangerous Derek Kevan but right on half-time, KEVAN escaped his grip to score after good work by Jackson and Allen.
The second half opened with Albion bombarding the North End goal. Jackson shot wide from a narrow angle and Allen hit a pile-driver inches off target. It was not long until West Brom. went 4-0 up with ALLEN scoring a brilliant goal.
Hogg on the left-wing started to give stand-in full-back Wilson a torrid time with his pace and crosses causing Preston problems. Robson hit the cross-bar and Jackson and Williams had shots go over the bar before Albion finally eased off.
Finney almost pulled a goal back late in the game when he beat Robson then saw his shot cleared off the line by Williams for the second time in the game.
The only Preston players to come out of the game with any credit were Else, Thompson and Finney. This result saw North End drop to third place in the table and they have now not won in their last six games.

A notable feature of the weekend games in Division 1 was the number of goals scored-49 in eleven matches.
Newcastle United hammered Manchester United 7-3 at St. James' Park with Len White scoring a hat-trick in front of the biggest crowd of the day. It was United's heaviest defeat since losing 7-1 at Charlton in 1938/39.
At Highbury, Arsenal and Wolves shared eight goals with 8 different goal scorers. Whereas at Upton Park, Burnley showed that they were serious Championship contenders by thrashing West Ham United 5-2. Ian Lawson proving a capable deputy for the injured Jimmy McIlroy by scoring two goals as the Burnley forward line sliced through the Hammer's defence.
There were also four goals for Manchester City and West Bromwich Albion in home victories.
North End Reserves beat Barnsley Reserves 2-1 at Deepdale with goals from Farrall and O'Farrell. Joe Dunn's presence bolstered the defence and he came through the game with no ill effects and could be fit to return to the first team in the Cup tie at Stoke.

JAN. 2ND DIVISION 1 RESULTS

ARSENAL	*4*	*WOLVES*	*4*
BIRMINGHAM C.	*0*	*TOTTENHAM H.*	*1*
BLACKBURN R.	*1*	*NOTTINGHAM F.*	*2*
BLACKPOOL	*3*	*FULHAM*	*1*
CHELSEA	*2*	*LEICESTER C.*	*2*
EVERTON	*0*	*BOLTON W.*	*1*
LEEDS UNITED	*1*	*LUTON TOWN*	*1*
MANCHESTER C.	*4*	*SHEFFIELD W.*	*1*
NEWCASTLE U.	*7*	*MANCHESTER U.*	*3*
WEST BROM. A.	*4*	*PRESTON N.E.*	*0*
WEST HAM U.	*2*	*BURNLEY*	*5*

					Goals		
	P.	W.	D.	L.	F.	A.	Pts.
Tottenham H.	25	13	8	4	54	30	34
Burnley	25	14	3	8	60	42	31
North End	**25**	**12**	**7**	**6**	**49**	**43**	**31**
Wolves	25	13	3	9	63	49	29
Blackburn R.	25	13	3	9	45	37	29
West Ham	25	13	3	9	49	47	29
Fulham..............	25	12	4	9	47	49	29
Bolton W.	25	12	4	9	33	29	28
Sheffield W.	25	11	5	9	46	31	27
West Brom.........	25	10	6	9	49	39	26
Newcastle U.	25	10	5	10	54	52	25
Manchester U. ...	25	10	5	10	62	54	25
Manchester C. ...	25	11	2	12	56	53	24
Chelsea	25	9	6	10	48	55	24
Blackpool	25	9	5	11	37	38	23
Arsenal	25	8	6	11	42	53	22
Leicester City......	25	6	9	10	50	54	21
Nottingham F. ...	25	9	3	13	31	47	21
Everton	25	7	6	12	37	47	20
Leeds United	25	6	7	12	40	59	19
Birmingham	25	6	5	14	32	48	17
Luton Town	25	5	7	13	28	46	17

LEADING SCORERS (JAN. 2ND 1960)

VIOLLET	Man. Utd.	25
GREAVES	Chelsea	20
McADAMS	Man. City	19
McCOLE	Leeds Utd.	17
WHITE	Newcastle United	17
MURRAY	Wolves.	16
DOBING	Blackburn Rovers	15
CONNELLY	Burnley	15
SMITH	Tottenham Hotspur	15
POINTER	Burnley	13
ROBSON	Burnley	13

Mon.4th Jan.-North End's wing-half, John Wylie, who has not kicked a ball since September in the reserves, was admitted to hospital for fourteen days for observation on his back problem.
Gil Lambert is back in light training but is still some way off full fitness.

Tues.5th-Leicester City wing-half, J. Newman, who has made nine appearances this season was transferred to Plymouth Argyle.
Wed.6th-Maurice Setters, the W.B.A. wing-half, was transferred to Manchester United for £30,000.
Nat Lofthouse, Bolton Wanderers and England centre-forward, was forced to retire from all football due to an ankle injury.
Cliff Britton stated that Willie Cunningham has a wrenched knee and strained ligaments and will not be fit for the Cup Tie at Stoke.
Fri.8th-After a week of dense fog, the Met. Office has stated that although it will remain cold, most of the Cup ties tomorrow should go ahead. Dunn will return to the P.N.E. side after missing six games with a shoulder injury. North End have sold 4,000 tickets for the game. Stoke City goalkeeper, Bill Robertson, will return to the side.

SATURDAY 9TH JANUARY

F.A.CUP THIRD ROUND

ASTON VILLA	**2**	**LEEDS UNITED**	**1**	
McParland, Wylie		McCole		43,474
BATH CITY	**0**	**BRIGHTON & HOVE ALBION**	**1**	
		Tiddy		18,015
BLACKPOOL	**3**	**MANSFIELD TOWN**	**0**	
Durie 3				18,812
BOURNEMOUTH	**1**	**YORK CITY**	**0**	
Southren				14,749
BRADFORD CITY	**3**	**EVERTON**	**0**	
Jackson, Reid, Stokes				23,550
BRISTOL CITY	**2**	**CHARLTON ATHLETIC**	**3**	
Atyeo, Cavanagh		Lawrie 3 (1 pen.)		18,400
BRISTOL ROVERS	**0**	**DONCASTER ROVERS**	**0**	
				15,522
BURY	**1**	**BOLTON WANDERERS**	**1**	
Higgins (og)		Parry		35,000
CARDIFF CITY	**0**	**PORT VALE**	**2**	
		Steele, Portwood		25,500
CHELSEA	**5**	**BRADFORD PARK AVENUE**	**1**	
Blunstone, Greaves, Brabrook 2, Livesey		Allan		32,212
CREWE ALEXANDRA	**2**	**WORKINGTON**	**0**	
Llewellyn 2				9,427
DERBY COUNTY	**2**	**MANCHESTER UNITED**	**4**	
Thompson, Barrowcliffe		Scanlon 2, Goodwin, Charlton		33,297
EXETER CITY	**1**	**LUTON TOWN**	**2**	
Daniel (og)		Turner 2		20,193
FULHAM	**5**	**HULL CITY**	**0**	
Chamberlain, Hill, Leggat 2, Cook				22,157
GILLINGHAM	**1**	**SWANSEA TOWN**	**4**	
Griffiths (og)		Williams H. 2, Jones B, Hughes		15,301
HUDDERSFIELD TOWN	**1**	**WEST HAM UNITED**	**1**	
Law		Dick		30,526
IPSWICH TOWN	**2**	**PETERBOROUGH UNITED**	**3**	
Millward, Phillips		Emery 2, Rayner		26,000
LINCOLN CITY	**1**	**BURNLEY**	**1**	
Harbertson		Pointer		21,693
LIVERPOOL	**2**	**LEYTON ORIENT**	**1**	
Hunt 2		Foster		40,343
MANCHESTER CITY	**1**	**SOUTHAMPTON**	**5**	
Barlow		Reeves 4, O'Brien		42,065
NEWCASTLE UNITED	**2**	**WOVERHAMPTON WANDERERS**	**2**	
Allchurch, Eastham		Flowers, Clamp (pen),		62,443
NEWPORT COUNTY	**0**	**TOTTENHAM HOTSPUR**	**4**	
		Blanchflower, Allen 2, Smith		22,655
NOTTINGHAM FOREST	**1**	**READING**	**0**	
Iley				28,579
ROTHERHAM UNITED	**2**	**ARSENAL**	**2**	
Sawyer, Myerscough (pen)		Julians, Williams D. (og)		24,447
SCUNTHORPE UNITED	**1**	**CRYSTAL PALACE**	**0**	
Middleton				12,561
SHEFFIELD UNITED	**3**	**PORTSMOUTH**	**0**	
Pace 2, Lewis				19,528

SHEFFIELD WEDNESDAY	**2**	**MIDDLESBROUGH**	**1**
McAnearney T. (pen), Ellis		**Clough**	**49,580**
STOKE CITY	**1**	**PRESTON NORTH END**	**1**
Howitt		**Sneddon**	**38,465**
SUNDERLAND	**1**	**BLACKBURN ROVERS**	**1**
Lawther		**Dobing**	**34,129**
WATFORD	**2**	**BIRMINGHAM CITY**	**1**
Uphill, Holton		**Hooper**	**31,500**
WEST BROMWICH ALBION	**3**	**PLYMOUTH ARGYLE**	**2**
Kevan 3		**Anderson, Penk**	**27,548**
WREXHAM	**1**	**LEICESTER CITY**	**2**
Weston		**Cheesebrough, Leek**	**22,560**

++++++++++++++++++++++

STOKE CITY V PRESTON NORTH END

STOKE C.-*Robertson, McCue, Allen, Asprey, Andrew, Cairns, Newlands, Wilson, King, Wilshaw, Howitt.*

P.N.E.-*Else, Wilson, Walton, Milne, Dunn, Smith, Mayers, Thompson, Finney, Sneddon, Taylor.*

Stoke started the game determined to put on a show for their supporters in a crowd double the size of the normal gate at the Victoria Ground and surprised P.N.E. with their early onslaught. Once again North End conceded an early goal with a gift to the opposition. Walton attempted to play a simple back pass to Else but under-hit the ball and HOWITT intercepted the pass and gleefully tapped the ball into the empty net with Else stranded.

The clinging mud made playing 'touch football' difficult but North End soon started to look more solid and imposed themselves on the game. Wilson had a much better game than last week at W.B.A. and Dunn added strength and experience to the defence.

Sneddon was everywhere, holding the ball, placing passes and waiting for the slightest chance. Eventually Preston equalised and Finney was at the heart of the move. He drew the centre-half out wide and then dribbled the ball past him before two other defenders converged on him. With precision timing he centred the ball to SNEDDON in acres of space, to head home an equaliser.

Taylor had the beating of the full-back down the left wing but Mayers was unable to make any progress against Allen on the right side. This resulted in the North End attack looking decidedly lob-sided with most balls being played to the left wing in order to make progress.

Both teams cancelled each other out in the second half with Preston's best chances falling to Thompson and Finney. The main talking point was when experienced referee Arthur Ellis awarded an indirect free-kick to Preston in the penalty area for obstruction. Finney had played the ball between two Stoke defenders and as he attempted to run around them to collect the ball, he was tripped by Allen. Finney after the game said that this should have been a certain penalty but Ellis viewed the incident differently.

Late in the match, Stoke had an opportunity to win the game but Else leapt sideways to knock the ball around the post from a shot by Cunliffe.

The replay will be at 7.15pm on Tuesday at Deepdale.

STOKE CITY

Back row left to right- Ford, Wilshaw, Asprey, Robertson, Hall, Andrews, Allen, Ratcliffe.

Front row- Howitt, Cairns, Newlands, Thomson, King, Bowyer.

THE SHOCK OF THE DAY was at Maine Road where Third Division Southampton pulled off an astonishing 5-1 victory to knock Manchester City out of the Cup.
When Colin Barlow put City ahead the fans must have thought a victory was on the cards, but they did not account for Derek Reeves scoring four goals to shatter their dreams.
Reeves had already scored twenty-eight League goals and two Cup goals prior to the game.

Preston brought the Reserve game against Burnley forward from the 15th April and the teams fought out an entertaining 1-1 draw at Deepdale. Campbell scored for Preston but the stars of the game were goalkeepers Kelly and McDonald who both pulled off some brilliant saves.

Mon.11th-In the F.A. Cup 4th Round draw, North End will play Bristol Rovers or Doncaster Rovers on 30th January if they can overcome Stoke City in tomorrow night's replay.

Tues.12th-The early team news is that North End will be unchanged but Stoke make one change with 38 year old Frank Bowyer replacing Wilshaw at inside-forward.

TUESDAY 12TH JANUARY
F.A.CUP THIRD ROUND REPLAY

PRESTON NORTH END 3 STOKE CITY 1

Finney, Thompson, Mayers Bowyer Att.35,352

P.N.E.-*Else, Wilson, Walton, Milne, Dunn, Smith, Mayers, Thompson, Finney, Sneddon, Taylor.*

STOKE C.-*Robertson, McCue, Allen, Asprey, Andrew, Cairns, Newlands, Bowyer, King, Wilson, Howitt.*

Tom Finney was the inspiration and the catalyst behind this Preston victory against a gallant Stoke City side.

A crowd of over 35,000 witnessed North End play their most convincing football for some time in recording a first victory in competitive football since 28th November 1959.

The pitch was in superb condition for the time of year, which enabled both sides to keep the ball on the ground, creating a fast flowing game. For once North End 'drew first blood' and what a goal it was. After 19 minutes of 'nip and tuck' football FINNEY put Preston ahead with a brilliant solo goal to turn back the clock and remind people of his mesmerising skills. He gathered the ball on the left wing and Andrew tried to tackle him, but Finney just side-stepped the player and with two other Stoke defenders converging on him, unleashed an unstoppable shot from a narrow angle into the net. The crowd went wild with

TOM FINNEY
Was involved in all three goals

admiration and the Stoke players looked on in bewilderment.
A quarter of an hour later, Finney was fouled by Andrew, he rose to his feet quickly and placed the free kick directly into the path of THOMPSON who hit a low ground shot from twenty yards to increase Preston's lead. In the second-half North End went 3-0 up when, after 68 minutes, Robertson could not hold a powerful shot from Finney and MAYERS had the simple task of scoring.
Despite trailing since early in the game, Stoke still caused plenty of problems for the Preston defence.
Wilson and Walton had to be at their best to prevent the speedy Stoke wingers making progress and Joe Dunn had a 'battle royal' with centre-forward King but just about came out on top. Smith and Milne did well in their defensive roles but found time to support the forwards.
When Stoke did eventually break through, they found Else in immaculate form. He dealt with everything that was thrown at him and his performance can best be summed up by one particular save. King was clean through on goal and hit a thunderbolt which Else deflected wide with one hand, diving full length across his goal. The crowd roared their appreciation of the save and watched as the forward sat on the ground and shook his head in wonderment. Then in spontaneous admiration he joined in the applause.
Eventually Stoke did pull a goal back through BOWYER but it was too late.
The Daily Mirror headline 'FINNEY WONDER GOAL-Tantalising Tom turns on a Cup Display fit for Wembley', sums up the game completely.

....

Other F.A. Cup 3rd Round Replay Results

Tues. 12th Jan.

BURNLEY	**2**	**LINCOLN CITY**	**0**
DONCASTER ROVERS	**1**	**BRISTOL ROVERS**	**2**

Wed. 13th

ARSENAL	**1**	**ROTHERHAM UNITED**	**1**
BLACKBURN ROVERS	**4**	**SUNDERLAND**	**1**
BOLTON WANDERERS	**4**	**BURY**	**2**
WEST HAM UNITED	**1**	**HUDDERSFIELD TOWN**	**5**
WOLVERHAMPTON W.	**4**	**NEWCASTLE UNITED**	**2**

SHOCK OF THE NIGHT-Second Division Huddersfield Town 'hammered' West Ham United 5-1 at Upton Park. Nineteen years old Dennis Law was the star of the game and despite the fact that he did not score, he certainly inspired his team to achieve a famous victory.

Thurs.14th-After scoring thirteen goals in twenty-one League games for Wrexham in Division 3, D. Weston joined Birmingham City for £14,000.

Fri. 15th-Cunningham is fit and will return to the North End team in place of Wilson for tomorrow's home game against Newcastle United. This will bring together, for the first time in many weeks, the same team that took P.N.E. to the top of Division 1 last November. The Reserve game at W.B.A. has been postponed due to the state of the ground.

A number of League games have already been called off, including the Division 1 game at Bolton v Luton and many more are doubtful due to the snow and ice around the country.

SATURDAY 16TH JANUARY

PRESTON NORTH END 1 NEWCASTLE UTD 2

Finney — Cunningham (og), Eastham

Att.24,353

P.N.E.-*Else, Cunningham, Walton, Milne, Dunn, Smith, Mayers, Thompson, Finney, Sneddon, Taylor*

NEWCASTLE UTD.-*Harvey, Keith, McMichael, Scoular, Heslop, Bell, Hughes, Eastham, White, Allchurch, Luke*

North End dropped down to fourth place after suffering their third home defeat of the season and they have now gone seven League games without a win. In a poor game neither side really deserved the two points.

It was a fine, bright and cold afternoon at Deepdale with some late winter sunshine just about taking a little of the frost hardness out of the pitch. A keen north-westerly wind blew from end to end and Newcastle had the advantage of it behind them in the first half.

P.N.E.'s approach work in the opening 15 minutes was good but the finishing was very poor. Thompson sliced a shot wide and Smith hit a rising drive too high. Finney was tightly marked by young Heslop and was given little or no room to impose himself on the game.

The basic football on display was lacklustre due to the difficulty of controlling the ball on the hard surface and the problem of judging the bounce.

Virtually all the scoring attempts by Newcastle in the first half came from Allchurch but on each occasion he failed to find the target. Eventually after 30 minutes the same player drove the ball at goal only to see Else catch it cleanly just under the crossbar.

The only other real action at the other end came from a Thompson through ball to Finney, who could not bring it under control quickly enough and Harvey dived to take the ball from his feet.

The teams left the field with the game goal-less and supporters feeling that they had been 'short changed'.

Cunningham returned for the second half with his left knee heavily strapped and he soon looked in some discomfort when running for the ball.

The second period started much better with both teams ‘stepping up a gear’. Allchurch once more had a header and shot saved by Else but really should have done better from the number of opportunities that had fallen to him. Scoular and Eastham began to orchestrate all the penetrating moves for Newcastle and their influence was to prove the difference between the two teams.
For Preston, Finney for once broke free of his marker and drilled a perfect ball to the feet of Thompson but the forward hesitated and the chance was lost.
After 54 minutes North End took the lead with a typical Finney goal. Thompson played the ball to him and FINNEY hit an unerring left foot shot into the net.

GEORGE EASTHAM **IVOR ALLCHURCH**

North End strived for a second goal to kill the game off and Finney shot just inches too high after cutting in from the right wing.
Newcastle began to ‘wobble’ but Finney ended up as a one man attack with little support. Mayers on the right-wing had a nightmare game and was completely out of form. Every time the ball was played out to him the move broke down.
Newcastle United eventually ‘weathered the storm’ and pressed forward for an equaliser. Eastham centred the ball causing panic in the Preston penalty area. CUNNINGHAM attempted to clear the danger but only managed to deflect the ball into his own net.
Shortly afterwards, EASTHAM had a shot which struck Dunn and wrong-footed Else to give Newcastle the lead. He claimed afterwards

that the goal should be credited to him.
Amazingly Preston almost conceded another own goal in the final minutes when a shot bounced off Cunningham onto the cross-bar to be cleared by the defence.
For once North End had created very few chances during a game and this combined with the number of goals conceded recently, must be a worry for management and fans.

SAT.16TH JAN. DIV. 1 RESULTS

BOLTON W.	*P*	*LUTON TOWN*	*P*
BURNLEY	*2*	*CHELSEA*	*1*
FULHAM	*2*	*EVERTON*	*0*
LEEDS UTD.	*3*	*WEST HAM U.*	*0*
LEICESTER C.	*0*	*WEST BROM. A.*	*1*
MANCHESTER U.	*2*	*BIRMINGHAM C.*	*1*
NOTTINGHAM F.	*0*	*BLACKPOOL*	*0*
PRESTON N.E.	*1*	*NEWCASTLE U.*	*2*
SHEFFIELD W.	*3*	*BLACKBURN R.*	*0*
TOTTENHAM H.	*3*	*ARSENAL*	*0*
WOLVES.	*4*	*MANCHESTER C.*	*2*

TOP HALF OF DIV. 1

					Goals		
	P.	*W.*	*L.*	*D.*	*F.*	*A.*	*P.*
Tottenham H. ..	26	14	4	8	57	30	36
Burnley........	26	15	8	3	62	43	33
Wolves	26	14	9	3	67	51	31
Preston N.E. ..	26	12	7	7	50	45	31
Fulham........	26	13	9	4	49	49	30
Sheffield W.	26	12	9	5	49	31	29
Blackburn R. ..	26	13	10	3	45	40	29
West Ham U. ..	26	13	10	3	49	50	29
W.B. Albion ..	26	11	9	6	50	39	28
Bolton W.	25	12	9	4	33	29	28
Manchester U...	26	11	10	5	64	55	27

Mon.18th-In the F.A.Cup 3rd Round second replay at Hillsborough, Rotherham United shocked the football world by beating Arsenal 2-0. Kettleborough and Sawyer scored the goals in front of a crowd of 56,290. Over 138,000 spectators had watched the three games.
Tues.19th-T. Ring, the Scottish International outside-left, moved from Clyde to Everton.
In the F.A. Youth Cup 4th round tie at Deepdale, North End beat Birmingham City 2-0 in front of 5,825 spectators on a bitterly cold evening. Preston provided their brave supporters with a spectacle of controlled football played at pace with unlimited enthusiasm.
Laing and Thompson scored the goals in a thoroughly deserved victory against a strong Birmingham side. Barton, in goal, and Hart, at left-half, gave the Youth Team invaluable experience having played at Reserve Team level.
Fri.22nd-Cunningham will miss the game at Birmingham tomorrow after injuring his left knee and Wilson will again deputise.

SATURDAY 23RD JANUARY

BIRMINGHAM CITY 2 PRESTON NORTH END 1

Larkin, Neal Sneddon Att.24,160

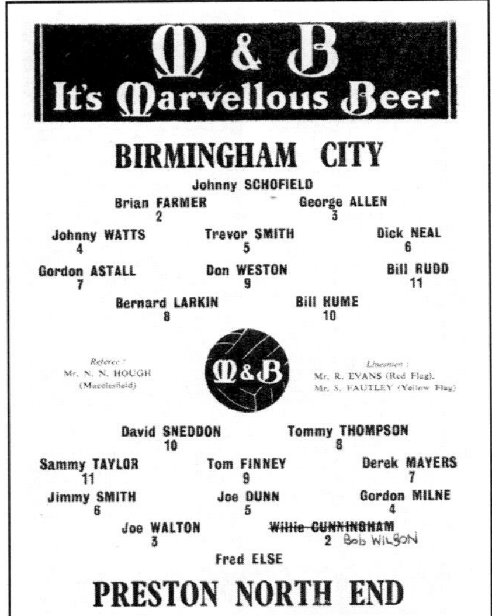

North End arrived at St. Andrew's ground to find water covering large areas of the pitch and the ground staff hard at work trying to drain the surface by forking.

Match referee, Mr Hough from Macclesfield, decided the pitch was playable but it soon became obvious that it would not take long for the affected area to become a greasy, slippery churned up quagmire.

Tom Finney was given loud applause by the Birmingham supporters as he led his team out following the announcement that he had completed twenty years service at Preston on that day.

What a start to the game. In the opening attack, Finney hit a pass to Thompson who had the ball in the net inside of 60 seconds, only to be ruled offside. Then two minutes later, Birmingham were awarded a penalty after Milne fouled Rudd. Astall hit a powerful shot from the 'spot' but Else tipped the ball over the crossbar.

After five minutes Birmingham took the lead when LARKIN turned quickly in the area and placed a low drive just inside the post. Else got a hand to the ball but could not keep it out.

The game settled down with Preston having difficulty trying to play their passing game in the clinging mud, whereas Birmingham were far happier just 'booting' the ball as far forward as possible.

Players from both sides had problems keeping on their feet and the ball was forever 'stopping dead' in the mud. At times it seemed impossible to move the ball from the bog in the centre of the pitch.

Chances were scarce. Jimmy Smith prevented Larkin reaching a cross by heading the ball away for a corner. Then Finney had a powerful left foot shot blocked on its path to goal by Trevor Smith who let it hit his body without flinching.

North End almost went further behind when Wilson's back pass stuck in the mud but Fred Else was just able to block the shot from Weston who was making his home debut.

D. SNEDDON

The mud eventually worked in Preston's favour when, after 37 minutes SNEDDON pounced on an attempted back pass to the keeper, took the ball to the right of goal onto a firmer part of the pitch and shot into the net.

The second half saw Birmingham given two early corners which the P.N.E. defence cleared without much problem but passing the ball continued to pose problems for everyone.

Else coped well in the Preston goal, blocking shots with his body and punching balls clear to keep North End in the game.

The taller, stronger Birmingham players had more success in the dire conditions than their shorter, frailer counterparts in the Preston team. The North End wingers were never able to make a telling contribution to the game and early in the half Mayers was injured following a late challenge. He still managed to drop a centre across goal to Sneddon who laid the ball back to Finney. As Finney attempted to run clear and shoot he was pulled back by his shirt by Neal but the referee did not award a penalty but waved play on.

After 63 minutes Finney almost brought the house down with a glorious individual effort after he picked up a clearance on the half way line. He burst through the defence down the right side and raced the full half of the field fending off challenges before seeing his shot flash inches wide with Schofield beaten.

Birmingham pushed forward and following a corner the ball dropped

BIRMINGHAM CITY 1959-60
Standing: B. Farmer, T. Smith, J. Schofield, R. Neal, J. Watts.
Seated: H. Hooper, B. Larkin, J. Gordon, R. Stubbs, B. Orritt, G. Allen..

to NEAL thirty yards from goal. He hit the ball on the volley into the top corner to give Birmingham the lead.
There were very few incidents over the last 20 minutes and hard as Preston tried they could make no impact on the Birmingham defence.
Another defeat and the eighth game without a win has resulted in many observers questioning whether the Preston side is really good enough to make a serious challenge for the Championship.
The Times newspaper reported, 'Preston North End and West Ham United, both leaders of the Championship at one point, have now skidded to 5th and 10th positions respectively. Not even Finney, celebrating his twentieth anniversary with Preston, seems capable of putting the brakes on the Lancastrians' fall for the moment.'

North End Reserves drew 2-2 at home to Newcastle United with goals from Dagger and Hatsell to remain in eighth position in the Central League.

At Goodison Park, Thomas scored a hat-trick for Everton in the 6-1 demolition of Nottingham Forest.

Cliff Britton, missed the Preston game to watch Cup opponents, Bristol Rovers and must have been impressed with what he saw in their 3-1 win against Sunderland. Alfie Biggs scored his fifteenth goal of the season in the home victory.

SAT. 23RD JAN. DIV. 1 RESULTS

BIRMINGHAM C.	*2*	*PRESTON N.E.*	*1*
BLACKBURN R.	*0*	*WOLVES.*	*1*
BLACKPOOL	*0*	*SHEFFIELD W.*	*2*
CHELSEA	*1*	*LEEDS UTD.*	*3*
EVERTON	*6*	*NOTTINGHAM F.*	*1*
LUTON TOWN	*4*	*FULHAM*	*1*
MANCHESTER C.	*1*	*ARSENAL*	*2*
NEWCASTLE U.	*0*	*LEICESTER C.*	*2*
TOTTENHAM H.	*2*	*MANCHESTER U.*	*1*
WEST BROM. A.	*0*	*BURNLEY*	*0*
WEST HAM U.	*1*	*BOLTON W.*	*2*

FIRST DIVISION

	P.	W.	D.	L.	Goals F.	Goals A.	Pts.
Tottenham H.......	27	15	8	4	59	31	38
Burnley	27	15	4	8	62	43	34
Wolves	27	15	3	9	68	51	33
Sheffield W	27	13	5	9	51	31	31
North End	**27**	**12**	**7**	**8**	**51**	**47**	**31**
Fulham..............	27	13	4	10	50	53	30
Bolton W.	26	13	4	9	35	30	30
West Ham	27	13	3	11	50	52	29
Blackburn R.	27	13	3	11	45	41	29
West Brom.........	27	11	7	9	50	39	29
Manchester U. ...	27	11	5	11	65	57	27
Newcastle U. ...	27	11	5	11	56	55	27
Chelsea	27	9	6	12	50	60	24
Manchester C. ...	27	11	2	14	59	59	24
Arsenal	27	9	6	12	44	57	24
Blackpool	27	9	6	12	37	40	24
Leeds United	27	8	7	12	46	60	23
Leicester City......	27	7	9	11	42	55	23
Everton	27	8	6	13	43	50	22
Nottingham F. ...	27	9	4	14	32	53	22
Luton Town	26	6	7	13	32	47	19
Birmingham C. ...	27	7	5	15	35	51	19

....

Tues 26th –***P.N.E. BOARD MEETING-agreed that a letter should be sent to Tom Finney placing on record the Board's appreciation of his services to the Club over the last 20 years.***

Wed. 27th- Cliff Britton took the players to Blackpool for a break from the normal training routine prior to Saturday's F.A. Cup Tie at Bristol. Some of the players took a brisk three mile walk whilst other did light work on the sands in misty and damp conditions. The players then had lunch at the Norbreck Hydro before returning by coach to Deepdale.

Thurs.28th-H. McCreadie, who had scored ten goals for Accrington Stanley in Division 3, transferred to Luton Town.

Les Dagger (pictured left) will play his first game of the season at Bristol tomorrow in place of Derek Mayers who is injured.

Torrential rain in Bristol has resulted in the pitch being 'very heavy'.

Cliff Britton is looking forward to returning to the club where he began his career in 1928 playing fifty games before moving to Everton in 1930. His father still lives in the area and has supported Bristol Rovers for many years so does not know who to cheer for on the day.

Sat. 30th- The weekly 'Soccer Star' magazine published on the day of the game contained the following editorial:-

'THIRTY SEVEN YEAR OLD Tom Finney, the pride of Preston, his only club in twenty years of competitive soccer, will be pulling out all the stops this weekend in the Fourth Round Cup-tie against Bristol Rovers at Eastville. This might be his last season in League football-although certainly his play does not suggest that. It could also be his last chance to get a Cup-winners' medal.

Strange how some of sports biggest honours seem to avoid those who strive longest for them. With Sir Gordon Richards it was winning the Derby, with Stanley Matthews it was a Cup-winners' medal- and , happily, both these sportsmen succeeded in the end.

How fitting it would be for the 76-times capped Preston plumber to clinch his ambition at the second attempt. Remember, his first and only chance came in 1954 when Preston met West Bromwich Albion at Wembley, only to lose 2-3 at the end.

Finney's 'second wind' has come at precisely the right moment. Though, naturally enough, somewhat slower these days, he has lost none of his old masterly touches. Indeed there are some who would say that, by altering his style to accommodate advancing years, he has achieved a happy, fluent understanding with his inside men, 'Topper' Thompson and David Sneddon. This fact is clearly indicated in the current League position of the club and in the scoring lists. As we write, this penetrating trio have scored twenty-eight League and Cup goals between them, of which Finney's personal contribution is thirteen.

If Preston can deal with Bristol Rovers on Saturday as they did in the competition in 1957 (when Finney ran riot in their 4-1 victory), then this gentleman of soccer will be one step nearer to the honour he would dearly like to have before he decides to retire.'

SATURDAY 30TH JANUARY

F.A. CUP FOURTH ROUND

BLACKBURN ROVERS	**1**	**BLACKPOOL**		**1**
McGrath		**Kaye**	**51,223**	
BRADFORD CITY	**3**	**BOURNEMOUTH**		**1**
D. Jackson, Stokes 2		**Lawlor (og)**	**19,701**	
BRISTOL ROVERS	**3**	**PRESTON NORTH END**		**3**
Biggs 2, Smith (og)		**Finney, Sneddon, Taylor**	**38,472**	
CHELSEA	**1**	**ASTON VILLA**		**2**
P. Sillett (pen)		**McParland, Thomson**	**66,671**	
CREWE ALEXANDRA	**2**	**TOTTENHAM HOTSPUR**		**2**
Llewellyn, M. Jones		**Allen, C. Jones**	**20,000**	
HUDDERSFIELD TOWN	**0**	**LUTON TOWN**		**1**
		Gregory	**28,220**	
LEICESTER CITY	**2**	**FULHAM**		**1**
McDonald, Wills		**Cunningham (og)**	**34,229**	
LIVERPOOL	**1**	**MANCHESTER UNITED**		**3**
Wheeler		**Charlton 2, Bradley**	**56,736**	
ROTHERHAM UNITED	**1**	**BRIGHTON & HOVE ALBION**		**1**
Kirkman		**Thorne**	**24,500**	
SCUNTHORPE UNITED	**0**	**PORT VALE**		**1**
		Portwood	**14,043**	
SHEFFIELD UNITED	**3**	**NOTTINGHAM FOREST**		**0**
Pace 3			**33,567**	
SHEFFIELD WEDNESDAY	**2**	**PETERBOROUGH UNITED**		**0**
Craig 2			**51,114**	
SOUTHAMPTON	**2**	**WATFORD**		**2**
O'Brien 2		**Holton, Page (og)**	**28,619**	
SWANSEA TOWN	**0**	**BURNLEY**		**0**
			30,060	
WEST BROMWICH ALBION	**2**	**BOLTON WANDERERS**		**0**
Jackson, Burnside			**36,201**	
WOLVERHAMPTON WANDERERS	**2**	**CHARLTON ATHLETIC**		**1**
Broadbent, Horne		**Summers**	**37,026**	

F.A. CUP—4th Round KICK-OFF 3.0 p.m.

BRISTOL ROVERS v. PRESTON NORTH END

R. BRISTOL ROVERS L.

Colours—Blue and White Quarters, White Shorts

NORMAN

HILLARD (2) WATLING (Captain) (3)

SYKES (4) FROWEN (5) MABBUTT (6)

PETHERBRIDGE (7) BIGGS (8) BRADFORD (9) WARD (10) HOOPER (11)

Referee: Mr. J. K. Taylor (Wolverhampton)

Linesmen: Mr. F. G. Alford (Red Flag), Mr. W. H. J. Cole (Yellow Flag)

TAYLOR (11) SNEDDON (10) FINNEY (9) THOMPSON (8) ~~MAYERS~~ DAGGER (7)

SMITH (6) DUNN (5) MILNE (4)

WALTON (3) WILSON (2)

ELSE

L. PRESTON NORTH END R.

THIS GAME RELAYED TO 22 HOSPITALS BY "HOSPITALS BROADCASTS"

BRISTOL ROVERS V PRESTON NORTH END

Once again North End made a dreadful start to a game by conceding an unfortunate goal after only 3 minutes. Ward crossed the ball and SMITH, under challenge from Biggs, headed the ball past Else into his own goal.

Preston soon began to dictate the play and Thompson saw his header strike the cross bar and drop to safety. Taylor was inches wide with one effort and Thompson twice shot narrowly wide from good positions. A goal had to come from the pressure and neat approach work resulted in an equaliser by SNEDDON.

Despite the continued pressure, North End found themselves 2-1 down at half-time when the dangerous BIGGS cracked another Ward cross into the net.

The pitch had 'played well' and the expected quagmire did not materialise. The wings were firm and North End used them to their advantage in the second half. Taylor on the left-wing gave his best display for many weeks constantly threatening the Rovers defence with his clever ball play.

On the other flank, in his first game, Les Dagger impressed onlookers with his accurate crosses, one of which led to FINNEY scoring an early equaliser.

Against the run of play Bristol Rovers took the lead for the third time when BIGGS headed home from a pass by Sykes with the North End defenders claiming for off-side.

P.N.E. did not panic and continued to play thoughtful, artistic football which resulted in an equaliser for the third time when another pass from Dagger was hit home by TAYLOR.

JIMMY SMITH

Scored an unlucky own goal

After a thrilling game neither side deserved to lose but Rovers had one last chance to clinch victory in the dying seconds of the game. Centre-forward, Bradford, hit a powerful shot heading for goal but Fred Else made a spine twisting save to deny the player and the referee immediately blew for full time. Else had previously made a similar late save in the last minute of the Cup Tie at Stoke to keep North End's Cup interests alive.

Preston gave a quality performance despite conceding three goals and will need to ensure that they maintain the same level if the are to progress to the next round in Tuesday night's replay.

The attendance of 38,472 was the highest ever crowd for a game at Eastville beating the previous best of 35,972 for a Cup game against Chelsea in 1955.

FRED ELSE
A brilliant last minute save kept Preston in the Cup

THE SHOCK OF THE DAY was at Gresty Road where Fourth Division Crewe Alexandra held Championship leaders Tottenham Hotspur to a 2-2 draw.
Second Division, Sheffield United had an outstanding victory at home against Cup holders Nottingham Forest with Pace scoring a hat-trick in a 3-0 win.

FEBRUARY 1960

Mon. 1st Feb.- Both P.N.E. and Bristol Rovers have announced unchanged teams for tomorrow night's replay. Fans have had to queue in heavy rain at Deepdale to buy tickets. In the F.A. Cup draw made today, the winners of the game will play at home against Rotherham United or Brighton & Hove Albion in the 5th Round on February 20th.

Stanley Matthews celebrated his 45th birthday today training at Blackpool. He has only appeared in four league games this season and has not played since 21st November 1959. He is nearing full fitness and could feature in the game at Wolves on Saturday.

TUESDAY 2ND FEBRUARY
F.A.CUP FOURTH ROUND REPLAY

PRESTON NORTH END 5 BRISTOL ROVERS 1

Finney 2, Taylor 2, Thompson Hooper Att.33,164

P.N.E.-*Else, Wilson, Walton, Milne, Dunn, Smith, Dagger, Thompson, Finney, Sneddon, Taylor.*

BRISTOL R.-*Norman, Hillard, Watling, Sykes, Frowen, Mabbutt, Petherbridge, Biggs, Bradford, Ward, Hooper.*

On a dreadful night at Deepdale the rain sodden North End fans in a crowd of over 33,000 saw Preston awarded a penalty after only two minutes. A goal-bound shot from Finney was handled on the line by Hillard. Finney stepped up to take the kick but did not connect properly with the ball which went straight to the 'keeper.

Both sides then had chances to take the lead. Biggs shot over and then had another effort diverted for a corner by Else. Biggs missed the target with a diving header and Smith headed a dangerous shot clear. Else made further saves from Petheridge and Bradford before Sykes shot wide of the post.

At the other end Sneddon wasted a good opportunity and Taylor had a shot saved. After 17 minutes the deadlock was finally broken and it was P.N.E. who edged in front when FINNEY rose highest to head home a free-kick from Walton.

After 30 minutes Preston doubled their lead after good work by Dagger on the right wing. His cross was met by Milne but the goalkeeper parried the ball only for THOMPSON to tap into the net from close range.

Despite being two goals down Rovers were still very much in the game and continued to attack with a series of incisive raids. Sykes and Bradford both hit shots off target and Biggs had an attempt blocked by Walton. North End went into the interval with a 2-0 lead but Else had been the far busier of the two goalkeepers.

Bristol started the second half on the offensive and Petherbridge hit the crossbar in the first minute. This missed chance seemed to stir Preston into action and at last the team started to play some smooth, quick flowing football to entrance the crowd.

Finney opened the scoring with a magnificent header from a Walton free-kick.

In the 50th minute Finney came in from the right-wing and pulled back a centre for TAYLOR to slam into the net.

Finney was now 'on fire' and his persistence and variety of skills inspired the team. It was FINNEY who scored the fourth goal with a glorious solo effort.

He received the ball from a clearance and from the half way line, side stepped a defender and shook off two more in a thirty yard run. He suddenly surged forward and at speed switched the ball from his right to his left foot before hammering a 'daisy cutter' into the net to bring the house down. Many Preston fans said afterwards that this was one of the best goals they had ever seen him score.

Bristol Rovers were rewarded for their contribution to a wonderful sporting contest when HOOPER pulled a goal back with a shot, which went in off the post.

Chances still came thick and fast at both ends with Finney beating the goalkeeper with a header only to see his effort cleared off the line and Thompson missed an open goal. Else had also to make three good saves to prevent Bristol reducing the lead further.

Preston finally sealed the game with a fifth goal. Following a move involving five players, TAYLOR ferociously smashed the ball home to a tremendous roar from the jubilant Preston fans.

There was still time for Dagger to shoot straight at Norman and then over the bar in a game where Preston's excellent football had created enough chances to win five games.
The Lancashire Evening Post carried the headline 'The Finney of old bewilders Bristol'.
North End face league leaders Spurs at Deepdale on Saturday and need to perform at the same level as in this game to return to winning ways.

....

Other F.A. Cup 4th Round Replay Results
Tues. 2nd Feb

BURNLEY	**2**	**SWANSEA TOWN**	**1**
WATFORD	**1**	**SOUTHAMPTON**	**0**

Wed. 3rd Feb

BLACKPOOL	**0**	**BLACKBURN ROVERS**	**3**
BRIGHTON & HOVE ALBION	**1**	**ROTHERHAM UNITED**	**1**
TOTTENHAM HOTSPUR	**13**	**CREWE ALEXANDRA**	**2**

The most amazing replay result came at White Hart Lane when, after playing so well in the first game, Fourth Division Crewe Alexandra could just not cope with the rampant Championship leaders. Goals from: Allen 5, Smith 4, Jones 3 (1 pen.) and Harmer made it a thoroughly miserable night for the visitors.
Leading 10-1 at half-time, the 'anoraks' at the game began to wonder if Spurs could beat the F.A. Cup record score of 26-0 when Preston beat Hyde in the 1887 competition. However, Crewe played a lot tighter in the second half, limiting Spurs to just three goals.
There is some consolation for the 'Railwaymen' as they will receive a share of the £8,875 gate from the crowd of 64,365.

Thurs 4th-George Farm, the Blackpool and Scottish International goalkeeper, was transferred to Queen of the South after requesting that he finish his career back in Scotland. The promising Tony Waiters will take his place in the first team.

Fri. 5th-Jim Smith of Preston and John White of Spurs, undergoing National Service, will both miss tomorrow's game at Deepdale as they have been selected for the British Army v Belgian Army in Brussels on Sunday. John Fullam will deputise for Smith playing his third game of the season whilst Medwin replaces White.
Bobby Smith suffered a twisted knee against Crewe and Dunmore will take his place as centre-forward.

JOHN FULLAM

SATURDAY 6TH FEBRUARY

PRESTON NORTH END 1 TOTTENHAM H. 1

Thompson | Mackay | Att.33,039

P.N.E.-*Else, Wilson, Walton, Milne, Dunn, Fullam, Dagger, Thompson, Finney, Sneddon, Taylor.*
SPURS-*Brown, Hills, Henry, Blanchflower, Norman, Mackay, Medwin, Harmer, Dunmore, Allen, Jones.*

Following their thirteen goals in midweek, Tottenham Hotspur found North End a much tougher proposition. Preston dominated the first half playing some attractive football against the aristocrats of the English game but could not break the deadlock.
Tottenham had two half chances but on each occasion Jones shot wildly.
Norman was outstanding in his duels with Finney and three times in quick succession he denied the North End player with well-timed tackles. The Spurs half-back line of Blanchflower, Norman and Mackay kept Preston at bay with relative ease in a well drilled defence.
The best chance of the half fell to Thompson who headed over an open goal after receiving an inch perfect cross from Finney.
Despite North End's domination it was Spurs who took the lead after 56 minutes. Dunmore was fouled just outside the penalty area and Blanchflower tapped the free kick to MACKAY who hit a terrific drive into the roof of the net.
Dunmore then missed a chance to increase the lead when he ballooned the ball over the bar after a shot from Cliff Jones had rebounded from an upright.
At times P.N.E.'s approach work was too complicated and the wingers were guilty of lofting the ball into the middle only to watch Norman head it clear time and time again.
Thompson missed a golden chance when he shot wide and Taylor came close to scoring but Spurs hung onto their lead.
At the other end Else made a great save from Dunmore. Preston's determination and spirit could not be questioned and the crowd

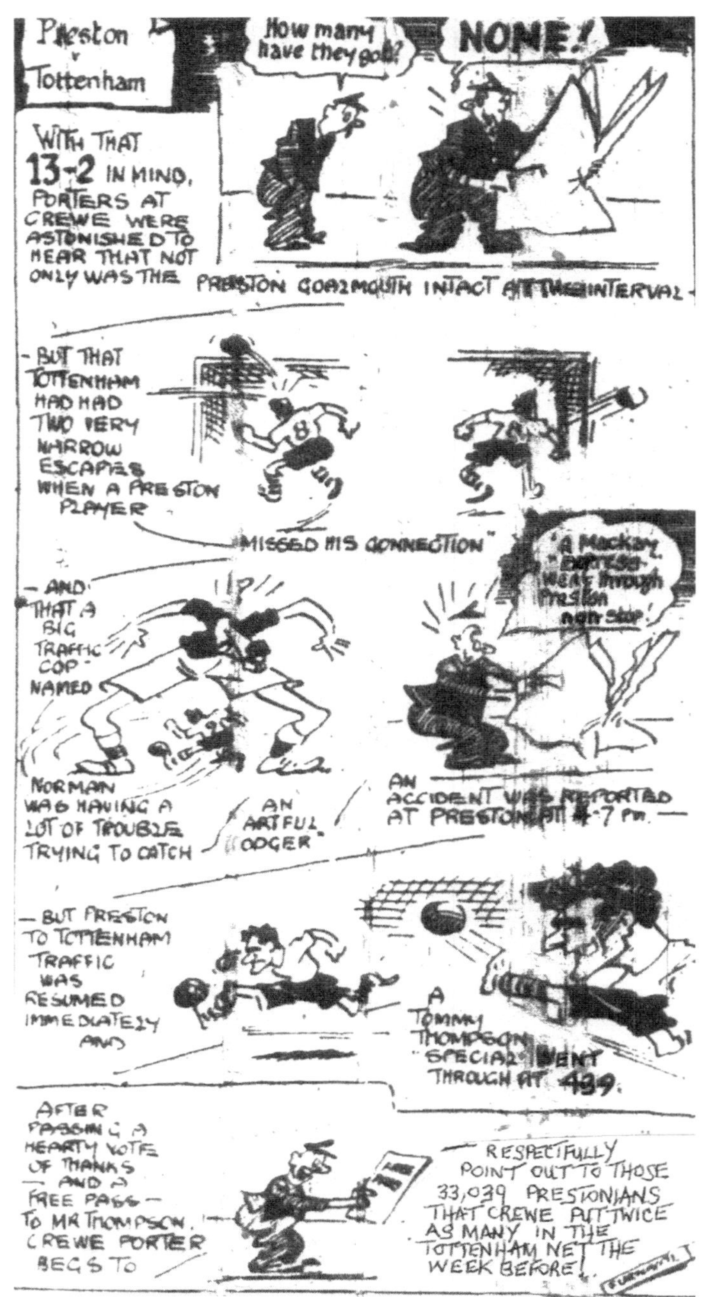

'TWICE AS MANY'
FURNIVAL CARTOON FROM THE L. E. P. 8TH FEBRUARY 1960

MAURICE NORMAN

appreciated their efforts as Tottenham 'rode their luck' during the second half onslaught.

In the closing stages Spurs reeled under the persistent Preston pressure and two minutes from time, North End scored a deserved equaliser. Finney started the move with a delightful pass to Taylor on the left-wing. For once the winger hit the ball directly to a forward and THOMPSON found the back of the net.

It had never been a classic game but P. N. E. did not deserve to lose to the League leaders. Young Fullam at wing-half gave a highly satisfactory performance and subdued the dangerous scheming of Harmer.

FEB. 6TH DIVISION 1 RESULTS

ARSENAL	*5*	*BLACKBURN R*	*2*
BURNLEY	*2*	*NEWCASTLE U.*	*1*
FULHAM	*1*	*BOLTON WAND.*	*1*
LEEDS UNITED	*1*	*WEST BROM. ALB*	*4*
LEICESTER CITY	*1*	*BIRMINGHAM C.*	*3*
MANCHESTER U.	*0*	*MANCHESTER C.*	*0*
NOTTINGHAM F.	*2*	*LUTON TOWN*	*0*
PRESTON N. E.	*1*	*TOTTENHAM H.*	*1*
SHEFFIELD W.	*2*	*EVERTON*	*2*
WEST HAM UTD.	*4*	*CHELSEA*	*2*
WOLVES.	*1*	*BLACKPOOL*	*1*

TOP OF DIVISION 1

					Goals		
	P.	W.	L.	D.	F.	A.	Pts.
Tottenham Hotspur ...	28	15	4	9	60	32	39
Burnley	28	16	8	4	64	44	36
Wolverhampton Wanderers	28	15	9	4	69	52	34
Sheffield Wednesday ...	28	13	9	6	53	33	32
Preston North End	28	12	8	8	52	48	32
West Bromwich Albion ...	28	12	9	7	54	40	31
Bolton Wanderers	27	13	9	5	36	31	31
West Ham United	28	14	11	3	54	54	31
Fulham	28	13	10	5	51	54	31
Blackburn Rovers	28	13	12	3	47	46	29

After some impressive games in the Youth side, Jimmy Humes, made his debut in the Reserve team at outside-right but could make little impression in the 3-0 defeat away to Sheffield United. North End Reserve's are now tenth in the Central League. Manchester United top the table having scored 85 goals in 28 games. Young Alex Dawson, who played at Deepdale for the United first team in the 4-0 defeat last September, has scored 29 goals in just 14 Reserve games this season.

Three teenagers made their debuts in West Ham United's 4-2 defeat of Chelsea. Nineteen year old Johnny Lyall, at left-back, and eighteen year old Tony Scott at outside-right for W.H.U. and seventeen year old Terry Venables at right-half for Chelsea. The outstanding player of the three was Scott who gave Peter Sillett a torrid time and his accurate crosses created two goals for Bond who went on to score a hat trick.

A goal-less draw in the Manchester derby was mainly due to the performance of Bert Trautmann in the City goal who pulled off some breathtaking saves.

Stanley Matthews had a quiet game in his return to action at Wolves but when he had the ball he certainly had the beating of Gwyn Jones almost every time. He made a number of chances and Blackpool eventually scored an equaliser.

Mon.8th Feb.- In the F.A. Cup 4th Round second replay at Highbury, Brighton & Hove Albion beat Rotherham United 6-0 with goals from Curry 3, Thorne 2 and Jones in front of a crowd of 32,864. Brighton will now play P.N.E. at Deepdale on 20th February.

Tues.9th- ***P.N.E. BOARD MEETING-J. Byrne (Reserve team player) has approached the manager regarding a return to Scotland. It was agreed that his name should be circulated to Scottish Clubs.***
Pathe News were given permission to take News Reel Pictures at the Cup Tie v Brighton.

Wed.10th- Roy Vernon, who has scored eight goals in eighteen League and Cup games for Blackburn Rovers, was transferred to Everton in exchange for E. Thomas plus £20,000. Thomas has been in good form at Everton scoring twelve goals.

The F.A. Youth Cup quarter final draw

Manchester United	v	Stoke City
West Ham United	v	Bristol City
Chelsea	v	Aston Villa
Swansea Town	v	**Preston North End**

North End Youth team will play at Swansea on Thursday 17th March with a 4.45pm kick-off as the ground has no floodlights.

Thurs. 11th- The F.A. have sent the following letter to all clubs still involved in the F.A. Cup following the threat of a rail strike.
'No doubt you will consider the possibility of a railway strike interfering with your travel arrangements for the match, or for a replay if one becomes necessary, during the following week.
It is the wish of the Challenge Cup Committee that ties should take place as arranged, and it is hoped that you will plan alternative transport well in advance to be available if required, to convey your players to and from the games if rail transport is not available'.

KEN HEYES

Fri.12th- Jim Smith is available again from his National Service and will return at left-half in place of Fullam for tomorrow's game at Old Trafford. Wilson is unfit and his place at right-back will be taken by Ken Heyes. The twenty four year old defender from Everton (who formerly worked as a wagon builder at a foundry near Haydock) will make his debut after some impressive performances in the reserve team. P.N.E. have a poor record at Old Trafford having won only twice in eleven post-war visits whilst never scoring more than two goals in a game.

Brighton have announced that in the event of a draw in the F.A. Cup Tie next Saturday, the replay will take place on Wednesday 24th February at 2.45 pm.

Snow and ice around the country has resulted in a number of early postponements including the Division1 games at Birmingham and West Brom.

SATURDAY 13TH FEBRUARY

MANCHESTER UTD. 1 PRESTON N. E. 1

Viollet Finney Att. 44,014

MAN. UTD.-*Gregg, Foulkes, Carolan, Setters, Cope, Brennan, Bradley, Quixall, Viollet, Charlton, Scanlon.*

P.N.E.-*Else, Heyes, Walton, Milne, Dunn, Smith, Dagger, Thompson, Finney, Sneddon, Taylor.*

Over the years, Manchester United v Preston North End games have often been classic encounters with flowing football and glorious goals. This game was the complete opposite with both sides playing well below their normal level, no doubt with an eye on next Saturday's home F.A. Cup Ties against Sheffield Wednesday and Brighton & Hove Albion respectively.

It was perhaps fitting that the goal scorers in the game were also the leading scorers at each club, Viollet and Finney, who both had tried to provide some entertainment for the crowd.

The opening goal came after 5 minutes following a break away instigated by Bobby Charlton. He seized onto a loose ball after a Preston throw-in went astray and raced thirty yards to put Viollet in possession.

Viollet passed the ball onto Bradley, who at first appeared to have held the ball too long, but then hit a pin point centre into the six yard area for VIOLLET to head the ball just inside the post for his twenty-seventh league goal of the season.

North End equalised after 70 minutes when Gregg was penalised for carrying the ball outside his penalty area. United formed a wall to protect their keeper and Taylor shaped to shoot. Instead he passed the ball to Thompson who hit a strong shot into 'the wall' and the ball rebounded to FINNEY who scored from six yards.

DENIS VIOLLET

Else was always the busier of the two 'keepers and made four magnificent saves from Scanlon, Charlton, Bradley and Viollet. There were many other efforts which were 'off target' especially from Charlton, who on a number of occasions hit powerful long distance shots wide of the post.
Finney had the best of the chances for Preston firstly shooting over the bar and then having another attempt saved by Gregg with his legs.
Joe Walton gave an excellent display at full-back before his old home crowd. His cool and composed performance together with the domination of Joe Dunn in the centre of the defence ensured that Preston came away with a point.
North End have now gone ten League games without a win, although six have been drawn, since the day they beat Luton to top the table on 28th November 1959.

....

North End Reserves lost 2-3 at home to Derby County Reserves in a below par performance. All the goals came in the second half with Alston opening the scoring and then two miss-timed back passes gifted goals to Derby. Farrall netted a late consolation.

Wolves made up ground on Spurs in the race for the Championship after a good performance at Everton gave them two points. Tottenham inexplicably lost 2-1 at home to lowly Leicester City. With Burnley's game postponed they are still three points behind Spurs but now have a game in hand.

13TH FEB. DIVISION 1 RESULTS

BIRMINGHAM C.	*P*	*BURNLEY*	*P*
BLACKBURN R.	*2*	*MANCHESTER C.*	*1*
BLACKPOOL	*2*	*ARSENAL*	*1*
BOLTON W.	*1*	*NOTTINGHAM F.*	*1*
CHELSEA	*4*	*FULHAM*	*2*
EVERTON	*0*	*WOLVES.*	*2*
LUTON TOWN	*0*	*SHEFFIELD WED.*	*1*
MANCHESTER U.	*1*	*PRESTON N.E.*	*1*
NEWCASTLE U.	*2*	*LEEDS UNITED*	*1*
TOTTENHAM H.	*1*	*LEICESTER C.*	*2*
WEST BROM. A.	*P*	*WEST HAM UTD.*	*P*

	P.	W.	D.	L.	F.	A.	W.	D.	L.	F.	A.	Pts.
Tottenham H'spur	29	8	4	3	33	18	7	5	2	28	16	39
Burnley	28	10	0	4	39	23	6	4	4	25	21	36
Wolverhampt'nW.	29	10	2	2	39	17	6	2	7	32	35	36
Sheffield Wed. ..	29	8	5	1	35	11	6	1	8	19	22	34
Preston N.E. ..	29	6	5	3	24	21	6	4	5	29	28	33
Bolton Wand. ..	28	7	4	3	23	17	6	2	6	14	15	32
West Bromwich A.	28	7	2	5	31	18	5	5	4	23	22	31
Blackburn Rovers	29	10	2	3	32	19	4	1	9	17	28	31
West Ham Utd. ..	28	10	0	4	36	21	4	3	7	18	33	31
Fulham	29	9	2	4	29	19	4	3	7	24	39	31
Manchester Utd.	29	8	3	4	37	24	3	4	7	29	34	29
Newcastle United	29	7	3	5	31	24	5	2	7	28	34	29
Blackpool ..	29	7	4	4	26	22	3	3	8	14	20	27
Chelsea	29	5	3	6	31	36	5	3	7	25	30	26
Arsenal	29	5	3	6	26	29	5	3	7	24	32	26
Manchester City	29	7	2	5	35	26	4	1	10	25	35	25
Leicester City ..	29	4	5	5	22	23	4	4	7	23	36	25
Nottingham F. ..	29	6	3	5	20	20	4	2	9	15	34	25
Everton	30	8	3	4	32	16	0	4	10	13	38	23
Leeds United ..	29	3	4	7	24	32	5	3	7	24	34	23
Birmingham City	28	6	4	4	24	20	2	1	11	14	32	21
Luton Town ..	28	4	2	9	16	23	2	5	6	16	27	19

Tues.16th- Willie Cunningham could be out for at least six weeks after being diagnosed with a cartilage problem which will require an operation on his left knee.

Wed.17th- Brighton expect to be unchanged for Saturday's Cup Tie at Deepdale. According to reports they had four scouts in different parts of the ground at Old Trafford watching North End. Manager, Billy Lane, stated that he believes his side can gain at least a draw and insists Brighton will play attacking football and will make no special plans to deal with Tom Finney.

Thurs.18th- Everton signed M. Lill the Wolves outside-right who had scored two goals in eleven games.

Fri.19th- A seventeen strong party travelled from Brighton and will stay at the Palace Hotel in Southport tonight. They have brought two types of boots and three sets of studs for each player in readiness for any ground condition. There has been some snow locally but the ground staff have swept the playing area which is firm but playable. Bobby Wilson has received treatment for a thigh injury and will return to the side in place of Heyes.

SATURDAY 20TH FEBRUARY

F. A. CUP FIFTH ROUND

BRADFORD CITY	**2**	**BURNLEY**	**2**	
Webb, Stokes		**Connelly 2**		**26,227**
LEICESTER CITY	**2**	**WEST BROMWICH ALBION**	**1**	
Walsh, Cheesebrough		**Kennedy**		**37,753**
LUTON TOWN	**1**	**WOLVERHAMPTON WANDERERS**	**4**	
Turner		**Mason 2, Murray, Clamp**		**25,714**
MANCHESTER UNITED	**0**	**SHEFFIELD WEDNESDAY**	**1**	
		McAnearney(pen)		**66,350**
PORT VALE	**1**	**ASTON VILLA**	**2**	
Jackson(pen)		**Hitchens, Thomson**		**49,768**
PRESTON NORTH END	**2**	**BRIGHTON & HOVE ALBION**	**1**	
Taylor, Sneddon		**Wilson(pen)**		**35,543**
SHEFFIELD UNITED	**3**	**WATFORD**	**2**	
Pace 3		**Holton 2**		**38,574**
TOTTENHAM HOTSPUR	**1**	**BLACKBURN ROVERS**	**3**	
Jones		**Woods, Bimpson 2**		**54,745**

PRESTON N.E. V BRIGHTON & H.A.

P.N.E.-*Else, Wilson, Walton, Milne, Dunn, Smith, Dagger, Thompson, Finney, Sneddon, Taylor.*

BRIGHTON-*Hollins, Bissett, Little, Bertolini, Jennings, Wilson, Tiddy, McNeill, Curry, Thorne, Jones.*

North End started the game strongly and after only half-an-hour, with a two goal lead, the match was effectively over as a contest.

Brighton were not sufficiently accomplished to give their First Division opponents a real test and had little to offer except courage, bustle and determination.

Roy Jennings, Brighton's tall centre-half, was so anxious to curb Tom Finney's skills that he gave away a number of free kicks, two of which resulted in goals.

In the fourth minute, Smith hit the free kick to Dagger who crossed the ball for TAYLOR to score. Then in the 32nd minute, Dagger took the kick, placing the ball to Thompson who tapped it onto SNEDDON to crack into the net.

From this point onwards Preston only exerted themselves as much as they needed to do and became indifferent in front of goal. Finney was the main culprit missing at least three clear-cut opportunities in a manner not normally associated with such a proven goalscorer. Taylor and Sneddon also wasted good chances.

BRIGHTON HOVE ALBION
Back Row left to right-Burtenshaw, Bissett, Bertolini, Hollins, Jennings, Wilson, Little.
Front Row-Abbiss, McNeill, Curry, Thorne, Tiddy, Jones.

Les Dagger was the outstanding forward always keeping things simple but rarely giving the ball away.
In defence Dunn kerbed the dashing Curry and North End's full-backs did well to contain the dangerous Brighton wing-men with shrewd positioning and covering. As always, Else dealt with everything that came his way in his usual calm and cool manner.
Brighton scored a consolation goal in the last minute from a penalty taken by club captain WILSON, but it was too late.
The win ensured that Preston would be in Monday's quarter final draw for the fourth time since the war.

"WHY WALK IT?"

FURNIVAL CARTOON FROM THE L.E.P. 22ND FEBRUARY 1960

Daily Telegraph Monday 22nd February carried the following headline 'Finney lets Brighton off lightly'. The article stated- 'Finney on whom so much reliance is placed by Preston was their biggest offender as a marksman-that is on the few occasions when he and his colleagues deigned to shoot. He shot wide of an open goal with Preston a goal ahead. Just before the interval he was through twice within a minute. Each time he shot straight at the helpless goal keeper. Not long afterwards he turned a backward centre from Taylor outside the post from six yards.'

Mr Jack Husband, the referee in the Leicester City v West Bromwich Albion Cup game, was found dead in his dressing room during the half-time interval. Mr Husband, aged 44, a Gas Board official at Wandsworth, had apparently collapsed and struck his head in falling. Although the second half started seven minutes late, with the senior linesman Mr Walker of Bristol taking charge, the players and spectators were completely unaware of what had happened. The clubs jointly sent a cheque for £200 to his widow and it is expected that other clubs will also make donations to his family. Mr Husband was strongly fancied to referee the Cup Final this season.

Derek Pace scored a hat-trick for Sheffield United in their 3-2 win over Watford having also scored a hat-trick in their previous Cup Tie against Nottingham Forest. Pace scored two goals in the third round game so has a total of eight F.A. Cup goals in three matches.

FEB. 20TH DIVISION 1 RESULTS

ARSENAL	*2*	*EVERTON*	*1*
LEEDS UNITED	*P*	*BIRMINGHAM C.*	*P*
MANCHESTER C.	*P*	*BLACKPOOL*	*P*
NOTTINGHAM F.	*2*	*FULHAM*	*2*
WEST HAM UTD.	*3*	*NEWCASTLE U.*	*5*

	P.	W.	D.	L.	F.	A.	PTS.
Tottenham	29	15	9	5	61	34	39
Burnley	28	16	4	8	64	44	36
Wolves	29	16	4	9	71	52	36
Sheffield W.	29	14	6	9	54	33	34
Preston	29	12	9	8	53	49	33
Bolton W.	28	13	6	9	37	32	32
Fulham	30	13	6	11	55	60	32
West Brom.	28	12	7	9	54	40	31
Blackburn R.	29	14	3	12	49	47	31
West Ham U.	29	14	3	12	57	59	31
Newcastle U.	30	13	5	12	64	61	31
Manchester U.	29	11	7	11	66	58	29
Arsenal	30	11	6	13	52	62	28
Blackpool	29	10	7	12	40	42	27
Chelsea	29	10	6	13	56	66	26
Notts Forest	30	10	6	14	37	56	26
Manchester C.	29	11	3	15	60	61	25
Leicester	29	8	9	12	45	59	25
Everton	30	8	7	15	46	56	23
Leeds U.	29	8	7	14	48	66	23
Birmingham	28	8	5	15	38	52	21
Luton T.	28	6	7	15	32	50	19

LEADING SCORERS
(Including League and Cup)

27	VIOLLET	Man. Utd.
24	SMITH	Spurs
23	GREAVES	Chelsea
22	McCOLE	Leeds Utd.
	MURRAY	Wolves.
21	WHITE	Newcastle
20	McADAMS	Man. City
19	DOBING	Blackburn
18	ROBSON	Burnley
17	CONNELLY	Burnley
	FINNEY	**P.N.E.**
	JONES	Spurs.
16	WESTON	Birmingham
	EASTHAM	Newcastle

England Under 23 Team to meet Scotland at Ibrox on March 2nd.

MARSHALL	(Hearts)
ANGUS	(Burnley)
ALLEN	(Stoke City)
SETTERS	(Manchester United)
SWAN	(Sheffield Wed.)
KAY	(Sheffield Wed.)
CROWE	(Leeds United)
EASTHAM	(Newcastle United)
BAKER	(Hibernian)
CHARLTON	(Manchester United)
SYDENHAM	(Southampton)

Mon. 22nd-F.A. Cup quarter final draw

Leicester City	v	Wolverhampton Wanderers
Aston Villa	v	Preston North End
Sheffield United	v	Sheffield Wednesday
Bradford City or Burnley	v	Blackburn Rovers

Tues.23rd-In the F.A. Cup 5th round replay, Burnley beat Bradford City 5-0 with goals from Pointer 2, Robson 2 and Connelly.

P.N.E. BOARD MEETING-Informed that Willie Cunningham has had a cartilage operation and Derek Mayers is back in full training.

Wed.24th- Alex Farrall, who has made 3 appearances this season, has requested a transfer.

Thurs.25th- J. Bollands, centre-forward of Sunderland, transferred to Everton.

Aston Villa announced that the quarter final on 12th March will be all ticket. Preston have been allocated 17,125 tickets out of the 68,500 available. Tickets are priced:

46,000 at 2/-
14,000 at 3/6
8,500 stand seats at 6/- or 8/6

Fri 26th- P. N.E. will be unchanged for the game at Goodison Park tomorrow. Dunlop returns in goal for Everton and Harris replaces Shackleton at centre-forward.

Peter Thompson will make his Central League debut in the home game v Blackburn Rovers Reserves with Jimmy Humes getting another game.

Joe McBride, centre-forward from Wolves, transferred to Luton Town.

SATURDAY 27TH FEBRUARY

EVERTON 4 PRESTON NORTH END 0

Vernon 2, J. Harris, Lill Att. 50,990

EVERTON-*Dunlop, Parker, Bramwell, Harris B., Labone, Meagan, Lill, Collins, Harris J., Vernon, Ring.*

P.N.E .-*Else, Wilson, Walton, Milne, Dunn, Smith, Dagger, Thompson, Finney, Sneddon, Taylor.*

North End's disastrous run in the League, since the end of November last year, continued at Goodison Park were they were completely outplayed by an Everton side who are only two points above the relegation zone.

But this is now a rejuvenated Everton team with a number of new signings and on this form they will surprise many of their opponents between now and the end of the season with their flowing attacking football.

On a mild afternoon with a fresh wind, Everton were soon into their stride and took the lead after only 5 minutes. Recent signing , ROY VERNON from Blackburn Rovers, hit a rasping drive which glanced off a defender before nestling in the goal.

The home side were easily the better team and fought for every ball as though their lives depended on it. The 'Toffeemen' scored again after 18 minutes when Vernon resisted two tackles before passing to JIMMY HARRIS who slammed the ball home.

Little was seen of the North End attack in the first half and only Dagger showed any urgency, using a direct approach crossing the ball quickly whenever possible. For some reason as the game progressed, he was starved of the ball for long periods.

Sneddon and Thompson were too easily brushed aside by the Everton defenders and Finney was tightly marshalled by Brian Labone who also won every ball in the air.

Preston were lucky to go into the interval only two goals down and had to thank Else for keeping them in the game with some terrific saves.

The second half continued just as the first had ended with Everton far superior in teamwork, skill and enthusiasm. Vernon was a constant

ROY VERNON

JIMMY HARRIS

thorn in the Preston defence with his persistence making it difficult to shake him off the ball.
North End did not have a worthwhile attempt on goal until the 55th minute when Sneddon almost surprised Dunlop with a hook shot. It was a collective off-day for the P.N.E. players who showed a lack of thrust and determination. Preston only had three other attempts on goal during the half.
In contrast, Everton's attack, strengthened by recent costly acquisitions, combined to perfection playing hard for the full 90 minutes. It was a blend of power and artistry with Ring and Collins providing the ammunition and Harris, Lill and Vernon shooting the goals. Wilson just could not cope with the quick footed Ring who ran him dizzy throughout the game.
It was no surprise when Everton increased their lead through VERNON and LILL to give them a comfortable victory over a lack-lustre P.N.E. side.
Preston have now gone eleven consecutive league games without a win, drawing six and losing five. Their confidence is completely shattered and it must be very worrying that the team has now lost four games by a margin of 4 or more goals.
Any thoughts of winning the Championship have now completely evaporated and only their involvement in the F.A. Cup is keeping the season alive.

FEB. 27TH DIVISION 1 RESULTS

ARSENAL	*1*	*NEWCASTLE U.*	*0*
BLACKBURN R.	*1*	*TOTTENHAM H*	*4*
BLACKPOOL	*0*	*MANCHESTER U*	*6*
BOLTON WAND.	*2*	*BURNLEY*	*1*
EVERTON	*4*	*PRESTON N.E.*	*0*
FULHAM	*5*	*LEEDS UTD.*	*0*
LUTON TOWN	*2*	*LEICESTER CITY*	*0*
MANCHESTER C.	*3*	*BIRMINGHAM C.*	*0*
NOTTINGHAM F.	*3*	*WEST HAM UTD.*	*1*
SHEFFIELD W.	*1*	*CHELSEA*	*1*
WOLVES.	*3*	*WEST BROM. ALB.*	*1*

TOP SIX

	P	W	D	L	F	A	Pts
SPURS	30	16	9	5	65	25	41
WOLVES	31	18	4	9	77	55	40
SHEFF. W.	31	15	7	9	56	34	37
BURNLEY	29	16	4	9	65	46	36
BOLTON W.	30	14	6	10	39	34	34
FULHAM	31	14	6	11	60	60	34

Although they beat Blackburn Rovers Reserves 1-0 at Deepdale, North End Reserves were far from convincing. Some of their passing was very poor and if Rovers had taken their chances, they would have won easily.
Peter Thompson had an encouraging debut and created a number of openings, many of which were wasted by Alston being caught off-side. Humes had a good game on the right wing.

Joe McBride was an instant hit at Luton after scoring with a diving header on his debut the day after signing from Wolves. Luton's 2-0 win over Leicester City gave their supporters hope that they may escape relegation.
Graham Leggat scored four goals in Fulham's 5-0 home win against Leeds United.
Bobby Charlton grabbed a hat-trick in United's 6-0 drubbing of Blackpool at Bloomfield Road. The first half was uninspiring and United led 1-0 at half-time. However, during a dazzling four minute spell in the second half United scored three goals, then later added two more.
Mon.29th Feb.-In the rearranged fixture at Deepdale tomorrow evening, North End have been forced to make two changes as Wilson and Dunn are absent with flu. Heyes will make his home debut at full-back whilst Richardson will play at centre-half. Blackburn Rovers have announced an unchanged team despite losing 4-1 at home to Spurs last Saturday.

MARCH 1960

TUESDAY 1ST MARCH

PRESTON NORTH END 5 BLACKBURN ROV. 3

Thompson 2, Smith, Dagger, Sneddon Douglas 2 (1pen.) MacLeod

Att. 26,781

P.N.E.-*Else, Heyes, Walton, Milne, Richardson, Smith, Dagger, Thompson, Finney, Sneddon, Taylor.*
BLACKBURN-*Leyland, Bray, Whelan, Clayton, Woods, McGrath, Bimpson, Dobing, Dougan, Douglas, McLeod.*

LEAGUE WIN AT LAST FOR P.N.E. WITH DAGGER THE INSPIRATION

After twelve games since their last league win at Luton Town, North End finally gained two points in an emphatic style against local rivals Blackburn Rovers.
The game opened with Preston on the attack and a pin point corner delivered by Dagger resulted in Thompson seeing his drive well saved by Leyland. Almost immediately Dagger had a shot that sailed over the cross-bar. It was then Rovers turn to thrill the crowd when a Douglas effort missed by inches.
North End seemed to be hurting after recent criticism of their performance at Everton and responded by adopting a more direct approach which certainly paid dividends.
On a rainy night at Deepdale, the surface was greasy with the ball skidding off the pitch at pace, and after 7 minutes Preston took the lead. Finney escaped Woods' attention and laid a ball to Thompson who miss-hit his shot allowing DAGGER to gain possession. He beat a defender before confidently stroking the ball home.
The chances were coming 'thick and fast' and Dougan missed one opportunity before Finney darted past Woods only to be brought down just outside the penalty area. Leyland made a good save from Taylor before North End increased their lead after 13 minutes. The move once again involved Dagger whose perfect centre was headed home by THOMPSON.

Dagger's confidence was now 'sky high' and his willingness to run at defenders and hit crosses quickly and accurately caused the Rovers defence problems.

BLACKBURN ROVERS
Back row left to right-Whelan, Woods, Bimpson, Leyland, Dougan, Bray
Front row-Douglas, Dobing, Clayton, McGrath, McLeod.

Blackburn's forwards lacked cohesion and rarely troubled Preston despite the probing runs of Douglas, as Bimpson and Dobing were well marshalled by the defence. Else did have one save to make from Dougan following a glorious pass by Douglas. After 25 minutes, against the run of play, Rovers reduced the deficit when a free kick was deflected into the path of McLEOD who scored easily.
The goal encouraged Blackburn and they nearly scored again when Dougan headed wide from a corner. North End responded by crisply knocking the ball about. Finney was just unable to reach a centre from Dagger after Thompson had set him free. With the half drawing to a close a beautiful passing movement involving Sneddon, Finney and Thompson ended with the ball at Dagger's feet. He hit yet another

cross, this time to SMITH who beat the keeper from close range.
The second half began with Woods again fouling Finney but the free kick came to nothing. After 51 minutes, P.N.E. scored a fourth goal when superlative ball play by Finney enabled SNEDDON to finish the move with a sharp hook shot into the net.
Despite being 4-1 down Rovers refused to concede the game and Douglas created two chances which Else was able to keep out.
Douglas himself, then had a short-range shot saved, but Rovers pressure produced a goal after 81 minutes. Richardson fouled DOUGLAS in the penalty area and the same player took the spot kick to make the score 4-2.
Blackburn continued to press forward and could have pulled another goal back with better finishing. Dagger had a 'goal' disallowed for offside before THOMPSON scored the fifth from a Dagger cross in the 89th minute.
Rovers went straight down to the other end and Douglas 'waltzed' past Richardson to make the final score 5-3.
As a local lad in a big derby game Dagger was the man of the match closely followed by Douglas and Finney who both hit a number of decisive passes to create goal scoring opportunities for other players.
The win secured a double for P.N.E. over Blackburn and renewed hope that North End could move back up the table with more performances like this one.

....

Tues 1st (cont.)-***P.N.E. BOARD MEETING- Mr H .Cartmell brought forward the question of a reported approach by W. Barnes to Tom Finney on behalf of the New York Soccer Club. It was agreed that enquiries should be made to find out more details.***

Burnley had a great 2-0 victory against League leaders Spurs at Turf Moor scoring both goals in a six minute spell in the second half. In the 64th minute Pointer headed powerfully into the net following good work by Connelly on the wing. Connelly then scored himself with a fine individual effort.
A crowd of almost 33,000 saw Burnley reduce the gap at the top of the table to three points with a 'game in hand'.

Wed.2nd- Jimmy Gabriel, Dundee United's wing half was transferred to Everton for £25,000.

Wolves were knocked out of the European Cup at the Quarter-Finals stage by Barcelona after losing 5-2 at home; 9-2 on aggegate.

North End Reserves had an outstanding win against Central League leaders Manchester United at Old Trafford.

Despite losing Mayers after 40 minutes and playing the rest of the game with ten men Preston went on to win 2-1 with goals from Farrall and Alston. Kelly and Singleton had great games in the P.N.E. defence.

Thurs. 3rd-Nat Lofthouse was appointed assistant coach at Bolton.

The press reported that Tom Finney may play in South Africa this summer. He is apparently considering an offer to play for a National League side in Johannesburg. Stanley Matthews has already accepted an invitation.

Fri.4th- Tommy Thompson has a slight thigh strain and will miss tomorrow's game against Arsenal at Deepdale. His place will be taken by transfer listed Farrall. Sammy Taylor also has an injury so Les Campbell will play his third game of the season at outside-left. Arsenal will have Bloomfield in the side in place of Barnwell.

LES CAMPBELL

ALEC FARRALL

SATURDAY 5TH MARCH

PRESTON N. E. 0 ARSENAL 3

Haverty, Bloomfield, Henderson

Att. 23,635

P.N.E.-*Else, Heyes, Walton, Milne, Richardson, Smith, Dagger, Farrall, Finney, Sneddon, Campbell.*

ARSENAL-*Kelsey, Magill, McCullough, Ward, Dodgin, Docherty, Henderson, Groves, Charles, Bloomfield, Haverty.*

P.N.E. SOON BACK TO LOSING WAYS

Tommy Docherty made his first appearance back at Deepdale against his former club and was given the honour of captaining Arsenal for the day. It was perhaps fitting that as the game progressed, Docherty had a fine match in both defence and attack, with his enthusiasm and determination shining through. He received warm applause from the home fans, many of whom did not want him to leave in the first place. The pitch was slippery and the ball very lively on a spring like day. Most of the early play consisted of spoiling movements with the defences well on top and the forwards unable to gain any leeway. After 14 minutes Kelsey cleared the ball from the advancing Dagger to put Arsenal on the attack, resulting in a surprise goal when HAVERTY let fly from twenty-five yards to completely deceive Else, who made no attempt to prevent the ball from entering the top corner of the net.

Shortly afterwards Bloomfield aimed wide from long range and then Haverty skipped past Heyes but screwed his shot off target.

Finney, Milne and Dagger initiated a Preston attack but Ward intercepted to divert Dagger's centre out of harm's way. Just before half-time Mel Charles beat Richardson in the air to get in a really dangerous header which Else did well to save.

North End began the second half by winning two corners but both were easily dealt with by the defence. Vic Groves 'man marked' Tom Finney all over the pitch and combined with the dominance of Dodgin in the air, the Preston maestro was unable to stamp his authority on the game.

Preston gave a drab, spiritless and disjointed display and always looked second best.

Goal No. 1. Joe Haverty's shot from well out sails into the top of the net

In the 60th minute, Heyes conceded a corner when he intercepted a long cross by Henderson. From the corner Charles shot from the edge of the penalty area and the ball rebounded off Heyes straight to BLOOMFIELD who scored from three yards out.

Goal No. 2. After a shot by Mel Charles had been blocked, Jimmy Bloomfield was on the spot to drive the ball home

Arsenal continued in a workmanlike, industrious and efficient manner unlike the glamorous, accomplished side of a few seasons ago but they were still good enough to win at a canter. The nearest Preston came to scoring was when Kelsey pounced on a fast centre from Farrall, with Sneddon running in. After 70 minutes HENDERSON scored Arsenal's third goal. Haverty began the move by giving the ball to Charles who found Henderson unmarked. The winger cut in to pick his spot and score with a well directed shot. Before the end Charles looked a certain scorer but his diving header struck the cross bar. Kelsey saved a header when Smith ran in to meet a centre from Sneddon and in the final action of the game, Else dived full length to beat out a forceful shot by Groves.

Goal No. 3. Jackie Henderson beats Walton and puts the ball past Else

It was a case of 'after the Lord Mayor's Show' following North End's great display on Tuesday evening and many spectators thought that the players minds were too firmly focused on the Cup quarter-final next weekend.

NATIONAL PRESS HEADLINES FOLLOWING THE GAME:
'Finney is well held by Arsenal';
"Policeman" Groves keeps Finney shackled';
'Pathetic Preston give Arsenal little to beat.'

In the North End Reserve match at Huddersfield Town, Gil Lambert played his first game since fracturing his ankle at Spurs in September. Alan Spavin was given his Central League debut but North End lost the game 2-1 when they should have at least got a draw.

MARCH 5TH DIVISION 1 RESULTS

BIRMINGHAM C.	*4*	*NOTTINGHAM F.*	*1*
BURNLEY	*1*	*BLACKBURN R.*	*0*
CHELSEA	*3*	*LUTON TOWN*	*0*
LEEDS UNITED	*2*	*BLACKPOOL*	*4*
LEICESTER CITY	*5*	*MANCHESTER C.*	*0*
MANCHESTER U.	*0*	*WOLVES.*	*2*
NEWCASTLE U.	*3*	*FULHAM*	*1*
PRESTON N.E.	*0*	*ARSENAL*	*3*
TOTTENHAM H.	*4*	*SHEFFIELD WED.*	*1*
WEST BROM. A.	*1*	*BOLTON WAND.*	*1*
WEST HAM UTD.	*2*	*EVERTON*	*2*

		Home					Away					
	P.	W.	D.	L.	F.	A.	W.	D.	L.	F.	A.	Pts.
Tottenham H'spur	32	9	4	3	37	19	8	5	3	32	19	43
Wolverh'mptonW.	32	12	2	2	45	20	7	2	7	34	35	42
Burnley ..	31	12	0	4	42	23	6	4	5	26	23	40
Sheffield W'day ..	32	9	6	1	37	12	6	1	9	20	26	37
Bolton Wanderers	31	8	4	3	25	18	6	3	7	15	17	35
Preston N. E. ..	32	7	5	4	29	27	6	4	6	29	32	35
Fulham	32	10	2	4	34	19	4	4	8	27	44	34
West Bromwich A.	31	7	3	5	32	19	5	6	5	26	27	33
Newcastle United	32	8	3	5	34	25	6	2	8	33	38	33
West Ham United	31	10	1	5	41	28	4	3	8	19	36	32
Arsenal	32	7	3	6	29	30	6	3	7	27	32	32
Manchester Utd.	32	8	3	5	37	26	4	4	8	36	37	31
Blackburn Rovers	32	10	2	4	33	23	4	1	11	20	34	31
Chelsea	32	6	4	6	36	38	5	4	7	36	31	30
Blackpool ..	31	7	4	5	26	28	4	3	8	18	22	29
Leicester City ..	32	6	5	5	30	24	4	4	8	23	38	29
Nottingham For.	32	7	4	5	25	23	4	2	10	16	38	28
Manchester City	31	8	2	5	38	26	4	1	11	25	40	27
Everton ..	32	9	3	4	36	16	0	5	11	16	42	26
Birmingham City	30	7	4	4	28	21	2	1	12	14	35	23
Leeds United ..	31	3	4	8	26	36	5	3	8	24	30	23
Luton Town ..	31	5	2	9	18	23	2	5	8	18	33	21

Burnley beat Blackburn Rovers 1-0 with a goal by Robson in a dress rehearsal for next weeks F.A.Cup quarter-final against the same opposition at Turf Moor. The win also kept them in touch with League leaders Spurs and second placed Wolves who also won their games. *Ray Charnley scored a hat-trick in Blackpool's 4-2 win at relegation haunted Leeds United who are now second from the bottom of Division 1. Cliff Jones also scored a hat-trick for Spurs.*

+++++++++++++++++++++

Tues.8th-North End announced that Dunn, Wilson and Taylor have commenced training again and are likely to be available for the Cup game. Thompson is still suffering from some form of fibrositis in his lower back but is desperate to play against his former club at Villa Park and could yet still make the team.
Derek Mayers has chipped an ankle bone whilst playing in the reserve game against Manchester United and could be out of action for some weeks.

Wed.9th-The players trained on a bitterly cold day at Deepdale but Tom Finney told the press that, 'it is much healthier than the muggy stuff and better than snow'
North End manager, Mr Cliff Britton, stated that he would not be announcing the team until Friday because of the injury problems. He also said that the Preston party would set off for Birmingham on Friday because of snow in the local area.

WED. 9TH MARCH DIVISION 1 RESULTS

BOLTON WAND.	*2*	*LUTON TOWN*	*2*
LEEDS UNITED	*3*	*BIRMINGHAM C.*	*3*
MANCHESTER C.	*2*	*BLACKPOOL*	*3*
WEST BROM. A.	*3*	*WEST HAM UTD.*	*2*

Thurs.10th-Joe Mercer, the Aston Villa manager stated that goal-keeper Nigel Sims will face a late fitness test because of a troublesome shoulder injury. If he is unfit to play then 19 year old, Calcutta born, Kevin Keelan will play his second game for the club.

Fri.11th-The Birmingham press reported that Second Division Aston Villa are very confident of victory in tomorrow's game.
The surprise news from the Preston camp is that Joe Dunn is still suffering from influenza and Richardson will play his first Cup game. Wilson, Thompson and Taylor will all return to the team in place of Heyes, Farrall and Campbell.
Two thousand North End supporters will travel by rail on Saturday morning with an estimated 12-15,000 travelling by road.

Leeds United transferred forward Chris Crowe, who had scored eleven goals, to Blackburn Rovers for £25,000.

SATURDAY 12TH MARCH
F.A. CUP QUARTER FINALS

BURNLEY	**3**	**BLACKBURN ROVERS**	**3**
Pointer, Pilkington, Connelly		**Dobing, McGrath, Douglas (pen)**	**51,501**
ASTON VILLA	**2**	**PRESTON NORTH END**	**0**
Hitchens, McParland			**69,732**
LEICESTER CITY	**1**	**WOLVERHAMPTON WANDERERS**	**2**
McDonald		**Broadbent, Chalmers (og)**	**48,907**
SHEFFIELD UNITED	**0**	**SHEFFIELD WEDNESDAY**	**2**
		Wilkinson 2	**59,692**

ASTON VILLA V PRESTON NORTH END

ASTON VILLA-*Sims, Lynn, Neal, Crowe, Dugdale, Saward, MacEwan, Thomson, Hitchens, Wylie, McParland.*

P.N.E.-*Else, Wilson, Walton, Milne, Richardson, Smith, Dagger, Thompson, Finney, Sneddon, Taylor.*

NORTH END OUT OF CUP
Too frail in attack against Villa
By Walter Pilkington
(L.E.P. article Monday 14th March 1960)

Tradition was the victor at Villa Park. It ought not to influence any particular match but subconsciously, it does, especially a Cup-tie. Aston's record up to their clash with Preston North End of 16 semi-finals, nine appearances in Finals and nine Cup wins is unparalleled. It inspired the Villa to play with irresistible determination against their old rivals in League and Cup.

On the other hand their opponents performances at Villa Park for 40 years, with a solitary win in all that time, would make any player think beforehand "there's not much for us here."

North End, I grant did their utmost to refute the psychological inferences to be drawn from this dismal record. While not playing as well as against Blackburn Rovers recently, through failing to find the same rhythm and thrust they gave an improved display and could not be criticised for want of striving.

They did their best and it was not good enough. As a result they finished without a goal and Villa are in their 17th semi-final, worthy winners by 2-0.

A fairer reflection of the play would have been 3-2. Preston ought to have had at least two goals from the four acceptable scoring chances created by sustained rather than fitful endeavour in attack. Villa's opening goal was a luckless affair for North End in that Walton deflected Hitchens shot out of Else's reach when the goalkeeper had it covered. But Aston were always the more threatening and more forceful side and if they had scored three, irrespective of this fluke, no one could have been surprised.

McParland hit a post in addition to scoring the goal which settled the issue near the finish, and there were as many escapes for North End as for the Villa.

Ifs and buts

In inquests one inevitably thinks of what might have been-if Walton had not impulsively stuck out a foot and turned Hitchens scoring shot off its original course; if Dagger had not lost a clear opening when off balance on recovery from a foul in the penalty area; if he had gone down instead and stayed down; if Sneddon had not topped his shot at an open goal through being flurried; if the same forward had not sent the ball inches too high with Sims beaten; if Thompson had been nippy enough to beat Sims in a dash for possession instead of being toppled over by the onrushing goalkeeper ... so one could go on but that is football.

Lively, rugged

The opening goal was a tragedy for Preston, but the fact remains that North End with as much of the play as their opponents, could not subdue a strong lively attack and failed to beat a rugged, solid defence.

Apart from its being the same old story for North End at Villa Park, there was inadequate fire power in the frail Preston attack.

There was any amount of clever, intelligent play and good positioning and the midfield moves were attractive. They upheld North End's reputation as a footballing side but at times there were too many passes. These merely created difficult situations in a congested middle and made it easier for uncompromising defenders who relied on first time, decisive tackling.

Often the forwards fatally delayed parting, with Finney no exception, which meant that colleagues were covered or in trouble when the pass arrived. A push and run method, I feel would have been considerably more effective against this Villa defence without detracting from a cultivated style of football.

Above all there was little punch and no apparent sense of the urgency needed to beat a quick moving, resolute defence.

Weak finishing

Preston looked really good at times in a fascinating contrast of styles which captivated the biggest crowd seen at any match this season. Frequently they produced smooth looking, elegant moves and just as often took too long over them. The team effort was there without the necessary sharp edge. Between the two penalty zones North End, as most people acknowledge were the better craftsmen but one must admit they seldom encouraged any confident hope that they would score. The finishing was weak. Time after time they were lacking in punch and thrust when glimpses of it might have revealed that this Villa defence was vulnerable.

Forwards and especially inside-forwards, giving away as much in height and weight as Preston did to the Villa backs and the halves must be first class to have much hope of success. This is obvious from the fact that Preston's inside trio average 5ft 6in in height and 10st 4lbs in weight, compared with the opposing half back average of 5ft 11in and 11st 13lbs.

PRESTON NORTH END
Back row left to right-R. Wilson, G. Milne, F. Else, J. Walton, G. Richardson, J.Smith
Front row-D. Mayers, T. Thompson, T. Finney, D. Sneddon, S. Taylor.
(Les Dagger replaced Derek Mayers at Villa Park)

and on this occasion North End were not slick enough to compensate for their lack of physical strength.

By contrast Aston Villa were dynamic, relentless and irresistible, especially the match winning McParland.

They organised their strength to blend a modicum of ball skill with undeniable power and their reward was a Cup semi-final inspite of the stubborn resistance offered by Preston's defence. Smith especially played magnificently and Else, compared with some matches, had not a great deal to do such was the industry expended in striving to give him sound protection.

Even so, there were weak links, as was to be expected with Cunningham and Dunn absent and it was significant that both goals came via these suspect routes.

Everyone will sympathise with Tom Finney especially in his bitter disappointment in seeing the chance of at last gaining a Cup winner's medal disappear. But although he did his best to utilise his resource to advantage, the crowd did not see the Finney magic of old.

MAR. 12TH DIVISION 1 RESULTS			
BLACKPOOL	*3*	*WEST HAM UTD.*	*2*
BOLTON WAND.	*1*	*NEWCASTLE U.*	*4*
EVERTON	*6*	*CHELSEA*	*1*
FULHAM	*2*	*BIRMINGHAM C.*	*2*
LUTON TOWN	*0*	*WEST BROM. ALB.*	*0*
NOTTINGHAM F.	*1*	*TOTTENHAM H.*	*3*

North End Reserves beat Bolton Wanderers Reserves 4-2 at Deepdale. The first goal came after 25 minutes when Alston was fouled in the penalty area and Farrall scored from the spot. Seven minutes later Preston were awarded another penalty but this time Farrall missed. Bolton equalised before Hatsell restored the lead for Preston after excellent work by Lambert and Farrall. Bolton again equalised and a draw looked likely until two goals in the last 10 minutes by Hatsell and Farrall ensured the victory.

Mon.14th-The L.E.P. article written by Walter Pilkington.

Finney says: "I am not retiring".

TOM FINNEY is NOT retiring from football, or even thinking of doing so.

A famous American philosopher and wit, Mark Twain , was said to have walked into a newspaper office and informed the editor that the report of his death was greatly exaggerated.

A weekend statement that it is "evens" on Finney quitting football after this season may be put in the same category.

He is reported as saying, in one breath, that he may call it a day after his disappointment of seeing another Wembley Cup dream dashed and in another of declaring "I have not given a thought to retiring from football. I am too busy enjoying it."

This type of story was a hardy annual concerning Stanley Matthews until he finally won a Cup medal with Blackpool in 1953, when he had already turned 38. Finney will not be that age until April 5th.

In the seven succeeding years there have been more rumours

about Matthews hanging up his boots, but he is still playing. He was 45 on February 1st his argument is, "A man is as old as he feels and I feel fine."
Tom Finney's comment to me on the rumour of his impending retirement after 20 years service with Preston North End was :- "It's a fine time to talk of quitting after getting knocked out of the Cup. Naturally I was disappointed at seeing another chance of getting to Wembley disappear and by North End's defeat, but fans wouldn't think much of me if I gave up football because of it. It is altogether too premature. There is all the summer to decide whether to go on playing or not, even if the question arose.
My personal feeling is to continue as long as I am fit enough to hold my own and still enjoy the game as much as I do now."

F.A.CUP SEMI FINAL DRAW

Aston Villa	v	Wolverhampton Wanderers
Sheffield Wednesday	v	Burnley or Blackburn Rovers

Tues.15th-Finney has a slight groin strain and will miss tomorrow's game at second placed Wolves. Alston will take his place at centre-forward and Farrall will play at inside-right in place of Thompson who has an ankle injury.
Jim Smith is required by the Army for a game against the Navy at Aldershot and John Fullam will deputise for his fourth game of the season.
P.N.E. BOARD MEETING-The Manager read a letter from Brothers F.C. of Johannesburg regarding T. Finney being allowed to visit them for about a month at the end of May to take part in games there. It was agreed that it should be left to the Manager to point out the inadvisability of such a trip and to try and dissuade the player from going.
Injury report: Dunn improving, Mayers to start training, Thompson ankle trouble and Finney a groin injury. Cunningham making good progress.
Division 1 Result ARSENAL 1 LEICESTER CITY 1

WEDNESDAY 16TH MARCH

WOLVERHAMPTON W. 3 **PRESTON N. E. 3**

Stobart, Broadbent 2 Farrall, Dagger, Taylor

Att. 28,760

WOLVES.-*Sidebottom, Showell, Harris, Clamp, Slater, Kirkham, Mannion, Mason, Stobart, Broadbent, Deeley.*
P.N.E.-*Else, Wilson, Walton, Milne, Richardson, Fullam, Dagger, Farrall, Alston, Sneddon, Taylor.*

Following the game at Deepdale in October when North End beat Wolves 4-3 in a pulsating match it looked like the Wanderers would get their revenge when they raced into a 3-1 lead at half-time. However, Preston with a number of reserves in the side and missing the leadership and guidance of Tom Finney, surprised Wolves with their second half performance and in the end thoroughly deserved a share of the points.
Wolves were desperate to gain two points to keep pace with league leaders Spurs but Preston's young side at times played wonderful football despite at other times looking very ordinary.
After 27 minutes STOBART applied the finishing touch to score for Wolves after Broadbent had headed the ball over the advancing Else. North End equalised 2 minutes later when Taylor crossed for Dagger to head the ball into the path of FARRALL whose first shot cannoned back to him from the 'keeper and then rebounded off Farrall back into the net.
In the 36th minute BROADBENT was given too much room and hit a terrific shot home from the edge of the penalty area.
Two minutes before half-time Wolves were awarded a penalty for hand ball by Sneddon but Clamp lifted the ball over the bar from the spot kick. Undeterred the Wanderers continued to attack and in the 44th minute increased their lead after good work by Mason and Mannion gave BROADBENT the time to drill another pile-driver into the net to make the half-time score 3-1.
Preston could easily have gone into the interval level as both Dagger and Farrall missed good opportunities.

Early in the second half Broadbent had a 'goal' disallowed for off-side and Else tipped a Mason shot over the bar. It was then North End's

WOLVERHAMPTON WANDERERS
Back row left to right-E. Stuart, E. Clamp, M. Finlayson, J. Murray, R. Flowers, G. Sidebottom, G. Showell, G. Harris.
Middle row-S. Cullis (Manager), G. Mannion, P. Broadbent, B. Slater, R. Mason, N. Deeley, J. Gardiner (Trainer).
Front row-D. Horne, B. Stobart.

turn to be denied a goal when Taylor headed wide and Dagger had a left-foot shot saved. Then the breakthrough finally came for Preston. Twelve minutes from time Sneddon played the ball to Milne who placed an inch perfect pass for DAGGER to score with a fine shot. In the 80th minute North End deservedly pulled level with a glorious goal by Taylor. Dagger was again involved when he hit a long centre to the left side of the Wolves penalty area and TAYLOR met the ball on the volley from twenty yards out to give Sidebottom no chance. The draw was a great result for Preston after the disappointment of being knocked out of the F.A.Cup.

In the F.A. Cup quarter final replay at Ewood Park, Blackburn Rovers beat Burnley 2-0 with goals from Dobing and MacLeod in front of over 53,000 spectators.

Thurs.17th-The North End Youth Team won their F.A. Youth Cup quarter-final tie at the Vetch Field, 4-1 in front of a crowd of 6,100 but were slightly flattered by the score line.
As always Preston's Youths played some beautiful football and created plenty of chances but Swansea Town had just as much of the play. For 15 minutes in the second-half Swansea staged a magnificent rally which could have easily resulted in an equaliser.
Peter Thompson opened the scoring for Preston after five minutes when he cut inside from the left-wing cleverly beating two Swansea defenders before coolly tapping the ball into the net. Just before the interval North End increased their lead when Smith smashed the ball home.

PETER THOMPSON

The second half saw Swansea Town throw everything forward and they were rewarded with a goal in the 61st minute and continued to put the North End defence under pressure.
Preston weathered the storm and Peter Thompson scored twice more in the 71st and 72nd minutes to claim his own hat-trick and put North End safely in the semi-final draw.

....

TRANSFER NEWS

The British transfer record was broken this week when 20 year-old Denis Law moved from Huddersfield Town to Manchester City for £53,000. He will make his debut in Saturday's game at Elland Road and City hope that he will soon add to the eight League and Cup goals that he has already scored this season.
Other transfers this week included:
B. Larkin-Birmingham City to Norwich City;
J. Smith-West Ham United to Tottenham Hotspur;
D. Dunmore-Tottenham Hotspur to West Ham United;
F. Goodwin- Manchester United to Leeds United;
P. Fagan- Manchester City to Derby County.

Fri.18th-Preston announced that Tom Finney was still unfit and they will keep the same attack that secured a draw at Wolves for the game against Sheffield Wednesday at Deepdale tomorrow. Jim Smith will return at left-half in place of John Fullam.
Wednesday will be unchanged from the team that beat local rivals Sheffield United in the F.A. Cup.

SATURDAY 19TH MARCH

PRESTON N. E 3 SHEFFIELD WED. 4

Farrall 2 (1pen), Taylor — Wilkinson, Ellis 2, Craig.

Att. 16,497

P.N.E.-*Else, Wilson, Walton, Milne, Richardson, Smith, Dagger, Farrall, Alston, Sneddon, Taylor.*

SHEFFIELD WED.-*Springett, Martin, Megson, McAnearney, Swan, Kay, Wilkinson, Craig, Ellis, Fantham, Finney.*

Joe Walton captained North End in the absence of Tom Finney but Wednesday won the toss and elected to play into a stiff south-easterly wind on a firm, fairly dry pitch in front of a poor crowd of only 16,497.

In the opening stages play was scrappy with fouls by both sides preventing any continuity. Good passing by Dagger and Farrall resulted in a free-kick. The ball was squared to Dagger who shot straight at Springett. Megson then grounded Dagger and this cynical approach by Wednesday set the scene for the game.

North End continued to look dangerous, and after 12 minutes, following excellent work by Alston and Farrall, the ball was played to Sneddon who shrewdly pulled it back to FARRALL to sidefoot it past England's 'keeper.

Preston almost increased their lead immediately when Alston had an effort cleared off the line by Martin.

The game was entertaining and Richardson twice saved Preston with good strong tackles but the equaliser was not long coming. In the 17th minute a good open move by Sheffield ended in WILKINSON beating Else with a fast, low slanting shot into the corner of the net. Kay, Swan and Martin were difficult to beat and continued to work hard against the lively Preston attack. They needed to be at their best as first Alston headed against the cross-bar and Dagger had a shot blocked.

Although the crowd was relatively small they applauded North End's endeavour and enjoyed the freedom and style of the younger players. Wednesday always remained dangerous with their wingers causing plenty of problems for Wilson and Walton. Long cross-field passes

and fast open play provided a contrast to the neater style of North End. Preston restored their lead when, after 32 minutes, Springett failed to catch a long cross from Dagger and TAYLOR nipped in to score before the goalkeeper could recover.
The perseverance of the Wednesday wingers soon led to an equaliser in the 35th minute when Megson moved down the wing beating Wilson before delivering an accurate centre for ELLIS to turn into the net.
The teams went in at half-time with the score 2-2

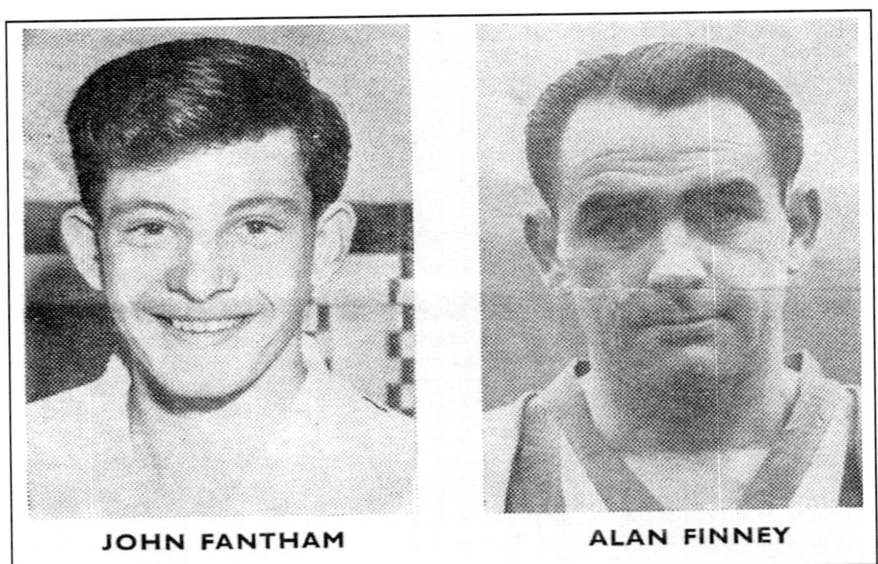
JOHN FANTHAM ALAN FINNEY

Wednesday came out for the second half in determined mood and within the first few minutes, Walton, Wilson and Richardson all had to beat off decisive raids. An injury to Taylor handicapped North End by reducing the effectiveness of the attack and Sheffield Wednesday's pressure was finally rewarded with two goals in two minutes. Wednesday took the lead for the first time in the game after 56 minutes when Else failed to deal with a high cross from CRAIG. The ball bounced off the 'keeper, hit the post and dropped into the net. Unfortunately for North End worse was to happen when a minute later, Else was deceived by the flight of a lob and could only knock the ball upwards and over his head. ELLIS had nothing to do but nod

it into the empty goal.
Richardson continued to have a tough game against Ellis, with both players often guilty of fouling each other. Megson and Alston were then involved in a melee and the referee took out his notebook. A minute later Milne was booked after flooring Swan. The game was fast deteriorating and Richardson fouled Wilkinson to add to the referee's list of bookings. The reckless tackles continued with Swan penalised for pushing Farrall. The Cup semi-finalists had no need to resort to the 'rough stuff' they dished out as they were well organised and had keen tackling wing-halves and dangerous forwards who were quick to probe any weakness in the home defence. It was a pity, because when both sides tried to play football, they had provided some good entertainment for the spectators.
The referee finally started to gain control of the game after being too lenient for long periods. Fouls had been frequent from the start and the tendency to play the man rather than the ball, especially by Sheffield Wednesday, led to ill feeling, loss of temper and friction as well as agitating the crowd.
Six minutes from time North End scored a consolation goal when Megson handled a centre from Dagger in the penalty area and FARRALL scored from the spot. In one final attempt Alston only gained a corner when he could possibly have scored and the final whistle signalled yet another North End home defeat.

MARCH 19TH DIVISION 1 RESULTS

BIRMINGHAM C.	*2*	*BOLTON WAND.*	*5*
BURNLEY	*3*	*ARSENAL*	*2*
CHELSEA	*2*	*BLACKPOOL*	*3*
LEEDS UTD.	*4*	*MANCHESTER CITY*	*3*
LEICESTER CITY	*2*	*WOLVES.*	*1*
MANCHESTER U.	*3*	*NOTTINGHAM F.*	*1*
NEWCASTLE U.	*3*	*LUTON TOWN*	*2*
PRESTON N.E.	*3*	*SHEFFIELD WED.*	*4*
TOTTENHAM H.	*1*	*FULHAM*	*1*
WEST BROM. A.	*6*	*EVERTON*	*2*
WEST HAM UTD.	*2*	*BLACKBURN ROV.*	*1*

TOP HALF OF TABLE

	P.	W.	D.	L.	F.	A.	P.
Tottenham H.	34	18	10	6	73	40	46
Wolves	34	19	5	10	83	60	43
Burnley	32	19	4	9	71	48	42
Sheff. Wed.	33	16	7	10	61	41	39
West Brom A.	34	14	10	10	67	50	38
Bolton Wand.	34	15	8	11	48	43	38
Newcastle U.	34	16	5	13	74	66	37
Fulham	34	14	8	12	64	66	36
Preston N. E.	**34**	**13**	**10**	**11**	**64**	**66**	**36**
Blackpool	34	14	7	13	53	56	35
West Ham U.	34	15	4	15	66	71	34

On a day when fifty-six goals were scored in the eleven Division 1 games, Derek Kevan led the way with five goals for West Bromwich Albion in their 6-2 defeat of Everton, to bring his season's total to twenty-three in League and Cup games.

North End Reserves drew 0-0 at Chesterfield Reserves in a keenly fought battle between two evenly matched sides. North End's team was as follows: Kelly, Heyes, O'Neill, Fullam, Singleton, O'Farrell, Campbell, Hatsell, Kerry, Byrne and Lambert.

The F.A. Youth Cup semi-final draw has ensured a North v South final. The matches which will be played over two legs on a home and away basis are;
Preston North End v Manchester United
West Ham United v Bristol City or Chelsea

Tues.22nd-SOCCER WAGES
Three days before the London meeting of the Football League Clubs' chairmen, the Professional Footballers' Association discussed last night the possibility of going to arbitration over money grievances.
After their annual general meeting in Manchester, the Association's secretary, Mr. Cliff Lloyd, said he would write to the League informing them of the meeting's unanimous decision to raise again the removal of the maximum wage clause, a percentage of transfer fees and the minimum wage of £12 for a player over 21 years old.
Mr. Lloyd stated that the League, at their last meeting with them, were unwilling to discuss these points again and unless this viewpoint was changed the Association would consider themselves in dispute, which would mean the matter going to arbitration.
League Champion's, Wolverhampton Wanderers, intend to advocate that there should be a higher maximum wage, graded according to status with increased bonuses and/or talent money.
It is understood that the League Management Committee will propose the introduction of a new League Cup Competition based on two-legged matches possibly from the 1961/2 season.

Fri.25th March-North End announced that the team for tomorrow's game away to Nottingham Forest will show two changes from that which lost last Saturday.

Fullam will play at right-half in place of Milne and 17 year-old Jimmy Humes (pictured below) becomes the second member of this season's successful Youth Team to make his debut in the first team. He will play at outside-left in place of Sammy Taylor.

Goalkeeper John Barton, from the Youth Team played three games in the first team last season.

Joe Dunn is fit again but will only travel as twelfth man.

The full casualty list is as follows: Milne (ankle), Finney (groin), Thompson (ankle), Hatsell (ankle), O'Farrell (knee), Mayers (ankle), Taylor (ankle) and Cunningham recovering from a cartilage operation.

Nottingham Forest will have Roy Dwight back in the side for the first time since breaking his leg in the Cup Final victory over Luton Town at Wembley last May.

SATURDAY 26TH MARCH
F.A.CUP SEMI FINALS

ASTON VILLA 0 WOLVERHAMPTON WANDERERS 1
Deeley (played at the Hawthorns)
Att. 55,596

SHEFFIELD WEDNESDAY 1 BLACKBURN ROVERS 2
Fantham
Dougan 2 (played at Maine Road)
Att. 74,135

++++++++++

NOTTINGHAM FOREST 1 PRESTON N. E. 1

Dwight
Sneddon Att. 19,855

NOTT'M. F.-*Armstrong, Thomas, McDonald, Whitefoot, McKinlay, Burkitt, Dwight, Booth, Wilson, Gray, Imlach.*

P.N.E.-*Else, Wilson, Walton, Fullam, Richardson, Smith, Dagger, Farrall, Alston, Sneddon, Humes.*

This was the classic game of two halves with the zestful, energetic, young North End attack being on top in the first half and the more experienced, methodical Forest forward line providing the danger in the second.

Despite Preston's early superiority they had only one goal to show for their efforts. This came after 16 minutes following a swift moving attack down the right flank. Sneddon sent the ball through to Alston who moved out to the right wing 'dragging' his marker with him before hitting the ball to the far post. Humes played the ball inside and Farrell helped it on to SNEDDON who ran in to drive a hard low shot into the net off the goalkeeper's legs. This was Sneddon's eleventh goal in league and cup this season.

The chances continued to fall to North End and Dagger had a soft header saved and just failed to connect with a crossfield ball with an open net awaiting.

Humes gave a confident display on the left wing and developed a good understanding with Sneddon. On one occasion he almost created a goal after intercepting a back pass meant for the goalkeeper. He passed the ball to Dagger who flicked it sideways but unfortunately no

one could take advantage of the cross.
At the other end, Else was mainly kept busy dealing with high balls and crosses. Richardson and Wilson had a private duel. After one pushing contest they were both sternly spoken to by referee Mr Woan.
Humes sent Sneddon away down the left side late in the half, but the Scot didn't hit the ball strongly enough and Armstrong was able to save.
Almost on half-time North End had a let off when Booth should have scored, following a free-kick, but shot wide of the post.

Forest began to push forward with more urgency in the second half and after 53 minutes they drew level.
Imlach went down the left-wing with an electrifying burst of speed and sold Wilson a 'dummy' in the process. He then hit a long cross field pass to Gray on the opposite wing. Gray squared the ball back into the middle where DWIGHT shot hard and low to beat Else. Dwight was overjoyed and celebrated with his team mates on scoring in his first game after his long absence through injury.

Not long afterwards the same player ran straight down the middle, out running the P.N.E. defenders, but saw his powerful shot pass inches outside the post.
Alston then provided the crowd with a glimpse of some wonderful ball skills. He back headed the ball over McKinlay and turned around to race towards goal leaving the centre-half helpless. Thomas then forced Alston to run wider allowing McKinlay to recover in time to foul Alston from behind and earn a lecture from the referee. Nothing

came from the free kick and little was seen of the North End forward line for the remainder of the game.
Forest forwards became far more penetrative and Gray proved troublesome down the right-wing forcing a corner after his shot had ricocheted off a Preston defender.

BOB WILSON

JOE WALTON

Else then made two saves in quick succession following desperate defending by Wilson and Walton who both nearly scored own goals whilst trying to block shots from the Forest forwards. Else was certainly back to his best and ensured that Preston hung on for a draw with some brilliant saves and clean handling.

North End Reserves had a good victory away at Wolverhampton Wanderers reserves with O'Neill scoring the only goal of the game to move the Reserves to ninth position in the Central League.

SAT. 26TH MAR. DIVISION 1 RESULTS

ARSENAL	*1*	*LEEDS UNITED*	*1*
BLACKPOOL	*2*	*WEST BROM. A.*	*0*
BOLTON WAND.	*2*	*TOTTENHAM H.*	*1*
FULHAM	*0*	*MANCHESTER U.*	*5*
LUTON TOWN	*1*	*BIRMINGHAM C.*	*1*
NOTTINGHAM F.	*1*	*PRESTON N.E.*	*1*

TOP 6 CLUBS

	P	W	D	L	F	A	Pts
Spurs	35	18	10	7	74	42	46
Wolves	34	19	5	10	83	60	43
Burnley	32	19	4	9	71	48	42
Bolton	35	16	8	11	50	44	40
Sheff.W	33	16	7	10	61	41	39
W.B.A.	35	14	10	11	67	52	38

Wed.30th-North End's game at Bolton Wanderers a week on Saturday has been put back from a 3pm kick-off to 7pm so as not to clash with the T.V. broadcast of the Scotland v England game. It will also avoid a clash with the Holcombe Point to Point race meeting.

WED. 30TH MARCH DIV. 1 RESULTS

BLACKBURN R.	*1*	*CHELSEA*	*0*
MANCHESTER C.	*3*	*WEST HAM UTD.*	*1*
SHEFFIELD W.	*4*	*MANCHESTER U.*	*2*
WOLVES.	*6*	*BURNLEY*	*1*

The most significant result of the evening was at Molineux where goals from Mannion 2, Mason, Broadbent, Murray and Horne put a severe dent in Burnley's title aspirations.

Thurs.31st Mar.-Youth will give way to experience for North End's home game against Fulham at Deepdale on Saturday. Dunn, Finney and Taylor return to the team in place of Richardson, Alston and Humes. Finney has missed the last three games due to a groin strain. Fulham will make a number of changes with Bentley moving back to centre-half after his emergency role at centre-forward. Cook is suspended and Lampe, Hill and Macedo are injured. Hawkins will take over in goal for his third League game of the season. Doherty will play at centre-forward and Key and Stokes will join him in the forward line.

APRIL 1960
SATURDAY 2ND APRIL

PRESTON NORTH END 4 FULHAM 1

Dagger, Sneddon, Finney 2 Haynes

Att. 15,007

P.N.E.-*Else, Wilson, Walton, Fullam, Dunn, Smith, Dagger, Farrall, Finney, Sneddon, Taylor.*

FULHAM-*Hawkins, Cohen, Langley, Mullery, Bentley, Lowe, Key, Stokes, Doherty, Haynes, Leggat.*

At last a performance by Preston to give their supporters something to cheer about. Fulham had two players, Haynes and Leggat, who will both play in next Saturday's International at Hampden Park, but it was North End who simply swept their opponents away and could have scored a bagfull of goals.

On a blustery, dull and chilly afternoon at Deepdale, Tom Finney was the inspiration behind the Preston victory on his return to the side. He gave a wonderful individual performance scoring two goals but also his general leadership and guile proved just too much for the Fulham defenders.

In the opening minutes, Finney put Taylor through with a neat back-pass. The winger crossed the ball and Fullam hit a rasping drive, which was turned round the post by the goalkeeper. Smith then shot narrowly wide from the corner.

Both sides played the ball on the ground and Else was next in action saving a crisp shot from Doherty and then another effort from Stokes. North End continued to look dangerous and following a save by Hawkins from Farrall, they took the lead in the 13th minute when DAGGER headed home a cross from Sneddon.

Almost immediately Dagger had a shot into the side netting and then Finney joined in the shooting practice by hitting a drive which flashed a yard wide.

After 19 minutes North End had an escape when Else caught a cross on the goal line and was charged by Doherty. Fortunately Else threw the ball clear before ending up in the back of the net himself from the

force of the collision.
The game moved on quickly and a minute later Preston increased their lead with a fine goal by SNEDDON. After receiving a pass from Finney, he swerved and dribbled past a defender before hitting a hard right foot shot into the far corner of the net.

FULHAM
Back row- G. Cohen, A. Mullery, E. Macedo, J. Stapleton, R. Lawler. Front row- G. Leggat, J. Hill, A. Stokes, J. Doherty, M. Johnson, J. Langley.

North End continued to be well on top and despite the smallest gate of the season so far at Deepdale, the crowd generated a good atmosphere. For once North End were not trying to walk the ball into the net and Hawkins, deputising for Macedo, was kept busy by the constant barrage of shots at his goal. He saved from Taylor and then saw a shot from Finney deflected.
Sneddon had his best game for some time and his constant probing and accurate passing was a joy to watch.

FURNIVAL CARTOON 'THE MASTER'

From the L.E.P. Monday 4th April 1960

The crowd could see the confidence returning to the Preston team and after 31 minutes they went 3-0 ahead. Smith hit a long pass to FINNEY, who ran through the Fulham defence, rounded the goalkeeper and tapped the ball into the empty net.
Haynes showed a touch of class with a first time shot which Else saved but in general Fulham were too busy defending to provide any real threat to the North End defence and went into the interval 3-0 down.
On the resumption, Fulham surprised Preston by pulling a goal back immediately, when HAYNES hit a shot, which rebounded into the net off a post. Although the linesman was flagging for off-side, the referee Mr Crawford, from Doncaster just ignored him and awarded a goal.
The goal gave Fulham a new lease of life and Stokes hit the base of the post and shortly afterwards Doherty headed against the underside of the cross-bar.
Almost on the hour mark Preston restored their three goal advantage when FINNEY took advantage of indecision in the shaky defence to pounce upon a diagonal pass from Sneddon and shoot into the net.
Time and time again North End could have increased their lead and Finney continued to tantalise the Fulham defenders, leading them astray and opening up a path for others.
Fifteen minutes from time Farrall sent Finney clear but he was unable to take advantage of the opportunity and the chance went begging.
In the closing stages Dagger missed two scoring opportunities and the final whistle ended a very satisfying afternoon for both the Preston team and their supporters.

....

With Spavin and Hume in the side North End Reserves gave one of their worst displays of the season in losing 4-0 away to Sheffield Wednesday Reserves.

SAT. 2ND APRIL DIV. 1 RESULTS

BIRMINGHAM C.	*2*	*EVERTON*	*2*
BURNLEY	*3*	*SHEFIELD W.*	*3*
CHELSEA	*3*	*MANCHESTER C.*	*0*
LEEDS UNITED	*0*	*WOLVES*	*3*
LEICESTER C.	*0*	*NOTTINGHAM F.*	*1*
MANCHESTER U.	*2*	*BOLTON WAND.*	*0*
NEWCASTLE U.	*1*	*BLACKPOOL*	*1*
PRESTON N.E.	*4*	*FULHAM*	*1*
TOTTENHAM H.	*1*	*LUTON TOWN*	*1*
WEST BROM. A.	*2*	*BLACKBURN R.*	*0*
WEST HAM U.	*0*	*ARSENAL*	*0*

		Home					Away					
	P.	W.	D.	L.	F.	A.	W.	D.	L.	F.	A.	Pts.
Tottenham H. ..	36	9	6	3	39	21	9	5	4	36	22	47
Wolverh'pton W.	36	13	3	2	54	24	8	2	8	38	37	47
Burnley	34	13	1	4	48	28	6	4	6	27	29	43
Sheffield Wed.	35	10	6	1	41	14	7	2	9	27	32	42
West Brom. A. ..	36	10	3	5	43	23	5	7	6	26	29	40
Newcastle United	36	9	4	5	38	28	8	2	8	39	40	40
Bolton Wanderers	36	9	5	4	30	25	7	3	8	20	21	40
Preston N.E. ..	36	8	5	5	36	32	6	6	6	33	36	39
Blackpool ..	36	9	4	5	31	30	6	4	8	25	27	38
Manchester Utd.	36	10	3	5	42	27	5	4	9	43	41	37
Fulham	36	10	3	5	36	26	4	5	9	29	49	36
West Ham Utd...	36	11	2	5	43	29	4	3	11	24	45	35
Arsenal	36	7	5	6	31	32	6	4	8	29	35	35
Blackburn Rovers	35	11	2	4	34	23	4	1	13	21	38	33
Leicester City ..	35	7	5	6	32	26	4	5	8	24	39	32
Chelsea	36	7	4	7	41	41	5	4	9	27	38	32
Nottingham For.	36	7	5	6	27	27	5	2	11	18	41	31
Manchester City	35	9	2	6	43	30	4	1	13	28	47	29
Everton	36	10	3	5	43	19	0	6	12	20	50	29
Birmingham City	35	7	5	5	32	28	2	4	12	20	41	27
Leeds United ..	35	4	5	9	33	45	5	4	8	25	40	27
Luton Town ..	36	5	4	9	19	24	2	7	9	23	39	25

LEADING SCORERS

Viollet	Man. U.	32
Greaves	Chelsea	28
White	Newcastle	26
Smith	Spurs	26
Murray	Wolves	26
McCole	Leeds	25
Kevan	W.B.A.	24
Connelly	Burnley	23
Dobing	Blackburn	21
Pointer	Burnley	21
Robson	Burnley	21
McAdams	Man. City	21
Leggat	Fulham	20
Charlton	Man. U.	19
Eastham	Newcastle	19
FINNEY	**PRESTON**	**19**
Weston	Birmingham	18

Mannion scored a hat-trick for Wolves in their 3-0 victory at Leeds United to move level on points with Spurs who could only manage a draw with bottom placed Luton Town at White Hart Lane.

Burnley dropped a point after drawing at home against Sheffield Wednesday but still have two games in hand on the top two teams.

Wed.6th April-Sheffield Wednesday drew 2-2 at home to Leicester City to leave them four points behind Spurs and Wolves with only six games to play.

Fri.8th –After being suspended for three games, John Higgins will return at centre-half for the local derby against North End at Burnden Park tomorrow. Deakin replaces Parry who is on International duty with England.
Following his two goals last Saturday, Tom Finney will again lead the Preston attack and for the first time since England resumed battle with Scotland at Hampden Park after World War II, he will not be in the England side.
Campbell will play in place of Taylor on the left-wing and Milne replaces Farrall.

SATURDAY 9TH APRIL

BOLTON WANDERERS 2 PRESTON N.E. 1

Stevens, Hartle (pen) — Finney

Att. 30,816

BOLTON-*Bollands, Hartle, Banks, Stanley, Higgins, Cunliffe, Bannister N., Hill, Stevens, Deakin, Holden*

P.N.E.-*Else, Wilson, Walton, Fullam, Dunn, Smith, Dagger, Milne, Finney, Sneddon, Campbell.*

GREAT HALF-CHANCE NORTH END GOAL

Bolton almost let Finney steal points

By John Taylor

(L.E.P. article Monday 11th April, 1960)

TOM FINNEY did his best to earn Preston North End two points they did not deserve, from their Saturday night out against Bolton Wanderers, at Burnden Park. When all is said and done about him holding the 'line up' because he is not as fast in the dart-through as he used to be, there remains the stark truth that there is no one on North End's books who can take chances as he can.

If it be true that this North End attack had not the speed of the opposition line to create chances for itself, then it is also certain that with only half a chance Finney gave his side an interval lead with a magnificent goal.

Barrier broken

No other North End forward, or indeed a Wanderers' attacker in this game, could have scored from this situation. In the middle, with a mountain of flesh of Higgins, Stanley and Hartle aligned in a protective barrier in front of him, Finney veered to the left-wing. A pass to Campbell looked likely. So the defending trio thought as each delayed his tackle.

Suddenly, in a move towards goal, Finney leapt forward, darted cheekily into a gap and when well within striking distance of two of them, cracked a hard left foot shot from the edge of the penalty area just inside the post, before a defending foot was lifted.

This in the 34th minute by which time Bolton ought to have had a hatful.

They flew from point-to-point with the urgency of Holcombe Hunt chasers, so often in the first half that chance creating was made to look easy. Just as simply, they threw them away. It was easy to see why Stevens, although he has scored twelve goals, since he filled this trouble-spot, is criticised as a poor successor to Lofthouse. It is an unfair comparison since the "Lion" was so adept with his head in meeting centres from all angles and at varying speeds.

Eight good opportunities had been scorned by Bolton when Finney gave his object lesson in the art. Deakin shot over from a good position, Stevens only deflected with his head a centre by Hill wide of the post, when had his judgement been that of a Lofthouse, Else must surely have been beaten. Then the North End 'keeper, who was in fine form, denied Deakin a goal with a spectacular save.

Few by comparison

Stevens then shot wide, Wilson I suspect handled Hill's shot as he stood on the line and immediately, from the same spot, kicked Holden's return clear in a scramble which North End were lucky to survive. Next, Dunn, also from the line, headed away for a corner Bannister's header after Else had dropped Hill's corner.

DENIS STEVENS

Trickery by this outstanding ball-player Hill left Smith beaten, and from the inside-right's centre Holden headed into Else's hands. All these before Finney scored.

By comparison Dagger had shot wide as had Milne following a misdirected attempt by Sneddon. These bids were all North End were allowed in a first half of pushing, ankle-tapping and temper which weak refereeing fostered.

The referee did his best in that first half to show that he was no "homer" as the saying is, for he leaned North End's way-to the crowd's annoyance naturally. Yet he was over sympathetic, for North End did their share.

The half of too many fouls would have been better for stricter control. At the interval one had fears that if the second half continued in like vein, the game would be out of hand.

Fortunately that never happened, for Bolton proceeded to tear away in great style with an urgency in playing the ball instead of the man that smacked of First Division talent money.

There was a suspicion of off-side when in a goal-mouth scramble after 50 minutes Stevens at last took a chance and equalised. Wanderers deserved to be level, mainly due to the industry and skill of their inside-forwards Hill and Deakin, who were never contained by Smith and Fullam. Their free moving line gave Dunn and company a hammering.

In the 74th minute Hartle settled the issue with a penalty.

Deakin was going through when Walton, coming across as the covering back, took the ball but floored the centre forward in the act.

A rare chance came to Milne, but from a good position he showed little balance and shot badly wide. In general, the young wing-half, tried again forward, did not add any punch to the line. But Else did into his goalkeeping. His save of Deakin's whizz bang, deflecting the shot onto the post and to safety was thrilling.

Yet, in the last minute, North End could have had a penalty.

Hartle, in going up high with Finney to meet one of Dagger's many accurate centres, clearly pulled the ball off Finney's head with a hand.

This was another official sin of omission and commission, some of which brought catcalls, whistles, and the slow hand clap from a 30,816 crowd.

Saturday evening football in Bolton is popular for this was higher than Wanderers' home Saturday afternoon average "gate".

ROY HARTLE

SAT. 9TH APRIL RESULTS

INTERNATIONAL MATCH

SCOTLAND	*1*	*ENGLAND*	*1*

DIVISION 1

ARSENAL	*1*	*CHELSEA*	*4*
BLACKBURN ROV.	*1*	*NEWCASTLE UTD.*	*1*
BLACKPOOL	*0*	*BIRMINGHAM C.*	*1*
BOLTON WAND.	*2*	*PRESTON N.E.*	*1*
EVERTON	*2*	*TOTTENHAM H.*	*1*
FULHAM	*1*	*LEICESTER CITY*	*1*
LUTON TOWN	*2*	*MANCHESTER U.*	*3*
MANCHESTER C.	*0*	*WEST BROM. ALB.*	*1*
NOTTINGHAM F.	*0*	*BURNLEY*	*1*
SHEFFIELD WED.	*1*	*LEEDS UNITED*	*0*

Scotland 1 England 1

Scotland Team-F. Haffey (Celtic), **D. Mackay** (Spurs), **E. Caldow** (Rangers), **J. Cumming** (Hearts), **R. Evans** (Celtic), **R. McCann** (Motherwell), **G. Leggat** (Fulham), **A. Young** (Hearts), **I. St. John** (Motherwell), **D. Law** (Manchester City), **A. Weir** (Motherwell).

England Team-R. Springett (Sheffield Wednesday), **J. Armfield** (Blackpool), **R. Wilson** (Huddersfield Town), **R. Clayton** (Blackburn Rovers), **W. Slater, R. Flowers** (Wolves), **J. Connelly** (Burnley), **P. Broadbent** (Wolves), **J. Baker** (Hibernian), **R. Parry** (Bolton Wanderers), **R. Charlton** (Manchester United).

A crowd of 100,000 at Hampden Park plus many more on T.V. saw one of the dullest Internationals between the two countries for many years. Leggat scored in the first half for Scotland and Charlton equalised with a penalty in the second.
The draw resulted in England Scotland and Wales having a triple tie with four points each in the Home International Championship table.

North End Reserves were beaten for the second week running by the same 4-0 score-line, this time at home to Aston Villa Reserves. The first half was very even with Preston unlucky to go in 1-0 down but in the second half they were completely outplayed.

Everton put a serious dent in Spurs Championship hopes when they beat them 2-1 at Goodison Park. The points were also vital for Everton's relegation battle and have enabled them to move four points clear of the second bottom club.
Burnley's away win at Nottingham Forest ensured that they remained in touch with the leading teams, still having two games in hand.

Mon.11th –Wolves had switched their home game against West Ham United to Monday night to ensure that Slater, Flowers and Broadbent, who played for England on Saturday, would all be available to play in the game. It proved to be a good move as Wolves over-ran the Hammers winning 5-0 with goals from Murray 2, Clamp, Horne and Mannion, to move into top spot in the table.

Deepdale was the scene of the semi-final first-leg of the F.A. Youth Cup between North End and Manchester United. Since the competition was introduced in the 1952/3 season, United had won

the Trophy on five occasions. Both teams fielded their regular and strongest teams.
Preston took the lead after 12 minutes through Peter Thompson who glanced home a free kick taken by Hart. Five minutes before half-time Preston increased their lead after a centre from Thompson was driven into the net by Jimmy Humes. John Barton, in the North End goal, dealt admirably with everything that United threw at him.
The tempo increased in the second half and United refrained from their previous rough tactics and started to play more attractive football to try and get back into the game. However, the Preston defence held firm, with Barton, Hart and Ross outstanding.
In the 85th minute Thompson scored a third goal with a fierce drive after cutting in from the left flank.
An excellent crowd of 18,430 (more than the gate for the last Division 1 game at Deepdale) witnessed a superb performance from the young P.N.E. side, who now have one foot in the final.

Tues.12th- ***P.N.E. BOARD MEETING-It was reported that Mr Cook, the referee from Saturday's game at Bolton had only been awarded 1 point. 'He was lacking in control, allowed himself to be influenced by the crowd and gave many inexplicable decisions.'***

Wed.13th- The Football League have told the Professional Footballers' Association that they do not consider that an industrial dispute exists between the members of the Association and their employers, as the Association claimed in a letter to the League last month.
The Association called for the abolition of the maximum wage-but the League reject this.
In an extract from his letter in reply, Mr Hardaker the Secretary of the Football League, said "My committee are concerned with the improvement of the League, to promote its success and the welfare of all its players and clubs. To achieve these objects the Committee relies upon certain well-recognised principles. One is that there should be a maximum wage and another a retain and transfer system.
In these ways, the committee seek to preserve balance and order between the star and other players and the wealthier and poorer clubs."

Mr Jimmy Hill, Chairman of the P.F.A., said "It seems from the League's reply that we are in dispute on the major issues. Our committee will be holding a meeting on Sunday week in Manchester to consider the situation."

FURNIVAL FROM L.E.P. APRIL 1960

Thurs.14th-The next five days over the Easter period are crucial, as all teams will play three games and the picture in terms of the Championship title and relegation places should become much clearer. North End have announced that the team will remain unchanged for their first Easter game against Blackpool at Deepdale on Saturday. This is the first time that this has been possible since mid-December. Durie will be in the Blackpool team on Saturday but is not available for the Good Friday game against Everton due to religious reasons. Below is shown the current League table together with details of the main games that will influence league positions.

DIVISION 1 PRIOR TO THE EASTER GAMES

		P	W	D	L	F	A	PTS
1	WOLVERHAMPTON W.	37	22	5	10	97	61	49
2	TOTTENHAM HOTSPUR	37	18	11	8	76	45	47
3	SHEFFIELD WED.	37	18	9	10	71	48	45
4	BURNLEY	35	20	5	10	76	57	45
5	WEST BROMWICH ALB	37	16	10	11	70	52	42
6	BOLTON WANDERERS	37	17	8	12	52	47	42
7	NEWCASTLE UNITED	37	17	7	13	78	69	41
8	MANCHESTER UNITED	37	16	7	14	88	70	39
9	**PRESTON NORTH END**	**37**	**14**	**11**	**12**	**70**	**70**	**39**
10	BLACKPOOL	37	15	8	14	56	58	38
11	FULHAM	37	14	9	14	66	76	37
12	WEST HAM UNITED	37	15	5	17	67	79	35
13	ARSENAL	37	13	9	15	61	71	35
14	BLACKBURN ROVERS	36	15	4	17	56	62	34
15	CHELSEA	37	13	8	16	72	80	34
16	LEICESTER CITY	37	11	12	14	59	68	34
17	EVERTON	37	11	9	17	65	70	31
18	NOTTINGHAM FOREST	37	12	7	18	45	69	31
19	BIRMINGHAM CITY	36	10	9	17	53	69	29
20	MANCHESTER CITY	36	13	3	20	71	78	29
21	LEEDS UNITED	36	9	9	18	58	86	27
22	LUTON TOWN	37	7	11	19	44	66	25

TOP OF DIVISION 1

	Fri.15th	Sat. 16th	Mon.18th	Tues. 19th
WOLVES	-	Newcastle (a)	Nott'm F.(h)	Nott'm F. (a)
SPURS	Chelsea (a)	Man. C. (h)	Chelsea (h)	-
SHEFF. W.	Newcastle (a)	W.B.A. (a)	Newcastle (h)	-
BURNLEY	Leicester (h)	Luton T. (h)	Leicester (a)	-
W.B.A.	-	Sheff. W. (h)	Birm. C. (a)	Birm. C. (h)
BOLTON W.	Man. C. (a)	Leeds U. (a)	Man. C. (h)	-

BOTTOM OF DIVISION 1

EVERTON	B'pool (h)	Leicester (a)	B'pool (a)	-
NOTT'M. F.	-	Chelsea (a)	Wolves (a)	Wolves (h)
BIRM. C.	-	Arsenal (h)	W.B.A. (h)	W.B.A. (a)
MAN. C.	Bolton W. (h)	Spurs (a)	Bolton W. (a)	-
LEEDS U.	-	Bolton W. (h)	P.N.E. (a)	P.N.E. (h)
LUTON T.	Blackburn (a)	Burnley (a)	Blackburn (h)	-

GOOD FRIDAY 15TH APRIL 1960
DIVISION 1 RESULTS AND SCORERS

ARSENAL *Henderson, Herd*	**2**	**FULHAM** *Att. 37,653*	**0**
BLACKBURN ROVERS	**0**	**LUTON TOWN** *McBride, Bingham* *Att. 22,714*	**2**
BURNLEY *Connelly*	**1**	**LEICESTER CITY** *Att. 23,777*	**0**
CHELSEA *Brabrook*	**1**	**TOTTENHAM HOTSPUR** *Smith 3.* *Att. 67,819*	**3**
EVERTON *Vernon 2, Collins, J. Harris*	**4**	**BLACKPOOL** *Att. 65,719*	**0**
MANCHESTER CITY *Barlow*	**1**	**BOLTON WANDERERS** *Att. 50,053*	**0**
NEWCASTLE UNITED *White 2, Bell*	**3**	**SHEFFIELD WED.** *Ellis, Fantham, Wilkinson* *Att. 39,942*	**3**
WEST HAM UNITED *Grice, Musgrove*	**2**	**MANCHESTER UNITED** *Dawson* *Att. 34,969*	**1**

EASTER SATURDAY 16TH APRIL

BIRMINGHAM CITY	**3**	**ARSENAL**	**0**
Murphy 2, Gordon			*Att. 27,201*
BURNLEY	**3**	**LUTON TOWN**	**0**
McIlroy (pen), Pointer, Robson			*Att. 20,893*
CHELSEA	**1**	**NOTTINGHAM FOREST**	**1**
Greaves		*Barton*	*Att. 24,542*
LEEDS UNITED	**1**	**BOLTON WANDERERS**	**0**
Charlton			*Att. 19,272*
LEICESTER CITY	**3**	**EVERTON**	**3**
Cheesebrough, McLintock, Chalmers (pen)		*Collins 2 (1pen), Lill*	*Att. 22,390*
MANCHESTER UNITED	**1**	**BLACKBURN ROVERS**	**0**
Dawson			*Att. 46,071*
NEWCASTLE UNITED	**1**	**WOLVERHAMPTON W.**	**0**
White			*Att. 47,409*
PRESTON NORTH END	**4**	**BLACKPOOL**	**1**
Campbell, Dagger, Finney, Sneddon		*Charnley*	*Att. 26,126*
TOTTENHAM HOTSPUR	**0**	**MANCHESTER CITY**	**1**
		McAdams	*Att. 49,767*
WEST BROMWICH ALBION	**3**	**SHEFFIELD WED.**	**1**
Burnside, Kevan, Jackson		*Griffin*	*Att. 27,806*
WEST HAM UNITED	**1**	**FULHAM**	**2**
Smillie		*Chamberlain, O'Connell*	*Att. 34,085*

PRESTON NORTH END 4 BLACKPOOL 1

P.N.E.-*Else, Wilson, Walton, Fullam, Dunn, Smith, Dagger, Milne, Finney, Sneddon, Campbell.*

BLACKPOOL-*Waiters, Armfield, Martin, Kelly J., Gratrix, Durie, Hill, Mudie, Charnley, Smethurst, Fawcett.*

After losing 4-0 at Everton yesterday Blackpool arrived at Deepdale hoping to gain their first points of the Easter period, but with an inexperienced attack they were no match for North End and conceded another four goals.

On a bright, sunny afternoon, a crowd of over 26,000 were disappointed that Stan Matthews was unfit, following a knock sustained yesterday and his place was taken by 19 years old, South African born Peter Smethurst for his League debut.

It was soon evident that the more experienced Preston side would prove too much of a handful for the Blackpool defence with their passing and move style being a joy to watch for the home crowd.

After only 15 minutes North End went ahead. Sneddon hit a strong volley which Waiters could only 'parry' into the path of CAMPBELL for him to easily score.

Five minutes later Preston went 2-0 up with a move started by schemer Finney. He played the ball to Milne who then laid it on to DAGGER for him to hit into the corner of the net.

Blackpool struggled 'up front' except for Ray Charnley who always kept the North End defenders on their toes with his strength and speed. It was CHARNLEY who pulled a goal back for the 'Seasider's' after 23 minutes with a fine header which Else completely misjudged.

A few minutes later, Charnley should have equalised when he ran onto a great pass by Durie but shot high over the cross-bar.

Blackpool started to apply more pressure and the game quickly moved from one end of the pitch to the other but it was Preston who always looked more dangerous especially when Finney had the ball. Two minutes before half-time Milne played a long through ball and FINNEY raced through the centre of the Blackpool defence before lobbing the ball over the advancing Waiters into the empty net, to give Preston a 3-1 interval lead.

Kelly did not return for Blackpool for the second-half after being concussed in a clash of heads just before half-time.

P·N·E.
v
Blackpool
Pleasant !!
What the heck's pleasant about it ?
This was a pleasant Saturday afternoon type of game
CAMPBELL
DAGGER
WELL, MAYBE IT WAS, BUT WE DOUBT IF THE BLACKPOOL 'KEEPER WOULD AGREE.
AFTER PICKING TWO OUT OF HIS NET IN THE FIRST 22 MINUTES
THE FIRST P.S.A. FEELING ONLY CAME WHEN CHARNLEY MADE IT 2-1
AT 3-45 HE CAME OUT TO GET A BETTER VIEW OF THE GAME — AND IMMEDIATELY A NEAT FINNEY LOB WENT OVER HIS HEAD INTO THE NET.
Was that pleasant ?
NO!
IN THE SECOND HALF, WHEN SNEDDON PUT ANOTHER IN
Did he wear a pleasant expression?
WELL, NOT PARTICULARLY.
I'm just back. We lost 4-1
NOT A "GREAT" DERBY GAME — DUE TO ABSENTEES, AND THE 'POOL BEING A MAN SHORT FOR THE SECOND HALF. — BUT WAS IT A "PLEASANT" ONE ?
WELL, IT ALL DEPENDS ON WHETHER THE 26,126 WHO SAW IT CAME FROM PRESTON — OR THE SEASIDE.

"QUERY"

Ray Charnley moved back into the defence leaving the forward line even more threadbare than before.
It was not long until North End scored again following good work by Milne down the right wing. His centre reached SNEDDON who scored with a low drive.
The ten men of Blackpool fought a rearguard action to try and prevent Preston from scoring again and in the end succeeded, partly because North End lost interest in killing the game off completely.

Following an inter-passing movement down the right-wing between Milne and Dagger, the winger cut in and beat Waiters with a hard shot just inside the near post for North End's second goal.

David Sneddon did hit the cross-bar and gave a thoroughly professional performance. Finney at times looked like the ball was fastened to him by a string, such was the mastery of his passing. Unfortunately at times his lack of acceleration enabled opponents to recover when he ran at the defence.
Smethurst, on his debut had two half chances for Blackpool but on each occasion failed to react quickly enough to take advantage of the situation.
A great victory for Preston giving them a 'double' over their local rivals from the seaside and a successful start to their Easter fixture programme. Leeds United are the next visitors to Deepdale on Easter Monday with an 11am kick-off.

North End Reserves suffered their third successive defeat when they lost 1-0 at Stoke City. Tommy Thompson played on his return from injury and gave an encouraging display.

Burnley made up ground on both Wolves and Spurs at the top of the table with an emphatic 3-0 home win over bottom club Luton Town. Wolves lost 1-0 at Newcastle and Spurs were surprisingly beaten by the same score at White Hart Lane against relegation threatened Manchester City.

Spurs should have had at least a point when, in injury time, at the end of the first-half they were awarded a penalty. Cliff Jones took the kick, which was saved by Trautmann, but the ball rebounded back to Jones who tapped it into the net. The referee correctly disallowed the goal as the rules state that the 45 minutes are completed as soon as the penalty kick either enters the net, misses the goal or is saved by the goalkeeper.

EASTER MONDAY 18TH APRIL

Home		Away	
BIRMINGHAM CITY	**1**	**WEST BROMWICH ALB.**	**7**
Gordon		*Allen 3(1pen),Jackson,Kevan 3*	
		Att. 28,685	
BLACKPOOL	**0**	**EVERTON**	**0**
		Att. 25,697	
BOLTON WANDERERS	**3**	**MANCHESTER CITY**	**1**
Holden, Stevens, Birch		*Barlow* *Att. 35,591*	
FULHAM	**3**	**ARSENAL**	**0**
Key, Jones, O'Connell		*Att. 31,058*	
LEICESTER CITY	**2**	**BURNLEY**	**1**
Cheesebrough, Wills		*Meredith* *Att. 24,429*	
LUTON TOWN	**1**	**BLACKBURN ROVERS**	**1**
Bingham		*Dobing* *Att. 14,167*	
MANCHESTER UNITED	**5**	**WEST HAM UNITED**	**3**
Charlton 2, Dawson 2, Quixall		*Cantwell (pen), Dunmore, Scott*	
		Att. 34,505	
PRESTON NORTH END	**1**	**LEEDS UNITED**	**1**
Sneddon		*Gibson* *Att. 15,879*	
SHEFFIELD WEDNESDAY	**2**	**NEWCASTLE UNITED**	**0**
Fantham, Froggat		*Att. 32,011*	
TOTTENHAM HOTSPUR	**0**	**CHELSEA**	**1**
		Greaves *Att. 37,205*	
WOLVERHAMPTON W.	**3**	**NOTTINGHAM FOREST**	**1**
Murray 2, McDonald (og)		*Younger* *Att. 39,834*	

PRESTON NORTH END 1 LEEDS UNITED 1

P.N.E.-*Else, Wilson, Walton, Fullam, Dunn, Smith, Dagger, Milne, Finney, Sneddon, Campbell.*
LEEDS U.-*Burgin, Ashall, Caldwell, Gibson, Charlton, Goodwin, Francis, Revie, McCole, Cush, Meek.*

On a bright, sunny Easter Monday morning at Deepdale a disappointing crowd of just fewer than 16,000 were present to witness a game of vital importance to Leeds United in their fight against relegation.

In the early stages, North End tried to play the ball along the ground, whereas Leeds played long balls down the middle, which Joe Dunn dealt with easily. The first attempt of the game fell to United but Francis shot wide of the post.

North End's passing was poor and Leeds were intent on playing a spoiling game, both facts resulting in a poor spectacle for the paying public.

After a quarter of an hour Campbell received an inch perfect pass from Finney, but although unmarked, screwed his shot wide. Finney was the next player to be guilty of wasting a good opportunity when he hit the ball high and wide.

The game was 'cat and mouse' and it was the 'Yorkshiremen' who had the next chance but Don Revie also shot wide.

At last something to stir the crowd. Finney headed goalwards only to see Goodwin head the ball off the line with the goalkeeper completely beaten. Then the ball went to the opposite penalty area and McCole shot straight at Else.

After 30 minutes Sneddon had a clash of heads with Gibson and was carried off the field. Despite only having ten men Preston should have gone ahead when a Finney pass to Milne was laid off to Campbell, who once again missed the target. Soon afterwards Milne drove a half volley over the bar.

Leeds also found themselves reduced to ten men when Meek had to leave the field after Wilson accidentally kicked him in the head just before half-time.

Sneddon resumed the second half with his head bandaged and 5 minutes later Meek reappeared for Leeds.

Revie had a right foot shot saved by Else and then a delightful move

involving Finney, Smith and Dagger resulted in Milne shooting over the bar.
A fierce cross-drive by McCole was diverted onto the cross-bar and Wilson hurriedly cleared the danger. A goal-less draw looked the most likely outcome. North End's play lacked the snap or decisiveness needed to control the game and Leeds became more positive. Else twice made brilliant saves to keep Preston in the match. Then in the 78th minute a goal finally came. Finney started the move from a throw in. Milne hit a fine square centre and the bandaged SNEDDON just managed to stick a foot out to divert the cross into the net.

Sneddon slides in to open the scoring for Preston

Finney then almost scored himself but the goalkeeper was able to divert the ball away and a defender cleared.
Just as Preston appeared to have the points in the bag Leeds snatched a life-line when 2 minutes from time Francis found GIBSON with a short pass and his low drive went into the corner of the net giving Else no chance.
It was a priceless point for Leeds in their relegation battle and yet another game of missed chances for Preston.

TUESDAY 19TH APRIL

LEEDS UNITED	**2**	**PRESTON NORTH END**	**1**
Charlton, Francis		*Campbell*	*Att. 23,764*
NOTTINGHAM FOREST	**0**	**WOLVERHAMPTON W.**	**0**
			Att. 42,335
WEST BROMWICH ALB.	**1**	**BIRMINGHAM CITY**	**1**
Kevan		*Gordon*	*Att. 37,894*

LEEDS UNITED 2 PRESTON NORTH END 1

LEEDS U.-*Burgin, Ashall, Caldwell, Gibson, Charlton, Goodwin, Francis, Revie, McCole, Cush, Meek.*
P.N.E.-*Else, Wilson, Walton, Fullam, Dunn, Smith, Dagger, Milne, Finney, Farrall, Campbell.*

NORTH END GIVE EASTER PRESENT

Leeds gained heart after Campbell miss

By John Taylor

(L.E.P. article Wednesday 20th April 1960)

PRESTON NORTH END adorned their Easter present in pink ribbon and presented it to Leeds United with the generosity of a fond parent to a child. The gift of a total three points from the two holiday encounters was timely for United and moved their vice-chairman, in his thankfulness, to an impromptu speech at Leeds yesterday.

Boarding the North End coach after the game at Elland Road where North End had just lost 2-1, Mr P.A. Woodward thanked the players for their sportsmanship. "Due to you, we shall be in the First Division next season. We know you were the better team but we got the points."

What he really meant was that Leeds should never have had those last two points. So completely dominated were Leeds in the first half after an early spell of fire that North End could have had the game securely arrayed in their Easter baskets by half-time.

Care-laden Leeds

At least they should have been ahead by 2-0, for it was most apparent that Leeds, in their anxiety, would then have been not only disheartened but a demoralised side.

United played like one heavily laden by the worry and awfulness of imminent relegation, and when Campbell put North End ahead by shooting in a lobbed centre by Finney which Milne, in the jaws of goal had missed badly, the inevitable defeat seemed to have been fashioned.

But for all their forthright football in the first half with good interchange of position, quick movement of the ball and some excellent support by wing-halves, Fullam and Smith, North End were restricted to a few good chances.

Farrall had a fine shot tipped over when it appeared to be about to stroke the bar. There was power in the drive, a quality lacking in other attempts by North End forwards whose timing in marksmanship was at fault repeatedly. One had to look to Leeds for power driving, if inaccurate in their early eagerness.

A shocking miss

But with North End one up and the first half about to end Campbell got the chance of the match. A quick ball came from the right into the middle to Finney. He completely bamboozled Charlton and company by stepping over the ball and allowing it to run through to Campbell.

No defender was within yards of the outside-left as he advanced towards Burgin. But at the six yard line, Campbell facing the 'keeper was presented with four, and too many, alternatives.

Burgin, on the ground, could have been beaten on his left or on his right. Campbell could have simply lobbed one over the prostrate body, or he could have rounded his adversary and walked it in. Spoiled for choice the winger hesitated, almost stopped, and then seemingly lost patience at his own indecision and tamely put the ball into the grateful 'keepers hands as he scrambled to his feet. It was an inexcusable miss. A goal here would have floored Leeds.

Then the tonic

Some thirteen minutes after the interval, Charlton went forward for a corner taken by Francis and from near the opposite post headed in Meek's centre, lobbed over the heads of a mass of players.

GEORGE MEEK

This was a great tonic for Leeds and how much they owe to their half-backs of late. Charlton scored a two point goal against Bolton, Gibson's one gave them a point at Deepdale and now Charlton had shown them the way. Leeds forwards may ponder on the moral of this.

United's enthusiasm and bite increased as North End's decreased. Gone were Preston's compactness and teamwork. The forward line of the first half was unrecognisable in the second. They were slow moving, failed too often to gain possession by permitting quick interceptions and primarily lost control of the ball.

There was no urgency in their work, as someone aptly remarked "it was a P.T.A.-a pleasant Tuesday afternoon."

The wing-halves 'went under' in the Leeds surges. Smith particularly, being repeatedly caught too far forward, imperilling those behind him. Fullam fought with a great show of spirit.

More missed

In front there was no bite particularly among the inside trio, although Finney did make a good second half chance for Farrall and Dagger, with his trusty right foot, had another both of which were 'foozled'.

Behind, under so much pressure, Dunn and company battled on not without committing errors. Inevitably, Francis, again given too much room in the second half by Walton after being contained in the first half, scored the winner after 68 minutes and jumped high for joy.

When a centre from Cush came to him, Francis seemed to have lost his chance by hesitating, yet he got in his scoring drive without being tackled.

DIVISION 1 AFTER THE EASTER GAMES

		P	W	D	L	F	A	PTS
1	WOLVERHAMPTON W.	40	23	6	11	100	63	52
2	TOTTENHAM HOTSPUR	40	19	11	10	79	48	49
3	BURNLEY.	38	22	5	11	81	59	49
4	SHEFFIELD WED.	40	19	10	11	77	54	48
5	WEST BROMWICH ALB	40	18	11	11	81	55	47
6	NEWCASTLE UNITED	40	18	8	14	82	74	44
7	BOLTON WANDERERS	40	18	8	14	55	50	44
8	MANCHESTER UNITED	40	18	7	15	95	75	43
9	**PRESTON NORTH END**	**40**	**15**	**12**	**13**	**76**	**74**	**42**
10	FULHAM	40	16	9	15	71	79	41
11	BLACKPOOL	40	15	9	16	57	66	39
12	WEST HAM UNITED	40	16	5	19	73	87	37
13	CHELSEA	40	14	9	17	75	84	37
14	LEICESTER CITY	40	12	13	15	64	73	37
15	ARSENAL	40	14	9	17	63	77	37
16	EVERTON	40	12	11	17	72	73	35
17	BLACKBURN ROVERS	39	15	5	19	57	66	35
18	MANCHESTER CITY	39	15	3	21	74	81	33
19	NOTTINGHAM FOREST	40	12	9	19	47	73	33
20	BIRMINGHAM CITY	39	11	10	18	58	77	32
21	LEEDS UNITED	39	11	10	18	62	88	32
22	LUTON TOWN	40	8	12	20	47	70	28

Wolves gained three points from the Easter programme and continue to head the table. A goal-less draw at Nottingham Forest in their final game has left them three points clear of Spurs and Burnley and within sight of their third consecutive title. Burnley, however, still have two games in hand of the leaders and could yet make a surprise leap to the top. The match between Wolves and Spurs at Molineux on Saturday now takes on added significance.
The situation at the foot of the table is equally tight. Luton, having played more games, are virtually relegated but the other team destined to go down is far from clear. Leeds United gained five points out of six and have given themselves a real chance of avoiding the drop, whereas Birmingham City suffered a 7-1 mauling at West Brom. and find themselves level on points with Leeds. Nottingham Forest and Manchester City are only one further point better off.

Wed. 20th- Bill Slater of Wolves and England was nominated as 'Footballer of the Year' by the Football Writer's Association.

Thurs. 21st- At Old Trafford in front of a crowd of 29,122 spectators North End's Youth team reached the final of the F.A.Youth Cup for the first time in the Club's history.
Although they lost 2-1 on the night they won through by a 4-2 aggregate and will now face Chelsea in the Final, again over two legs. After United took the lead after only 3 minutes with a great goal by Moir their joy was short lived when Peter Thompson equalised three minutes later. It was his thirteenth goal in the Competition and he has now scored in every game.
United put North End under tremendous pressure and the onslaught brought a second goal seven minutes from the interval from Ian Moir. Despite Preston being on the back foot for the whole of the second half, United were unable to score again and North End deservedly won their place in the Final.
At the Lancashire Evening Post Office's in Preston town centre approximately 2,000 people gathered at 9pm awaiting details of the result which was exhibited on a board as soon as it was received. They all went home happy.

NORTH END F.A. YOUTH CUP TEAM, 1959-60

Standing: ROSS, WEBB, BALDWIN, BARTON, WILL, LAING, HART.
Seated: SMITH, WILSON, THOMPSON, SPAVIN, HUMES, MATTHEWS.

Fri. 22nd- North End remain unchanged for the game at Maine Road tomorrow. Law is still unfit and misses the game but Leivers returns at full-back in what is a very important game for the Club in their fight against relegation.

SATURDAY 23RD APRIL

MANCHESTER CITY 2 PRESTON NORTH END 1

Colbridge, Barlow Dagger Att. 29,812

MAN. CITY-*Trautmann, Leivers, Leigh, Barnes, Ewing, Oakes, Barlow, Hannah, McAdams, Hayes, Colbridge.*

P.N.E.-*Else, Wilson, Walton, Fullam, Dunn, Smith, Dagger, Milne, Finney, Farrall, Campbell.*

Finney the Great

by ARTHUR WALMSLEY

(Evening Chronicle Sports Columnist)

Injury permitting, we shall see Tom Finney at Maine Road this afternoon. Most of us have, of course, seen Tom Finney play many times—but, as with Stanley Matthews, there is always something special about seeing the Pride of Preston. It is a prospect all the more to savour for the fact that we are now always wondering just how many times we shall see him again. Rumour and counter-rumour have had Tom "retiring" and making his "comeback" time and again over this last couple of years during which he has been plagued with obstinate groin injury. But this season has seen Tom as great as ever and, one fervently hopes, likely to go on as long as Stan Matthews.

Just how great a player is Tom Finney? Whenever the subject crops us there is always the inevitable comparison with Stan Matthews. I make no such comparison here. Both are great players and if I had to name a world eleven now Tom Finney would go down as my centre-forward for I rate him an even better player than Real Madrid's Di Stefano. I remember arriving in Glasgow for the 1954 Scotland v. England match at Hampden Park and being bombarded with queries from Scottish colleagues on the mystery of why Stan Matthews had been left out of the England team. The Scots just couldn't reason why we were crazy enough to ignore Stan and felt we had presented them with the match on a plate.

There was no implied criticism of Finney. The Scots expected Stan on the right wing and Tom on the left. As it was Finney was on the right wing and he cut and carved Scotland unmercifully, as almost single-handed, he inspired England to a 4-2 win—climaxing his great performance with a brilliant individual goal.

As we left the Press Box my downcast Scots colleagues said "It's not fair. You leave Matthews at home and bring up another like Finney." It is the measure of Finney's greatness that he could step into Matthews' "place" and do the job as well. Indeed, I think it is the measure of the greatness of both Matthews and Finney that whenever the name of one is mentioned it invites comparison with the other. There are precious few others I would care to mention in the same breath.

A great Finney performance this afternoon could turn out to be something of a mixed blessing for City supporters sweating out the relegation struggle. But Finney at his best—and a City victory. That would be something, indeed, for the Maine Road fans.

ARTICLE FROM MANCHESTER CITY PROGRAMME

On a dull, fine but warm afternoon at Maine Road, a crowd of just under 30,000 were present to see if City could gain the win they needed to keep above the relegation places.
North End's early approach play was disappointing with passes going astray and moves breaking down through not being brisk enough. City, with more incentive to win, held the initiative for long periods and after 17 minutes should have scored. Hayes was put clean through but Else was alert to the danger and smothered the shot.
Finney was similarly given a couple of yards start on two defenders but opted to pass the ball to Milne and the chance was lost. After 24 minutes Campbell crossed the ball but Milne just failed to get in a first time shot.
Fullam caught the eye with his neat and varied touches and was easily the best passer of the ball on view.
After 37 minutes City took the lead when Hannah hit a glorious pass to Barlow and his centre was missed by two North End defenders. The ball landed at the feet of COLBRIDGE who beat Else with a fast, low drive. City just about deserved to reach the half-time interval with a 1-0 lead.
From the outset of the second half Preston continued to look incapable of exerting themselves on, what for them, was just an end of season game. After an hour's play Trautmann had been virtually a spectator and probably had his easiest game of the season. City should have increased their lead at this point in the game when Barlow shot wide of an open goal.
North End finally created a couple of openings with Farrall shooting wide and Finney failing to reach a cross by inches. City began to appear edgy. Their play deteriorated and they began to concentrate on defending their lead in this vital game for the club. Then the inevitable happened. Five minutes from time a free kick cost City a goal. Walton hit a long ball into the penalty area and Finney headed it onto Smith, whose header was partially saved by Trautmann but DAGGER was on hand to score from close range.
City then threw everything at Preston and following a mad scramble in the North End area, BARLOW somehow squeezed the ball home for the winner. Two vital points for Manchester City in their fight against relegation and a lacklustre performance by Preston.

APRIL 23RD DIVISION 1 RESULTS

ARSENAL	*5*	*MANCHESTER U.*	*2*
BLACKBURN ROV.	*0*	*LEICESTER CITY*	*1*
BLACKPOOL	*1*	*BURNLEY*	*1*
BOLTON WAND.	*2*	*CHELSEA*	*0*
EVERTON	*1*	*LEEDS UNITED*	*0*
FULHAM	*2*	*WEST BROM. ALB.*	*1*
LUTON TOWN	*3*	*WEST HAM UTD.*	*1*
MANCHESTER C.	*2*	*PRESTON NORTH E.*	*1*
NOTTINGHAM F.	*3*	*NEWCASTLE UTD.*	*0*
SHEFFIELD WED.	*2*	*BIRMINGHAM CITY*	*4*
WOLVES	*1*	*TOTTENHAM H.*	*3*

North End Reserves lost 2-1 at home to Manchester City Reserves. A goal from Alston put Preston in the lead, but poor finishing cost them the game. Cunningham gave a steady display on his return from injury.

		Home					Away					
	P.	W.	D.	L.	F.	A.	W.	D.	L.	F.	A.	Pts.
Wolverh'pton W.	41	15	3	3	63	28	8	3	9	38	38	52
Tottenham H'spur	41	9	6	5	39	23	11	5	5	43	26	51
Burnley	39	15	1	4	52	28	7	5	7	30	32	50
Sheffield Wed. ..	41	12	7	2	48	20	7	3	10	31	38	48
West Bromwich A.	41	11	4	5	47	25	7	7	7	35	32	47
Bolton Wanderers	41	12	5	4	37	27	7	3	10	20	23	46
Newcastle United	41	10	5	5	42	31	8	3	10	40	46	44
Manchester Utd.	41	12	3	5	48	30	6	4	11	49	50	43
Fulham	41	12	4	5	42	28	5	5	10	31	52	43
Preston Nth. End	41	9	6	5	41	34	6	6	9	36	42	42
Blackpool ..	41	9	6	6	32	32	6	4	10	26	35	40
Leicester City ..	41	8	6	6	37	30	5	7	9	28	43	39
Arsenal	41	9	5	7	39	38	6	4	10	29	41	39
Everton	41	13	3	5	50	20	0	8	12	23	53	37
Chelsea .. .	41	7	5	8	43	45	7	4	10	32	41	37
West Ham United	41	12	2	6	46	32	4	3	14	28	58	37
Manchester City	40	11	2	7	46	32	5	1	14	30	50	35
Blackburn Rovers	40	11	3	6	35	27	4	2	14	22	40	35
Nottingham For.	41	8	6	7	30	28	5	3	12	20	45	35
Birmingham City	40	8	5	6	36	35	4	5	12	26	44	34
Leeds United ..	40	6	5	9	36	46	5	5	10	26	43	32
Luton Town ..	41	6	5	10	25	29	3	7	10	25	42	30

Bloomfield scored the only hat-trick in Division 1 for Arsenal in their 5-2 victory over Manchester United. Seventeen year old Alan Tyrer scored the only goal for Everton in their home win against Leeds United.

Although Luton Town beat West Ham United 3-1 at Kenilworth Road, results elsewhere doomed them to relegation. Syd Owen, their popular manager, could take no more and resigned after just one year in the post. Mathematically there are still five other clubs who could accompany them down into Division 2. Leeds United still look the most vulnerable as they are two points adrift, even though they have a game in hand on Nottingham Forest.

At the top of the table Wolves suffered a severe dent to their hopes of achieving the double after losing 3-1 at home to Spurs.

Burnley picked up a point at Blackpool and are still hot on the heels of the two top clubs with two games in hand.

Mon.25th-The Professional Footballers Association has, through Mr

Wilkins M.P., asked for a meeting with the Minister of Labour, Mr Edward Heath M.P. regarding their wage dispute with the Football League.
It is expected that the Minister will invite both parties to see him in order to put forward their conflicting points of view.

Mon.25th April (continued)-***P.N.E. BOARD MEETING-The Chairman informed the meeting that he had received the following letter from Tom Finney-***

Dear Mr Buck,
I find this letter difficult to write, but it is only a reflection of the problems that have confronted me in arriving at one of the major decisions of my life.
I have decided to retire from football, at least in the active sense, as from the end of this current season. I have given a lot of thought to this problem. I have discussed it with my wife and family and my business associates and I have had quite a few sleepless nights before finally making up my mind.
I came straight into North End's first team over 20 years ago. I have remained in it ever since and want to go out while still in good health, physical condition and playing ability. I do not want to drift out due to either deterioration arising from increasing age or the ever present possibility of injury, which could suddenly terminate my career and possibly have lasting effects on my future fitness.
As you know, I had a lot of trouble with my groin injury last season which fortunately has not recurred the present year. Nevertheless, I have had one or two twinges of pain which remind me that the possibility of a recurrence is still there and reinforced my desire not to tempt providence any further.
Football has provided me with a long, happy and enjoyable career, not without its material benefits. It has allowed me to travel all over the world, to meet people in all walks of life that, but for football, I should never had had the opportunity of knowing, and I want to go out with those recollections and memories untarnished.
I should like in this letter to say thank you to you, your predecessor, Mr Jim Taylor, your co-directors-and all who have assisted in the management of the club during the 21 years I have been associated with it, for your help and assistance throughout the period and the happy relationship which has always existed between us.

Comment is frequently made in the Press about a player remaining loyal to one club throughout his playing career, but in so far as it takes two to make a bargain, a relationship such as ours is reciprocal. It reflects loyalty on the part of the directorate and management to me and it is for this that I want to express my appreciation.
There is one other point on which I should like to comment. It may be presumption on my part to imagine that efforts may be made to bring about a change in my decision, but I would prefer that this should not be done and that my decision should be treated as irrevocable. As I said earlier in this letter, it has not been easy to contemplate retirement. It has taken me a long time to make up my mind. I have vacillated quite a lot and I do not want to go through a similar period of indecision again.
Finally, although retiring in the active sense, I would not like to think that I was severing my connection with football, the game that has given me so much enjoyment and to which I owe so much. Nor would I like to think that my association with my one and only club was coming to an end. If, therefore, I can continue to serve the interests of the club in any capacity whatsoever, I shall be only too happy so to do.
Yours very sincerely,
Tom Finney

The Board accepted his resignation with regret and agreed to send the following response-

Dear Tom,
Thank you for your letter which I read to my colleagues at our meeting tonight. My directors were naturally deeply shocked to learn of your desire to retire from the game at the end of the season.
At the same time they cannot but agree with the sentiments expressed in your letter and fully appreciate the decision you have taken.
I will be writing to you more fully in the near future, but in the meantime the board accept with deepest regrets your decision to leave the game you have graced for so many years.
They desire to place on record on behalf of Preston North End, their sincere appreciation of your unremitting efforts on the club's behalf for

so many years and your unsurpassed contribution to the game of football, not only in this country but throughout the world.
Kindest regards and every good wish for your future.
Yours sincerely,
Nat Buck, Chairman.

Tues.26th –The Press were informed of the decision by Tom Finney to retire and the local and national papers all carried similar articles expressing some surprise at the announcement and yet thanking Tom for the entertainment he has provided on the football field over the years.
The Lancashire Evening Post stated that Finney had a sore heel and had recently had a slight recurrence of his groin trouble, both of which cast some doubt as to whether or not he will be fit to play on Saturday. He will receive treatment during the week and has already stated that he is desperate to play in what would be his final game.

In the first leg of the F.A.Youth Cup at Stamford Bridge, Preston drew 1-1 with Chelsea. Jimmy Humes was injured and his place was taken by seventeen years old Ian Matthews. On his debut the youngster scored the opening goal after 85 minutes following a beautiful pass from Peter Thompson, but Chelsea hit back almost immediately to equalise.
Both sides had played entertaining football and although Chelsea had the edge, the Preston defence stood firm. It was a pity that only 9,037 spectators witnessed the game. North End are now favourites with the second leg at Deepdale next Tuesday.

Wed.27th-There were two important games in Division 1 –
Blackburn Rovers 3 Leeds United 2
Birmingham City 0 Burnley 1
The defeat for Leeds United has put them in real danger of relegation whereas the two points for Burnley has increased the pressure on Wolves and Spurs at the top of the table.

North End Reserves drew 0-0 away against West Bromwich Albion Reserves.

Thurs.28th-Johnny Fullam, North End's twenty-year old Irish wing-half, has been named as a reserve for the Republic of Ireland's tour games against Germany and Sweden in May.
Although he has only played eleven games in the Football League he has soon received recognition of his skills at international level.

Many North End supporters have expressed their disappointment at the decision of Tom Finney to retire from football, especially as he has played the majority of games this season and is the club's leading goalscorer. This general outcry in the Preston area has placed Finney under pressure but he is adamant that he has made the right decision.

Fri.29th-Great news from Deepdale-Tom Finney has passed a fitness test and, at his own request, will play at outside-right against Luton Town tomorrow in his final League game. This is the same position he played on his debut in 1946.
Alec Alston, David Sneddon and Sammy Taylor all return to the team. Brown and Bingham are named in the Luton Town team. Mike Tracey, the former Preston Catholic College schoolboy and English Amateur International will play at outside-left.

SATURDAY 30TH APRIL

PRESTON NORTH END 2 LUTON TOWN 0

Alston, Smith Att. 29,781

P.N.E.-*Else, Wilson, Walton, Fullam, Dunn, Smith, Finney, Milne, Alston, Sneddon, Taylor.*

LUTON T.-*Baynham, Dunne, Daniel, Morton, Kelly, Brown, Bingham, Turner, McBride, Cummins, Tracey.*

Finney star of his last game

By Walter Pilkington

(L.E.P. article Monday 2nd May 1960)

TOM FINNEY'S farewell appearance in a first-class match-it was his 570th since his debut in August 1946-was a poignant yet highly successful occasion, in that everything happened to make it memorable, except that the one goal needed by the man of the moment to round off a total of 250 just would not come.

It was a lovely day. North End won a sporting game with relegated Luton by 2-0; Finney delighted his admirers when the emotion he naturally felt at the outset had subsided; and everyone stayed to the finish, all 30,000 of them.

Many swarmed onto the pitch in spite of a request not to do so. Finney made a farewell speech, obviously from his heart, and few indeed of those who had seen his last game for North End could have been unaffected by the parting.

In the board-room afterwards there was another little ceremony largely free from the strain which most people had felt, even though it was still a decidedly personal occasion for Finney.

His family were guests of the club and he was the centre of attraction in a fitting break with the custom. I have never seen a player in the board-room before.

The chairman, Mr N. Buck said "This is a sad day for all of us. We are losing one of the greatest players of our time. In his case the old saying 'be a man and play the game' can be reversed, Tom Finney has played the game and been a man".

On behalf of the board, staff and all concerned with North End, Mr Buck thanked him for all the pleasure he had given.

The chairman's sentiments were endorsed by the Mayor (Mrs F. Hoskins) who echoed supporters sentiments in saying how proud the town was of a Prestonian who had made himself world famous by his achievements. Tom Finney suitably replied.

All circumstances considered, Finney played remarkably well especially in the second half. Apart from the farewell aspect of the occasion he was troubled by a sore heel which, had it not been so

"AND THE BEST OF LUCK"

necessary for him to appear, would have prevented him from playing. Many times he had to tread gingerly and when on the turn clearly felt sharp twinges of pain.

Alston pleases

Almost everyone worked with a will to ensure that Finney's last bow was worth watching. The Luton left-back challenged him for possession with spirit and fairness. He made the old master fight for the ball without spoiling his tenacity with foul tackles. Long before the game ended enthusiasts had seen how adept Finney still is at passing and centring and how immaculate his ball control. In fact it is a long time since the ball came across from the right wing as often and as effectively.

He contributed to the second goal, there would have been two or three more if colleagues had not been either impetuous or over eager in their finishing. Finney himself was robbed of a goal in the final minutes only by a desperate intervention.

A pleasing feature and, I hope a happy augury, was the lively thrustful foraging and opportunism of young Alston. He was a decided success in taking Finney's place at centre-forward.

Twice Alston was denied a goal solely through hurried finishing: twice he might have made two more if he had passed instead of shooting from a difficult angle-a fault which experience could correct- and his enterprise was responsible for both goals. He scored the first by forcing his way through with fine determination, and the second was due to his persistence when raiding on the left. In each instance an encouraging sign was that he did not get flustered.

The previous four photographs are from Finney's final game and are reproduced courtesy of The Lancashire Evening Post's book 'Sir Tom Finney-A Life in Pictures.'

SAT. 30TH APRIL DIV. 1 RESULTS

BIRMINGHAM C.	*1*	*BLACKBURN R.*	*0*
BURNLEY	*0*	*FULHAM*	*0*
CHELSEA	*1*	*WOLVES.*	*5*
LEEDS UNITED	*1*	*NOTTINGHAM F.*	*0*
LEICESTER C.	*1*	*BOLTON W.*	*2*
MANCHESTER U.	*5*	*EVERTON*	*0*
NEWCASTLE U.	*0*	*MANCHESTER C.*	*1*
PRESTON N.E.	*2*	*LUTON TOWN*	*0*
TOTTENHAM H.	*4*	*BLACKPOOL*	*1*
WEST BROM. A.	*1*	*ARSENAL*	*0*
WEST HAM UTD.	*1*	*SHEFFIELD WED.*	*1*

		Home					Away					
	P.	W.	D.	L.	F.	A.	W.	D.	L.	F.	A.	Pts
W'lverh'mpton W.	42	15	3	3	63	28	9	3	9	43	39	54
Tottennam H'spur	42	10	6	5	43	24	11	5	5	43	26	53
Burnley	41	15	2	4	52	28	8	5	7	31	32	53
West Bromwich A.	42	12	4	5	48	25	7	7	7	35	32	49
Sheffield W'day ..	42	12	7	2	48	20	7	4	10	32	39	49
Bolton Wanderers	42	12	5	4	37	27	8	3	10	22	24	48
Manchester Utd.	42	13	3	5	53	30	6	4	11	49	50	45
Newcastle Utd.	42	10	5	6	42	32	8	3	10	40	46	44
Preston N. E. ..	42	10	6	5	43	34	6	6	9	36	42	44
Fulham	42	12	4	5	42	28	5	6	10	31	52	44
Blackpool ..	42	9	6	6	32	32	6	4	11	27	39	40
Leicester City ..	42	8	6	7	38	32	5	7	9	28	43	39
Arsenal	42	9	5	7	39	38	6	4	11	29	42	39
West Ham Utd.	42	12	3	6	47	33	4	3	14	28	58	38
Manchester City	41	11	2	7	46	32	6	1	14	31	50	37
Everton	42	13	3	5	50	20	0	8	13	23	58	37
Blackburn Rovers	42	12	3	6	38	29	4	2	15	22	41	37
Chelsea	42	7	5	9	44	50	7	4	10	32	41	37
Birmingham City	42	9	5	7	37	36	4	5	12	26	44	36
Nottingham For.	42	8	6	7	30	28	5	3	13	20	46	35
Leeds United ..	42	7	5	9	37	46	5	5	11	28	46	34
Luton Town ..	42	6	5	10	25	29	3	7	11	25	44	30

North End Reserves ended the season in a disappointing fashion losing 3-0 away to Everton Reserves.
Cunningham again played in the side and appears to have made a very good recovery following his cartilage operation.

CENTRAL LEAGUE

					Goals		
	P.	W.	D.	L.	For	Agst	Pts
Manchester United	42	26	8	8	114	69	60
Liverpool	42	20	14	8	100	59	54
Sheffield United	42	22	10	10	81	65	54
Wolverhampton W.	42	21	10	11	90	56	52
Stoke City	42	21	9	12	78	54	51
Blackburn Rovers	42	21	9	12	85	65	51
Sheffield Wednesday	42	21	9	12	74	57	51
Newcastle United	42	18	12	12	94	58	48
Derby County	42	17	10	15	81	71	44
Everton	42	15	13	14	72	62	43
Burnley	42	18	7	17	66	68	43
West Bromwich Albion	42	18	6	18	83	68	42
Manchester City	42	16	8	18	81	88	40
Preston North End	42	13	14	15	63	73	40
Bury	42	12	14	16	66	70	38
Aston Villa	42	14	9	19	84	71	37
Huddersfield Town	42	11	15	16	53	76	37
Blackpool	42	13	7	22	81	93	33
Bolton Wanderers	42	9	11	22	53	97	29
Chesterfield	42	8	13	21	48	97	29
Barnsley	42	11	5	26	47	113	27
Leeds United	42	6	9	27	49	113	21

Burnley can still win the Championship providing they win against Manchester City at Maine Road on Monday evening.
Leeds United join Luton Town in the Second Division next season whilst Aston Villa and Cardiff City are promoted.
There was a hat-trick on the final Saturday of the League season for Alex Dawson at Old Trafford in United's 5-0 victory over Everton.

LEADING SCORERS UP TO AND INCLUDING 30TH APRIL

32-VIOLLET	Manchester United
31-MURRAY	Wolverhampton Wanderers
SMITH	Tottenham Hotspur
30-GREAVES	Chelsea
29-KEVAN	West Bromwich Albion
WHITE	Newcastle United
27-McCOLE	Leeds United
25-JONES	Tottenham Hotspur
24-CONNELLY	Burnley

MAY 1960

Mon.2nd-At Maine Road Burnley beat Manchester City by 2-1 to clinch the Division1 title in front of almost 66,000 spectators, with goals from Pilkington and Meredith in a very tense game. This was the only time in the whole season that Burnley went top of the table.

		Home					Away					Total		
	P.	W.	D.	L.	F.	A.	W.	D.	L.	F.	A.	F.	A.	Pts
Burnley	42	15	2	4	52	28	9	5	7	33	33	85	61	55
Wolverhampton Wand.....	42	15	3	3	63	28	9	3	9	43	39	106	67	54
Tottenham Hotspur	42	10	6	5	43	24	11	5	5	43	26	86	50	53
West Bromwich Albion....	42	12	4	5	48	25	7	7	7	35	32	83	57	49
Sheffield Wednesday	42	12	7	2	48	20	7	4	10	32	39	80	59	49
Bolton Wanderers	42	12	5	4	37	27	8	3	10	22	24	59	51	48
Manchester United	42	13	3	5	53	30	6	4	11	49	50	102	80	45
Newcastle United.........	42	10	5	6	42	32	8	3	10	40	46	82	78	44
Preston North End	42	10	6	5	43	34	6	6	9	36	42	79	76	44
Fulham	42	12	4	5	42	28	5	6	10	31	52	73	80	44
Blackpool	42	9	6	6	32	32	6	4	11	27	39	59	71	40
Leicester City	42	8	6	7	38	32	5	7	9	28	43	66	75	39
Arsenal	42	9	5	7	39	38	6	4	11	29	42	68	80	39
West Ham United	42	12	3	6	47	33	4	3	14	28	58	75	91	38
Everton	42	13	3	5	50	20	0	8	13	23	58	73	78	37
Manchester City..........	42	11	2	8	47	34	6	1	14	31	50	78	84	37
Blackburn Rovers	42	12	3	6	38	29	4	2	15	22	41	60	70	37
Chelsea	42	7	5	9	44	50	7	4	10	32	41	76	91	37
Birmingham City	42	9	5	7	37	36	4	5	12	26	44	63	80	36
Nottingham Forest	42	8	6	7	30	28	5	3	13	20	46	50	74	35
Leeds United	42	7	5	9	37	46	5	5	11	28	46	65	92	34
Luton Town	42	6	5	10	25	29	3	7	11	25	44	50	73	30

On the same day Preston North End announced that six players have not been offered terms for next season. Dennis Hatsell, Harry Mattinson, Les Campbell, Alex Farrall, Ken Heyes and Johnny Byrne have been placed on the transfer list.

Tues.3rd -In the second leg of the F.A.Youth Cup Final at Deepdale, Chelsea proved too strong for North End's youngsters winning the game 4-1 (5-2 on aggregate).
Chelsea scored twice in the first 15 minutes through Bobby Tambling, who then went on to score a hat-trick.
Terry Venables, in mid-field, had an outstanding game and his experience and passing skills far outshone any other player on view.
Matthews scored the consolation goal for Preston.
It was a disappointing end to a wonderful season for the Youth team but their brilliant football throughout the tournament was testament to why 27,000 spectators attended the game.

CHELSEA F.A. YOUTH CUP TEAM, 1959-60

Back: HARKNESS, MORE, VENABLES, RAY, CONROY, ROBINSON.
Standing: D. FOSS (Youth Manager), SMART, HANLEY, HARRIS, CARTER, BONETTI, H. MEDHURST (Trainer).
Seated: BUTLER, MURRAY, BOLLAND, BRIDGES, TAMBLING.

Sat.7th May-In the F.A. Cup Final at Wembley Wolves made up for the disappointment of losing out in the Championship to Burnley, by beating Blackburn Rovers by 3-0. It was unfortunate that David Whelan broke his leg when Rovers were looking like they could have drawn level. Norman Deeley scored two goals and the third came from a Mike McGrath own goal.

RESULTS, SCORERS & ATTENDANCES

Date	Opponent	Venue	Score	Attendance	Scorers
Aug-22	Chelsea	a	4-4	42,891	Finney,Thompson,Mayers,O'Farrell
25	WEST HAM UNITED	h	1-1	29,489	Thompson
29	WEST BROMWICH ALBION	h	1-1	24,876	Milne
31	West Ham United	a	1-2	31,916	Smith
Sep-05	Newcastle United	a	2-1	37,683	Finney, Milne
8	Burnley	a	1-2	29,195	Sneddon
12	BIRMINGHAM CITY	h	3-2	18,934	Taylor 2, Lambert
15	BURNLEY	h	1-0	27,299	Finney
19	Tottenham Hotspur	a	1-5	51,776	Lambert
26	MANCHESTER UNITED	h	4-0	35,016	Finney 2 (1pen), Sneddon, Taylor
Oct-03	Blackburn Rovers	a	4-1	41,694	Finney, Farrall, Sneddon, Taylor
10	MANCHESTER CITY	h	1-5	32,546	Finney
17	Arsenal	a	3-0	43,941	Sneddon, Walton, Alston
24	WOLVERHAMPTON W.	h	4-3	22,612	Finney (pen), Taylor, Thompson, Alston
31	Blackpool	a	2-0	27,796	Finney, Taylor
Nov-07	NOTTINGHAM FOREST	h	1-0	21,226	Cunningham
14	Fulham	a	2-1	26,432	Mayers, Taylor
21	BOLTON WANDERERS	h	1-0	28,723	Mayers
28	Luton Town	a	3-1	17,174	Thompson 2, Mayers
Dec-05	EVERTON	h	0-0	24,463	
12	Sheffield Wednesday	a	2-2	41,633	Finney 2
19	CHELSEA	h	4-5	15,775	Thompson 3, Sneddon
26	Leicester City	a	2-2	32,864	Taylor, Thompson
28	LEICESTER CITY	h	1-1	23,545	Knapp (og)
1960					
Jan-02	West Bromwich Albion	a	0-4	23,917	
9	F.A.Cup 3rd Rd Stoke City	a	1-1	38,465	Sneddon,
12	Replay STOKE CITY	h	3-1	35,352	Finney, Thompson, Mayers
16	NEWCASTLE UNITED	h	1-2	24,353	Finney
23	Birmingham City	a	1-2	24,160	Sneddon
30	F.A.Cup 4th Rd Bristol Rov.	a	3-3	38,472	Finney, Sneddon, Taylor
Feb-02	Replay BRISTOL ROVERS	h	5-1	33,164	Finney 2, Taylor 2, Thompson
Feb-06	TOTTENHAM HOTSPUR	h	1-1	33,039	Thompson
13	Manchester United	a	1-1	44,014	Finney
20	F.A.Cup 5th Rd. BRIGHTON	h	2-1	35,543	Taylor, Sneddon
27	Everton	a	0-4	50,990	
Mar-01	BLACKBURN ROVERS	h	5-3	26,781	Dagger, Thompson 2, Smith, Sneddon
Mar-05	ARSENAL	h	0-3	23,635	
12	F.A.Cup Q.F. Aston Villa	a	0-2	69,732	
16	Wolverhampton Wanderers	a	3-3	28,760	Farrall, Dagger, Taylor
19	SHEFFIELD WEDNESDAY	h	3-4	16,497	Farrall 2 (1pen.), Taylor
26	Nottingham Forest	a	1-1	19,855	Sneddon
Apr-02	FULHAM	h	4-1	15,007	Dagger, Sneddon, Finney 2
9	Bolton Wanderers	a	1-2	30,816	Finney
16	BLACKPOOL	h	4-1	26,126	Campbell, Dagger, Finney, Sneddon
18	LEEDS UNITED	h	1-1	15,879	Sneddon
19	Leeds United	a	1-2	23,764	Campbell
23	Manchester City	a	1-2	29,812	Dagger
30	LUTON TOWN	h	2-0	29,781	Alston, Smith

FIRST TEAM APPEARANCES

CUP		G	R.B.	L.B.	R.H.	C.H.	L.H.	O.R.	I.R.	C.F.	I.L.	O.L.
6	ELSE	42										
	CUNNINGHAM		24									
6	WALTON			42								
	O'FARRELL				4		6					
	FULLAM				10		2					
5	DUNN					29						
1	RICHARDSON					13						
6	SMITH						34					
2	MAYERS							18				1
6	FINNEY							6		31		
6	THOMPSON								21			
6	MILNE				28				10			
	HATSELL									3		
6	SNEDDON								3		37	
6	TAYLOR											34
	ALSTON							2		8		
	LAMBERT										3	
	FARRALL								8		2	
	CAMPBELL							2				6
6	WILSON		15									
4	DAGGER							14				
	HEYES		3									
	HUMES											1

LEAGUE AND CUP GOALSCORERS

FINNEY	21	SMITH	3
SNEDDON	14	CAMPBELL	2
TAYLOR	14	LAMBERT	2
THOMPSON	14	MILNE	2
DAGGER	5	CUNNINGHAM	1
MAYERS	5	O'FARRELL	1
FARRALL	4	WALTON	1
ALSTON	3	OWN GOAL	1

CONCLUSION

After researching the detail of the 1959/60 season, the question to be addressed is 'Did Sir Tom retire at the right time?'
There is no doubt that Tom Finney was still a feared opponent and most teams tried to plan a strategy to negate his impact on the game. But did they succeed?
The facts show that they didn't, as he still scored 21 League and Cup goals besides being the catalyst for many of the other goals scored during the season.
His move to centre-forward gave him the power to dictate the game by becoming the focal point from which he could control the pace and direction of play without the need to rely on his electrifying speed of earlier years.
North End supporters would argue that they saw Tom Finney play more games in his final season than they had in any other season and this must have been testament to his match fitness.
He scored a number of brilliant headed goals, some of which are depicted in photographs in the book. Preston supporter Jack Fahey, who saw Finney score a breathtaking header against Bristol Rovers in the F.A. Cup, told me that the goal was still the best 'header' that he had ever seen even compared against the superstars of the modern game.
Stanley Matthews in a newspaper article published at the time Sir Tom announced his retirement stated that he was surprised at the decision and thought Finney would 'play on' for another two or three years.
Finney had enjoyed a good season on the field as the Club's captain and leading goalscorer and for once had remained virtually injury free but he could no longer command a place in the England team.
Aged 38 he retired whilst still at the top of his game and at a time when he could also fully develop his outside business interests.
The Preston supporters only saw him perform at his best and this would also have been a reason for his decision as he would not want his performance to drop below his own high standards.
My own conclusion is that he retired at the right time but I leave you, the reader, to make up your own mind.

The effect on the Club was to prove devastating with the side relegated the following season. Although North End reached the F.A. Cup Final in 1964 as a Second Division team, they never returned to the top division over the intervening fifty years.

Tom Finney will probably become the last ever captain to lead Preston North End to the Number 1 position at the top of English Football.

ANORAK CORNER

TOM FINNEY played one more competitive match when in 1963 he was persuaded to play for Distillery against Lisbon in the European Cup. He gave a good display in a 3-3 draw but declined an invitation to play in the away leg which Lisbon won easily.

ALEX DAWSON, who played for Manchester United at Deepdale in September 1959, joined North End in October 1961 for £18,000. The 'Black Prince' became a cult figure at the Club scoring 132 goals in 235 games.

ALFIE BIGGS, having scored two goals against Preston for Bristol Rovers in the F.A. Cup Fourth Round game at Eastville, moved to Deepdale in 1961 scoring 24 goals in 60 games. He asked if he could return home and rejoined Bristol Rovers in 1962. He finished his career with a total of over 200 League goals.

FRANK O'FARRELL went on to become a famous football manager with Leicester City and Manchester United being his highest profile appointments.

JOHN FULLAM returned to Ireland in 1961 and continued playing until the age of 40. He was twice nominated as the Irish Soccer Writers' Personality of the Year and won eleven caps for the Republic of Ireland.

JIMMY HUMES never established himself in the first team at Deepdale and moved to Bristol Rovers in 1962, then onto Chester City and Barnsley. He scored a career total of 33 League goals in 152 appearances.

DAVID SNEDDON had one more season at Deepdale before going back to Scotland having scored 24 goals.

WILLIE CUNNINGHAM moved to Southport as Player-Manager in 1964 before returning to Preston as Reserve Team Trainer.

FRED ELSE played 238 games for North End before moving to Blackburn Rovers in 1961 going on to play 187 League games. He finished his career at Barrow.

JOE WALTON made over 400 appearances for P.N.E. before moving to Accrington Stanley weeks before they dropped out of the Football League in 1961.

At the end of the 1959/60 season **DENNIS HATSELL** moved to non-league Chelmsford City, whilst **KEN HEYES** and **GIL LAMBERT** played local non-league football. **ALEC FARRALL** went to Gillingham and then on to Lincoln City and Watford playing a total of over 300 League games.

BOBBY WILSON played 99 games over ten years before joining Tranmere Rovers in 1962.

ALEC ALSTON, having scored 30 goals for the Club, moved to Bury in 1963 and ended his career at Barrow.

GORDON MILNE transferred to Liverpool in 1960 and went on to gain 14 England Caps.

JIMMY SMITH remained at Deepdale until 1969 when he joined Stockport County having played over 350 games for North End.

JOHN BARTON, GEORGE ROSS, ALAN SPAVIN, DAVID WILSON and **PETER THOMPSON** from the successful Youth Team all had distinguished careers.
Ross and Spavin played a total of over 900 games for North End.
Peter Thompson moved to Liverpool in 1963 for £40,000 and gained 16 Caps for England.
David Wilson also went to Liverpool for one season in 1967 but could not establish himself in the team and returned to Deepdale the following season.
John Barton, having played 48 League games for Preston, moved to Blackburn Rovers in 1966 playing a further 68 games.

After Preston were relegated in 1961, **LES DAGGER** joined Carlisle United. **TOMMY THOMPSON** moved to Stoke City and **DEREK MAYERS** joined Leeds United.
SAMMY TAYLOR went to Carlisle United playing nearly 100 games.
JOE DUNN, after over 200 games for the Club, left League football.
LES CAMPBELL joined Blackpool for a season then Tranmere Rovers.
GARBUTT RICHARDSON went to Accrington Stanley.

In October 1959 Stanley Matthews and Tom Finney played against each other for the last time in the Football League Division 1 game at Bloomfield Road.